SIX PLAYS BY BLACK AND ASIAN WOMEN WRITERS

edited by Kadija George

Rukhsana Ahmad

Maya Chowdhry

Trish Cooke

Winsome Pinnock

Meera Syal

Zindika

AURORA METRO PRESS

We gratefully acknowledge financial assistance from the LONDON ARTS BOARD.

First published in 1993 by AURORA METRO PRESS

Copyright 1993 © Aurora Metro Publications Ltd. info@aurorametro.com

Reprinted and revised 2005

Production Editor   Simon Moore

Cover Design Copyright © 2005 Sanam Madjedi sanam.madjedi@voila.fr

Selection and Introduction Copyright © 2005 Kadija George

A Hero's Welcome   Copyright © 1993 Winsome Pinnock
Monsoon   Copyright © 1993 Maya Chowdhry
Leonora's Dance   Copyright © 1993 Zindika
My Sister-Wife   Copyright © 1993 Meera Syal
Song For A Sanctuary   Copyright © 1993 Rukhsana Ahmad
Running Dream   Copyright © 1993 Trish Cooke

ISBN   0–9515877–2–2

Printed by Ashford Colour Press Ltd. UK

Contents

Introduction

Kadija George

Earlier in the 20th century, Black women's theatre gained prominence with American playwrights documented by Kathy A. Perkins in the volume, *Black Female Playwrights Before 1950*. She informs us that before this date, Black women had over sixty plays and pageants published with many more probably remaining undiscovered. One 'undiscovered' that should be mentioned here, from an African-American playwright, now duly acknowledged as one of the greats, is *Polk County* by Zora Neale Hurston, recently unearthed after 53 years in Washington DC's Library of Congress and adapted and produced by Arena Stage to much acclaim in that city in 2002. In the same year, Suzan-Lori Parkes received the Pullitzer Prize for Drama for *Topdog/Underdog*, the first African-American woman to do so.

As Perkins documents, most of the writers were known as poets, novelists and essayists first, although their first love was drama, reflecting the historical tradition of the oral performance; in short, mini theatre. Early themes focused on issues that only Black women could express with regards to their situations. Perkins selected 19 plays from 7 writers, going as far back as the 1920's to include writers such as Zora Neale Hurston, Georgia Douglas Johnson and Shirley Graham. After the 1950's, the strength of their voices culminated in Lorraine Hansberry becoming the first woman of African descent to stage a production on Broadway and to win the New York Drama Critic Award for *Raisin in the Sun*, a play that continues to be staged today in both the US and the UK.

The British scene has mirrored the same difficulties, idiosyncracies and hypocrisies to writing by women of African and Asian descent being published and performed. Although anthologies of plays by writers of African descent have been published, *Six Plays by Black and Asian Women Writers* is the first anthology to represent women alone.

It is an exciting development, and heralds the significance that young women of African and Asian descent now have more role models to look towards, reinforced by actors and writers-in-residence going into educational institutions and even more diverse organisations and situations from, the BBC supporting writer-in-residence projects, with the likes of performer/artists Rommi Smith and Erika Tan to performance poet/multi-media artist Dorothea Smartt as the Brixton Market Poet-in-Residence. Indeed, since the first publication of this anthology, Meera Syal has become an international name, with novel, TV and stage credits including the popular musical, *Bombay Dreams*, debuting in the West End theatre. After receiving a writer-in-residence fellowship at Cambridge University, Winsome Pinnock has gone on to produce further plays staged at much respected fringe theatres such as the Tricycle Theatre. Maya Chowdhry continues to be experimental with her work in multi-media formats, has co-edited a book with Nina Rapi, *Acts of Passion: Sexuality, Gender and Performance* and is currently working on a co-edited anthology of women's writing in the North of England, '*Bitch Lit*'; Zindika has written for dance theatre, for Adzido, and co-edited a book, *When Will I See You Again* with Natalie Smith; Rukshana Ahmad has published a novel, *The Hope Chest*, and received a Royal Literary Fellowship and Trish Cooke has a successful career writing books for children.

Up and coming playwrights are taking more risks in terms of content, language and structure of their work. (Note: Deirdre Osborne's comments on Debbie Tucker Green in her essay). Another recent example is, Gurpreet Kaur-Bhatti's play *Behzti* (translated as, *Dishonour*) that instigated community furore with confrontations between Sikh protesters and police outside the Birmingham Repertory theatre, national media attention and death threats against the playwright at her portrayal of a rape scene in a Sikh Temple.

Women of Asian descent in Britain taking more centre stage has encouraged young women, such as Saman Shad, to set up her own production company, to take her first play to the Edinburgh Festival where her play, *Lingering Voices* was shortlisted for the first Amnesty International Freedom of Expression Award – a new award that recognises shows that highlight the plight of persecuted peoples around the world.

Yasmin Whittaker Khan's new work, *Bells*, (named after the mujra dancers' distinctive ankle straps) features what she describes as 'in-your-face' sex scenes and a homosexual Sikh character. The Birmingham Repertory Theatre has once again agreed to tour a controversial play by a woman of Asian descent.

This also highlights the fact that although London is the epicentre of dramatic and literary works, some of the most challenging and promising work is happening in the regions. Major theatres such as the Nottingham Playhouse and West Yorkshire Playhouse, have held training and writing programmes for playwrights of African and Asian descent out of which are emerging promising new writers such as Marcia Layne. But 'showcasing' their work is not enough and the major obstacle is moving from this fledgling position to fully-staged productions. Two companies that are working to strengthen their work and development are Laurence Batley Theatre and Red Ladder Theatre Company.

Two other developments have recently occurred of importance with regards to British Asian Theatre. The establishment of SALIDAA, whose digital archive is a free online resource featuring collections of South Asian literature, art, theatre, dance and music by British-based artists and organisations. The website carries a comprehensive and extremely informative history of South Asian theatre in Britain. It aims to provide a window on the development of South Asian arts and literature in Britain, highlighting the fact that new aesthetic forms have grown out of the interaction between more traditionally per-ceived 'Western' art forms and those of the Subcontinent, both classical and contemporary. Just as importantly, this testifies to the degree of new blood that South Asian artists have provided to English cultural, literary and artistic heritage. It aptly documents how the 'colour' of British art is changing. It seems to go unnoticed that one of Britain's most long-running and successful West End productions was written by a woman of Middle Eastern descent – *Art*, by Yasmina Reza.

The second development is the award of a major grant for research into the history of British Asian theatre and of Asian performers in Britain at the School of Performance Arts at the University of Exeter. The AHRB announced the four-year award in November 2003, and the project will run from October 2004 to September 2008. The project also has a funded PhD research studentship attached to it, which is held by Chandrika Patel.

Kali Theatre together with Tara Arts (founded in 1975 by Jatinder Verma) and Tamasha Theatre Company (set up in 1989 by a women's collective) continue to be the leading theatre companies that produce important work by Asian writers, particularly new writers. It should also be noted that many of the playwrights mentioned here, and other women playwrights of African and Asian descent have worked with Clean Break, a women's theatre company, that works with incarcerated women.

One characteristic of this anthology is the effortless depiction of characters devoid of stereotypical images and typecast roles. Another is the playwrights' approach to unconventional issues, for example in Chowdhry's *Monsoon,* in which Jalaarnava discovers her cultural and sexual identity on a trip to India. Against the backdrop of the monsoon, Chowdhry uses poetry to create a sense of beauty.

The conflicts of cultural identity are looked at in two different ways by Rukshana Ahmad and Meera Syal. Unresolved in *Song for a Sanctuary,* Ahmad heightens dramatic tension by using two characters to reveal conflict in prejudice. Rajinder is the orthodox middle-class Pakistani mother and Kamla the career minded British Asian with a deep-rooted prejudice arising form her secret embarrassment at her own cultural shortcomings.

Meera Syal's *My Sister Wife,* the first screenplay written by an Asian woman to be produced by the BBC, tells the bittersweet story of Farah's struggle to be both Indian and Western – trying to please everyone and failing to please anyone. It's a reflection of many of the conflicts faced by youth of African and Asian descent.

The representation of the spiritual influence appears common within many plays written by Black women. Zindika's *Leonora's Dance* renders various interpretations although the most dominant voice has proved to be the spirit Medusa. This presence is more subtle, although just as effective in Trish Cooke's *Running Dream.* She also expertly explores the mother/daughter relationship, pertinent to the current generation, when it has often been a long distance one. The spiritual influence decides the outcome.

The three young women portrayed in Winsome Pinnock's play, *A Hero's Welcome,* set in the Caribbean just after the Second World War, reveal the limited options available to women at that time. Getting married. Yet by the end of the play, none of them follow this route. Ishbel becomes an unmarried mother, resigned to the fact the she will never walk down the aisle, Sis takes to an education path, discovering and realising that this is an exciting option and Minda, outwardly the most confident at the beginning, runs away from a marriage to make a new start in a land of opportunity, but relies on the support of another man to do this.

This anthology represents just a few of the distinguished and nationally achieved writers who have had their work produced on stage, television and radio, with some of the most distinguished actors, directors and producers of African and Asian descent that the arts field in Britain has seen. Yet the struggle continues to have them taken from the margins and into the mainstream; this process continues to happen too slowly. More than ten years on from the publication of this anthology, the fight and funding for a 'Black' owned and managed theatre in Britain, is still being argued for, and unfortunately has barely moved.

Kadija George

Kadija is a literary activist, editor and publisher. A graduate of Birmingham University, she co-edited *IC3: The Penguin Book of New Black Writing in Britain* and is the publisher and editor of *Sable LitMag*.

The Importance Of Oral Tradition To Black Theatre

Valerie Small

The essence of theatre, according to Stuart Griffiths, lies not in the word so much as its ability to affect us, touch us so that we feel pleasure or pain, force us to identify with it by reflecting something which has significance to our life.

Black theatre in Britain is surviving. Though few plays have made it to West End stages, productions on the fringe have had continuing success. These plays attract a predominantly Black audience and contain all the elements of the greatest drama: symbolism, language conflict, rhythm. This is popular theatre at its best using every means necessary to awaken residues of oral traditions buried in the depths of the race memory.

Tradition

Such traditions are exemplified by the hereditary court performers or 'griots' of the Mandinka people of western Africa, enslaved African storytellers of southern United States, extempo calypsonians of the Caribbean and recently the dub poets of Britain. Griots, more than most, have straddled the chasm of tradition and contemporary theatre. They were and still are responsible for singing the praises of the king, recording his achievements and other important historical events and act as a reminder when he deviates from what is communally expected. Their dramatic skill and artistry can be experienced in the great Malian (Malinke) oral epic, *Sundiata,* which also demonstrates all the elements of good theatre.

Sundiata, recounts the legend of the 13th century crippled boy who grew up to become an outstanding military and political leader and founder of the Mali Empire. The most well-known version recorded by Djibril Tamsir Niane captures his heroism — the intrigue, magic, suspense, betrayal, suffering and eventual success. In *The Destruction of Sosso the Magnificent,* an excerpt recited by griot, Mamadou Kouyate, scenes of battle and the supernatural hold their own against any Shakespearian play. Other court poets included the 'kwadwuyo' of the Ashantis and the Zulus 'imbongi'. Apart from the court, religion provided the other great staging ground for the dramatic. Religion with its rituals, miracles and morality lends itself easily to dramatised performance. The present day Yoruba popular theatre, for instance, began with dramatisation of biblical stories. These plays grew out of the Mission school system and were made popular by the travelling theatre companies of Hubert Ogunde, Lola Ogunmola and Duro Lapido. They were in effect morality plays stressing a strong Christian ethic. They juxtaposed Yoruba myths, legends and historical facts with biblical stories and used a mixture of dance, prose and drama to get their message across.

Storytelling

Storytelling is the oral tradition which forms the basis for much of the passing down of our history, legends, myths and culture. It holds the memory band of tradition. To impress and retain the audience's interest, the storyteller would embellish the tale using any dramatic technique necessary including colourful language, big words, rhymes and exaggerated gestures. That storytelling was effective, one need only look at how Anansi stories proliferate throughout the African Diaspora.

These stories – brought to the cane fields and cotton plantations by enslaved West Africans, chronicle the exploits of Anansi, a disadvantaged but clever, lovable rascal who could always outwit the bossman. Anansi was more than just a spider to these people and their descendants, he is them – dislocated, disenfranchised and always up against the odds.

Louise Bennett, the doyenne of Jamaican folk theatre has performed Anansi stories in a variety of settings. And in *The Marriage of Annansewa,* Ghana's Efua Sutherland has successfully married the twin traditions of storytelling and dramatised stage performance to give theatrical expression to one of the most popular Anansi stories. Although it was written as a play for the modern stage, Sutherland has retained all the elements of a traditional oral performance: the musician and Mbongi, the storyteller who narrates and explains events while the audience join in.

Theatrical Heritage

Despite this long and continuous history of oral storytelling, it was not until it was shown that Homer, creator of the *Illiad* and the *Odyssey* and founder of the European literary tradition, was of the oral tradition too, that the value of this form of dramatic theatre began to be acknowledged. When it was discovered that the roots of all drama lay in the oral traditions of folklore, myth and ritual, a re-evaluation of the nature of drama became necessary.

In the past, historical accounts of the development of contemporary theatre often began with the Greeks and Romans. Where the efforts of other civilisations were mentioned, the Egyptians for example, it was to dismiss what they did as merely the religious and social ceremonies of primitive peoples. Consequently, traditional definitions of what constitutes theatre excluded all those elements which form the cornerstone of African theatre such as actors speaking or singing with the original unison chorus, an audience emotionally involved in and participating in the action and dialogue free from conflict.

Traditional performers assume the audience's right to participation and it responds by shouting encouragement, feigning disbelief and prompting even greater extravagant performances. This tradition of audience participation as well as public performance linked to public relevance highlights the continuous strands between African and Caribbean artistic heritage and tradition.

Carnival as portrayed in Trinidad, is probably the most complete example of participatory theatre. Carnival has everything – colour, pace, entertainment and commentary. It is not confined to a conventional stage, but running through it are the serious undertones of its origins. One of the least documented aspects of Black peoples' struggles has been their search for a distinctive cultural expression. In Africa, the Caribbean, Britain and the U.S.A., the response to eurocentric imperialistic hegemony has manifested in music, dance, art, drama and a defiant return to traditional ways of seeing things. In the case of dramatic arts, this has meant challenging the conventional western approach to form and structure which inevitably result in stretching the boundaries of 'theatre', removing drama from its rigid compartment and opening it up to include other art forms to provide a rich and vibrant source for staged performance.

Wole Soyinka's *The Road,* recognisably conventional theatre, does just that. It is the story of two convergent lives brought together by the spirit child, Murano. This is Soyinka at his most metaphysical and satirical. *The Road* combines naturalism, with symbolism, popular comedy with ritual, political satire with political reality. It is flexible and inventive. For example, two scenes, *The Narrow Escape* and *Driver's Festival,* are plays within the play employing cinematic flashback techniques. In the tradition of the best popular theatre, *The Road* is meandering without apparent end, not designed to be understood but to be experienced, just like 'the road of life', its original title.

Some African intellectuals are quick to point out that there was no theatre in Africa prior to colonisation. But by seeing their theatrical heritage only in terms of a written tradition and a building, they are themselves colluding with the denial of a dramatic tradition which existed long before there were Europeans.

Language

Faced with the problems of using an alien language, Black people have drawn on their own experience, traditional oral techniques, dialects and imagery to relate, explain and express the meaning of their lives. A great deal of oral poetry conforms to a particular artistic tradition devised to be sung or chanted often accompanied by dance and music.

Ntozake Shange has combined all these elements in her powerful choreopoem, *for coloured girls who have considered suicide/when the rainbow is enough.* This evolved out of a series of poems exploring the realities of seven nameless, faceless but easily recognisable Black women. Like Soyinka's *The Road,* Shange's poem can be adapted to suit the situation, or audience where it is being performed. Here, the 'lady in orange' is speaking against a background of sharp music to which each of the other ladies are dancing as if catching a disease from her neighbours;

'ever since i realized there was someone callt a colored girl an evil woman a bitch or a nag i been tryin not to be that and leave bitterness in somebody else's cup'

In the Caribbean, Jamaica's Louise Bennett and Barbadian Edward Kamau Braithwaithe wrote and performed their dialect poetry and here in Britain, Linton Kwesi Johnson continued the tradition with his 'dub' poems written exclusively in 'Nation' language and performed to the beat of heavy drumming music.

People's Theatre

But popular theatre for all its professionalism, vitality, and robustness does not have the same ranking as that based on a literary tradition of great writers and of texts. Hence the continued devaluation of theatre in Africa and the Diaspora. Yet Ama Ata Aidoo, Cyprian Ekwensi,

Derek Walcott, and others have proven time and again that Black playwrights can indeed produce dramatic text on par with anything from Europe. Walcott's *Joker of Seville* was written for the Royal Shakespeare Company and although it has a Caribbean flavour, it is not as accessible to Caribbean audiences as *Ti-jean and His Brothers*. Here is a play they can relate to: a poor single mother, talking animals, magic, fantasy and a battle royal with the devil which Ti–Jean wins by using his wits. Echoes of Anansi.

While Walcott uses the surreal to reach his Black audience, Black British playwright Maria Oshodi's *Blood, Sweat and Fears* is fairly based in the realities of the community. In her dramatisation of a young man with sickle cell anaemia, she explores the effects this has on his family, friends and himself.

So what is Black Theatre? Does a production of *Hamlet* or *King Lear* with an all Black cast constitute Black Theatre, or should the content of the play be recognisably Black? Is the 'mime' of the Black Mime Theatre simply minimalism or is it on the way to being a Black definition of mime? Is carnival theatre? Is the musical the future of Black Theatre as Derek Walcott suggests? Or must Black playwrights continue to emulate their white counterparts in order to gain recognition?

Black Theatre is constantly maturing. And with that comes the confidence to reclaim the past, experiment with form and structure and generally define for ourselves what we mean when we talk about theatre. So what if there is no great museum of written texts? Many have struggled to preserve and pass on the traditions. It is up to the present generation to carry it forward and try and merge the popular with the literary.

A Recent Look At Black Women Playwrights

Deirdre Osborne

From 2003, something unprecedented started to happen in mainstream London theatre that arguably reflects the current "state of the nation". A cluster of high profile plays by Black British dramatists were staged in a range of theatres from the Royal Court, to the Royal National Theatre, from Hampstead Theatre to the Soho Theatre.[1] However, with the exception of Paulette Randall, Josette Bushell-Mingo and Michael Buffong, all of the productions were directed by white directors – primarily men.

The new writing initiatives of the late 20th century grew out of a need to haul white elitist (male-dominated) theatre into a multicultural world wherein the plays staged were more accurately reflective of surrounding society, demographically and culturally. In fact after the funding decimation of many Black and Asian theatre groups in the late 1980s, the cultivation of writers from marginalised social groups comprised an aspect of dismantling institutional racism in a post-Macpherson Report, (1999) context. Funding of mainstream theatres became contingent upon demonstrating relevance to wider communities than had hitherto been the norm.

In a world where white men clearly dominate the theatrical terrain, the staging of Black British women's work still remains, at best, rare. In discourses relating to black identity in Britain, male subjectivity is primarily fore-grounded, not only in retrieved historical document-ation, but also in the drama produced. As May Joseph has pointed out, it was not until the late 20th century that "the absence of Black women

---

[1]The plays are: Royal Court Theatre: *crazyblackmuthaf***in'self* by DeObia Oparei (January 2003) *Fallout* by Roy Williams (June 2003), Hamptead Theatre: *born bad* by Debbie Tucker Green (April 2003), Royal National Theatre: *Elmina's Kitchen* by Kwame Kwei-Armah (May 2003), Soho Theatre: *dirty butterfly* by Debbie Tucker Green (February 2003) and *Wrong Place* by Mark Norfolk (October 2003), Theatre Royal Stratford East: *Urban Afro Saxons* by Kofi Agyemang and Patricia Elcock (November 2003). This continued throughout 2004 with the Royal Court Theatre staging *The Sons of Charlie Paora* by Lennie James (February) and *Blest Be the Tie* by Dona Daley (April), Theatre Royal Stratford East: *The Big Life* by Paul Sirett and Paul Joseph (April) and Royal National Theatre: *Sing Yer Heart Out for the Lads* by Roy Williams (April) and Kwei-Armah's *Fix Up* (December). Rhashan Stone's *Two Step* premiered at the Almeida as part of the September PUSH 04 season of black-led arts. In March 2005, Tucker Green's *Trade* (for the RSC) appeared at Soho as *Work in Progress* and *Stoning Mary* opened at the Royal Court in April. Winsome Pinnock's *One Under* at the Tricycle (March) marked the return of Britain's foremost black woman playwright. The Eclipse Theatre's premiere of Williams' latest work, *Little Sweet Thing* was staged at Hampstead Theatre in April after touring.

as subjects with agency" (Joseph 1998: 198) was challenged and countered by the work of black women playwrights. From the mid-80s Jacqueline Rudet, Winsome Pinnock[2], Trish Cooke, Jenny McLeod, Maria Oshodi and Jackie Kay entered the mainstream with varying degrees of longevity through performance and publication. Other plays (never mainstream), that were staged also mark key articulations of black women playwrights such as, Grace Dayley *Rose's Story* (1985), Killian M. Gideon *England is De Place for Me* (1987) Sandra Yew *Zerri's Choice* (1989), Lisselle Kayla *Don't Chat Me Business* (1990) and Valerie Mason-John *Brown Girl in the Ring* (1999). Moreover, the archiving of these women writers has been undertaken primarily by women editors in collections such as: *Plays by Women* Vol.IV. Wandor, (1985) *Plays by Women* Remnant, (1986, 1990) *Black Plays* Brewster, (1987, 1989, 1995), *Lesbian Plays* Davis, (1987), *First Run: New Plays by New Writers* Harwood, (1989), *Six Plays by Black and Asian Women Writers* George, (1993) and *Brown Girl in the Ring* Mason-John, (1999).

In polemic, Gabriele Griffin's *Contemporary Black and Asian Women Playwrights in Britain* (2003) successfully proclaims and charts the legacy of women playwrights' contributions in dramatising and staging the creative consequences of the African and Asian diasporas as they intersect with, inhabit and revise the British theatre-scape. The overarching merit of this monograph is that it contributes to the archiving process of work which has habitually had a precarious existence after staging and, as Griffin points out, 'Much more needs to be done publicly to preserve all of this material, including financial support and education of companies and playwrights regarding the process of publicly preserving their work and accessing funding to do so.' (Osborne forthcoming 2006, Griffin 2003: 31)

Two distinctive writers of the new millennium are Dona Daley *Weathering the Storm (1997), Blest be the Tie (2004)* and Debbie Tucker Green *Two Women (2003), born bad (2003), dirty butterfly (2003), Trade (2005), Stoning Mary (2005)*. Commissioned through new writing initiatives at the Royal Court and Hampstead theatres, these women dramatise articulations of the experientially

---

[2]Helen Kolawole has described Pinnock as "the godmother of black British playwrights" (Kolawole 2003). Her plays include: *The Wind of Change* (1987), *Picture Palace* (1988), *Leave Taking* (1988), *A Rock in Water* (1989), *A Hero's Welcome* (1989),*Talking in Tongues* (1991), *Mules* (1996), *Can You Keep a Secret* (1999), *Water* (2001), *One Under* (2005)

uncharacteristic in British theatre.[3] They produce sustained experimentation with form, style and subject matter to stage Black experience as universal – as rendered by black writers.

Paulette Randall directed Daley's *Blest be the Tie* as a co-production between the Royal Court and Talawa. A stalwart presence in the legacy of Black women's theatre in the UK from the 1980s Second Wave onwards, Randall continues to carve out her territory with exciting new work that interrogates the changing landscape of what defines Britishness, belonging and personal heritage across generations, race and culture. Although there have been many Black women directors in British theatre before her, it is the consolidation of their legacy (as with writers) that Randall cites as being hard to sustain. She views the impetus to "keep the door wide open for others to follow" as crucial to her artistic directorship of Talawa in its co-productions with traditional mainstream venues. As she reflects, black directors have suffered pigeon-holing, being called when a 'Black' play was on offer, as though only the political and emotional aspect, the experience of being Black equipped their practice rather than their artistic vision in the theatre.[4]

Daley's play was an appropriate artistic interface, a Black woman director staging the words of a Black woman writer, furthermore, experiences rarely seen in British theatre, those of women in their fifties (both black and white), what Jatinder Verma has called "the often 'hidden texts' of modern multicultural Britain." (Verma 1996:195 Osborne 2004: 58).

However, the expected exchange of voices and views characterising collaboration with a new writer was in this case, poignantly tempered. Daley died suddenly in 2002, well before seeing her play performed. In never having met the woman who wrote the words they worked with, Randall acknowledges the open-ended questions she and her cast posed. It was a rehearsal process with a very personal investment, what Randall terms "empowering and beautiful", a dialogue with Dona's artistic legacy and her cast's own heritage historically and theatrically. Randall and her actors relied upon the sharing of their Black diasporic inheritance which shapes not only their British

---

[3] Tucker Green noted that her commission with Hampstead (*born bad*) was a "strange marriage". Her own target audience would not be an audience typical to the theatre and Hampstead do not stage plays that interest her. "They didn't know what they would get, I didn't know what I would give." Talk with students MA Writing for Performance, Goldsmiths College 1st Feb. 2005.

[4] Randall, Paulette. Personal Interview. April 2004.

identities but also their experiences as friends, daughters and sisters and the fraught complexities of such ties.

It is the experience of love from all over the place, of having hearts big enough to hold more than one kind of love, that Randall sees as integral to the play's exploration of blood ties stretched to breaking point in the light of a cross-race friendship. In a reversal of *A Hero's Welcome,* the plot charts a reunion of two Jamaican sisters in England, Martha who stayed behind and Florence who emigrated and her friendship with the white Englishwoman Eunice. Refusing to go back to Jamaica with her sister, Florence states, "I can't leave Eunice" her friendship formed despite what Martha sees as an inferior quality of life where, "People pee inna de lift, fighting to keep warm. Small balcony fe a garden. Yu don't have to live like this". (Daley 2004:55)

The assertion of Britain as home echoes Leonora's rejection of the Caribbean to proclaim her independence from her mother in *Leonora's Dance,* "you can take your mothering and obeah back to the Caribbean with you. In fact on the way over, drop it in the ocean where it belongs."(George 1993:207) It is the disengagement of characters from customary significations as girlfriends, wives and mothers, that Randall sees as Daley's unique contribution to Black British theatre – residing in the dramatisation of a cross-race friendship of two women as a primary relationship rather than between a woman and a man, and a love-triangle not based upon a sexual relationship.

Whilst Daley employs unqualified naturalism in her dramatisation (using patois throughout), Tucker Green blows this apart with a blitz on the comfort zones of theatrical realism both in terms of linguistic creativity and taboo topics such as child abuse and domestic violence. Clearly it was her dialogue that presented the greatest challenge to critics who overwhelmingly sought to account for her work via what it was doing to Standard English rather than how Standard English as the habitual normative was irrelevant to Green's pared-down freefall in rendering the core of her characters. In *born bad* Dawta verbally lacerates Mum as she embarks upon her odyssey to name a sexually abusive father and colluding passive mother to the family, "If yu actin like a bitch/ I'm a call yu it/ if yu lookin like a bitch/ I'm a call yu it."(Tucker Green 2003: 4). Fiona Mountford notes, "Tucker Green continues to wage war on capital letters and conventional spelling" whilst Robert Hewison records that, "She writes in coarse contemporary patois, with a vocabulary of hardly more than 500 words, yet forces it into a high poetic rhetoric where rhythm and repetition carry the meaning." (Hewison 2003:25)[5]. Ian Johns observes how "Green uses fragmented, rhythmic, overlapping mono- logues to reflect her characters' sense of dislocation, but her mannered, poetic-demotic style risks making the audience feel equally disconnected with what's happening on stage."(Johns 2003:19) But does it? Claims for "the audience" are resoundingly reworked in the staging of these women's plays where,

> The importance of including and perpetuating indigenous Black British drama in the mainstream theatrescape can be neither under-estimated nor over-emphasised. It provides a key cultural site wherein ethnicities and experiences who may not otherwise meet are directly exposed to each other's cultural practices... Black drama exposes mainstream (predominantly white) theatre-goers to aspects of Black British cultural input that is *as* indigenous to contemporary British cultural identity as that provided by white playwrights. It provides Black audiences with authentically rendered cultural representations which have not as yet been able to develop a flourishing continuum in Britain's cultural psyche. (Osborne 2005).

Clearly the current 'new crop' of writers adding to the established legacy of Winsome Pinnock, Trish Cooke and Zindika provide further evidence to the key ways in which women dramatists articulate sensibilities and perspectives arising from their positions within culture and theatre. Whilst in 2000 Afia Nkrumah argued that "established theatres and new writing houses need to plan the long-term nurture of writers they are producing at present". (Robson 2000:9) In the subsequent five years, the sustained visibility and developing assurance of Black British drama is becoming increasingly apparent in ways not previously seen.

Works Cited

Daley, Dona. *Blest be the Tie* London: Royal Court, 2004.

Green, Debbie Tucker. *born bad* London: Nick Hern Books, 2003.

Griffin, Gabriele. *Contemporary Black and Asian Women Playwrights in Britain* Cambridge: Cambridge University Press, 2003.

Johns, Ian. *The Times* 6 March 2003 19

---

[5] Tucker Green has noted that in rehearsals for *Trade* there were problems with the actors being unable to deliver the text. (Feb. 2005)

Joseph, May. "Bodies outside the State: Black British Women Playwrights and the Limits of Citizenship" Peggy Phelan and Jill Lane eds. *The Ends of Performance* New York and London: New York University Press, 1998. 197-213

Kolawole, Helen. *The Guardian* Sat. July 26 2003

Mountford, Fiona *Evening Standard* 7th May 2003 n.p. *born bad* Hampstead Theatre Company Production File 17th May 2003 Theatre Museum, Covent Garden, London.

Nkrumah, Afia. "Introduction" in Robson, Cheryl. Ed. *Black and Asian Plays Anthology* London: Aurora Metro Press, 2000.

Osborne, Deirdre. "The State of the Nation: Voicing the Margins in the Staging of the UK". Proceedings of the Thirteenth Annual Conference of the German Society for Contemporary Theatre and Drama in English, June 3-6, 2004: Staging Displacement, Exile and Diaspora: eds.Christoph Houswitschka and Anja Muller-Muth. University of Bamberg, Germany, January 2005.

Osborne, Deirdre. "Writing Black Back: An Overview of Black Theatre and Performance in Britain" *Studies in Theatre and Performance*. Vol. 26. No.1 Jan. 2006(forthcoming)

Osborne, Deirdre. "Dona Daley: Inspirational Playwright and Educator (1956-2002)" *Sable: The Lit Mag for New Writing* Autumn 2004, Issue 5 (56-9)

Verma, Jatinder. "The Challenge of Binglish": Analysing Multi-Cultural Productions" in Campbell, Patrick ed. *Analysing Performance: A critical Reader* Manchester: Manchester University Press. 1996. 193-202

Zindika. *Leonora's Dance* in George, Kadija. Ed. *Six Plays by Black and Asian Women Writers* London: Aurora Metro Press, 1993 & 2005 76-110

THE PLAYS

A HERO'S WELCOME

Winsome Pinnock

A *Hero's Welcome* by Winsome Pinnock received its first performance at the Royal Court Theatre Upstairs in February 1989. Presented by The Women's Playhouse Trust in association with the Royal Court Theatre, London. It was directed by Jules Wright with design by Lucy Weller and lighting by Tina MacHugh.

CHARACTERS:

LEN	Brian Bovell
NANA	Mona Hammond
CHARLIE	Andrew Fraser
MINDA	Suzanne Packer
SIS	Pamela Nomvete
ISHBEL	Joanne Campbell
MRS. WALKER	Corinne Skinner-Carter
STANLEY	Gary McDonald

Setting: Small district on an island somewhere in the West Indies 1947.

ACT ONE, SCENE 1

Outside LEN'S house. Daytime. LEN with the sleeves of his white shirt rolled up, is washing clothes in a tin bath. NANA sits on a chair. CHARLIE, a young boy, sits on the ground a short distance from them staring at LEN.

LEN	You made up your mind to stay or what?
NANA	I'm thinking about it.
LEN	I'm making your favourite dinner, Nana. Ackee and saltfish.
NANA	How am I going to eat ackee and saltfish with no teeth?
LEN	You don't need teeth for ackee and saltfish.
NANA	You need teeth for everything.
LEN	What's that you reading?
NANA	Mind you business. *(Slight pause)* Boy, why didn't you just leave me alone?
LEN	One day, Nana, I ain't going to come and look for you. Next time I'm going to sit down, put me feet up, smoke a cigarette and just wait for you to come running back.

NANA   I din ask you to come look for me. I mean it ain't like I get lost or something.

LEN   Anything could happen to you out there.

NANA   Like what? I know this place like the back a me hand. I don't know why you just can't leave me alone. Just because I'm an old woman it don't mean that I don't want a life a me own, telling me what to do all the time.

LEN   Nobody telling you what to do, Nana. Hey, look at this shirt, Nana, nice and clean. Look at that white. Watch the way the sun shine on it. *(Slight pause)* Is about time you ge a new set ennit.

NANA   Set a what?

LEN   Teeth. Those old teeth won't last much longer.

NANA   Neither will I if you don't leave me alone.

LEN   I'm only trying to help.

NANA   Most of the old people round here does die from too much kindness. Look at poor Mrs B., the strongest woman I know. Everybody say she can't look after herself, sen' her to live with she daughter. Within two months the woman stone cold dead. Couldn't cope with the strain a pretending to be a poor helpless old woman.

LEN   That won't happen to you, Nana.

NANA *(To CHARLIE)* You all right Charlie boy? *(To LEN in half whisper)* Why that boy don't go home? *(LEN shrugs)* Him have parents don't it?

LEN   He likes it here, eh Charlie? *(CHARLIE says nothing, looks at the ground embarrassed)* He's a good boy.

NANA   Lord the day does run slow if you got people watching you every minute.

LEN   You make it sound as if I keeping you prisoner.

NANA   Thas' how I feel.

LEN   You free to come an' go as you please. As long as you don't go further than that line I mark out over there.

NANA   You might as well lock me up.

LEN   Is for your own good Nana. Anything could happen to you in the bush.

NANA   Not to me.

LEN   You not starting up that witchcraft nonsense again Nana? Is that you reading?

NANA   Mind you business. Can't I even read without you interfering?

LEN   Oh Nana. I thought you did give this up when you started going church again.

NANA   I can't give it up boy. Where's the harm in it? Is been in me family for years. Me great gran'mother did teach me and I'll teach your daughter.

LEN   I ain't no expert on these things, Nana, but it seems to me like you got to choose one or the other. The bible or this.

NANA   And what you know? Look, I know about these things. *(Imitating him)* 'The bible or this'. Is the same thing, boy.

LEN   How?

NANA   Didn't Pastor Broderick give Harris a dose a boils just by sitting in a churchyard on his old dead mother's tomb and praying all night.

LEN   Nonsense.

NANA   You look close at Harris face and see if it isn't truth I'm talking. Is a god given gift and I use it in the right and proper way.

LEN   I don't think that you going to get too many customer after what happen to little Rosie.

NANA   The girl was getting belly pains and I cured them.

LEN   Yes Nana but nine months later and the poor girl's holding a bawling baby in she arms.

NANA   She wanted that child. I know. *(Pause)*

LEN   Nana?

NANA   Yes?

LEN   Why you keep running away?

NANA   What?

LEN   You not happy here?

NAN   Happy enough boy, but I'm happier out there.

LEN   Don't you ever get frightened out there by yourself?

NANA   Not me. Women like me ain't frightened a nothing. In my day us women helped to build the world with our bare hands. The men worked hard in the field day and we worked hard back at home, scratching a living from the soil, bring up children. I tell you boy, those days was hard but we did it. And now you people mashing it up wit you bomb and you gun.

LEN   We ain't mash up nuttin. You have to fight for freedom sometimes, Nana.

NANA   Thou shalt not kill.

LEN   Sometimes you got to destroy before you progress – I call it constructive destruction.

NANA   It's murder. I never thought that I would end up livin' in a house with a murderer on land that was paid for with other men's blood.

LEN   Is that why you run away?

NANA   You joking boy? I leave because I've got something to run away to.

LEN   What Nana?

NANA *(Stands slowly)* You ask too many questions. You give me a pain in me head, I'm going inside.

LEN   You go inside and have a little lie down. If you need anything just call me. *(NANA kisses her teeth and exits inside the house. CHARLIE stares at LEN. Silence.)* Didn't your mother ever tell you that it was rude to stare?

CHARLIE *(Deadpan)* Man not supposed to wash clothes.

LEN   And why not Charlie?

CHARLIE Because it's woman's work that's why.

LEN   And what if you haven't got a woman? Eh? What then?

CHARLIE Easy enough to find one.

LEN   Really? Well how about you give me lessons then eh Charlie?

CHARLIE I'm not interested in women. *(Pause)*

LEN   Don't you ever go home boy?

CHARLIE Tell me about the war. Tell me how you get you limp.

LEN   You should know the story off by heart now Charlie.

CHARLIE Tell me again.

LEN   Some other time.

CHARLIE Tell me now.

LEN *(Relenting)* All right, but after you have to go home, y'hear? *(Slight pause, gets himself ready then begins)* It was one a those nights in the trenches. One a nights when you bin fighting all night. Everybody tired. I was near to dropping I tell you boy. All on a sudden me see a blinding light and I hear a loud bang. Then everything quiet except for a ringing in me ears. For a while I can't see nuttin.' Then me eyes get used to the dark again and I look round. Nothing. Everybody dead.

CHARLIE Everybody?

LEN   Every single one a them dead a dirt. And what's more looking straight in my face so that my nose nearly touching his nose, so that our eyelashes nearly touching is – guess who?

CHARLIE Who?

LEN   A German soldier.

CHARLIE Kiss me beak. What happened next?

LEN   He tell me to get out. He say –

CHARLIE Oh let me say it. Please –

LEN   All right boy. *(CHARLIE stands and points an imaginary gun at LEN)*

CHARLIE *(In West Indian sounding German accent)* Put you gun down and your hands up.

LEN   That's what the man said. *(Puts his hands up)* Then he turn around to signal to his friends. *(CHARLIE does so)* And I slowly, slowly pick up me gun, but him hear me. Him turn round quickly and shoot me.

CHARLIE Blam!

LEN   Right in me big toe! Pain shooting through me leg like electricity boy. But faster I than him. I let him have it. *(He does so with an imaginary machine gun. CHARLIE falls to the ground his body convulsing with multiple bullet wounds. After a while he lies completely still)* Him dead. Damn fool jerry stone cold dead.

CHARLIE *(Rises from the dead)* Man, you brave for sure Len.

LEN   You woulda done the same.

CHARLIE You did get a medal?

LEN   Yes. The War Office did send a medal. *(Slight pause smiling to himself)* But it get lost in the post.

CHARLIE Damn post office spies *(SIS, MINDA and ISHBEL enter laughing)*

MINDA *(To LEN)* You finish playing war games little boy?

LEN   Eh, eh boy we got visitors. And I didn't even notice. Hello Min. How you keeping?

MINDA   Fine. Till I see you. Miss Nana home?

LEN   You're like a drop a sunshine in my dull world Min.

MINDA   Dull not the word.

LEN   You alright Sis?

SIS   Yes thank you.

LEN   You finish the book I did lend you?

SIS   Nearly. I walk it round when I done wit it.

ISHBEL   Nana here?

LEN   What you want her for Ishbel?

ISHBEL   Is a secret.

LEN   What kind of secret?

ISHBEL   I can't tell you.

LEN   Oh Ish, don't be like that. And me your best friend. One a you in trouble?

ISHBEL   *(Giggles)* No. We just want to –

MINDA   Shut up Ish. Is none a his business.

LEN   You always ready wit a soft word eh Min?

MINDA   Just go an get Nana.

LEN   Not till you tell me what you want her for.

MINDA   You really want to know?

ISHBEL   Don't tell him Minda.

MINDA   Why not? We shouldn't keep secrets from him, ennit? Him
bound to find out after living so close with 'er an everything. Come let me
whisper. *(LEN bends down. MINDA whispers in his ear. It evidently
makes him feel uncomfortable, he squirms)*
LEN   That ain't funny Minda.
MINDA *(Laughing)* You said you wanted to know. Serve you right. Now go
and get Nana before I give you a limp in the next foot as well. *(LEN goes
off sheepishly)*
SIS   You shouldn't treat him like that Minda.
MINDA   Why not? The man is a fool.
SIS   He's no fool.
MINDA   How you know?
ISHBEL   I think he's kinda cute.
MINDA   My arse.
SIS   Always joking around an' things.
MINDA   Fool. How many men of that age do you know who still live with
their grandmother? He even wash clothes and cook dinner.
SIS   That's what makes him so different to the rest.
MINDA   You think?
SIS   Do you think we're doing the right thing coming here to see
Nana?
MINDA   Course we are.
SIS   I don't know... *(NANA and LEN enter)*
MINDA   Hello Nana.
NANA   Hello girl, you want me for something?
MINDA   Mama send me with this for you. *(Hands over a parcel)*
NANA   Your mother was always a kind woman Minda. Thank her for
me.
ISHBEL   My mother give me this to give you Nana.
NANA   What is this? Christmas?
SIS   Mama was saying she ain't see you around for a while Miss
Nana.
NANA   Is the boy. Keep me like a prisoner in me own home.
LEN   Is for you own good.
SIS   She woulda come round to see you sheself but she got too much
work to do.
NANA   She working?
SIS   She get a job up at the Hayman house. Two weeks now.
NANA   What? The foot get better?
SIS   Heal right up.

NANA   Praise the Lord. She use the balm I did sen' her?

SIS   Yes Nana. She did rub it in. She say it warm her foot and soothe it.

NANA   You see boy? Find me a doctor that could an' do that. Yes sir. I put my faith in the Lord.

LEN   Hallelujah. Praise the Lord. Amen.

NANA   You see how you stay? You watch yourself boy before God send down a flash a fork lightning come lick you in you backside.

SIS   She say I should give you this an' say thank you. *(Hands over parcel)*

NANA   Is my lucky day. You three really cheer me up. Thank you. *(Pause. The girls stand around, embarrassed)* You want something?

SIS   It's woman talk, Nana. Private.

NANA   I see. Go inside Len.

LEN   Nana.

NANA   Inside.

ISHBEL   And you Charlie.

CHARLIE What?

ISHBEL   Go away.

CHARLIE Why?

ISHBEL   Because we don't want you here boy.

CHARLIE Who want to stay anyway?

MINDA   Bye bye Charlie boy.

CHARLIE You all just wait. I hope you all rot in hell. *(CHARLIE runs off, stops, turns, blows a raspberry then exits quickly as MINDA makes to run at him)*

MINDA   Can't you control that brother a yours?

SIS   Oh. He don't mean nothing.

NANA   So. Girls, what you want me for?

MINDA   We need your help Nana.

SIS   Advice.

NANA   Man trouble?

ISHBEL *(To the others)* You hear that? She know already before we even open we mouth an' say anything. How you know?

NANA   Why else would three lively young girls wit plenty to fill them days come hotfoot come visit an old lady like me? Besides, by the time I was your age I was married three years.

MINDA   That was them days. The men so different now, Nana.

SIS   They don't want to settle down.

ISHBEL   If we're not careful we'll never get married.

SIS   These days it not enough to be able to cook an' keep a house clean.

MINDA   These days a woman has to know certain tricks.

SIS   Sssh.

NANA   I see. So you think that I can give you some kind a potion turn man fool in love with you?

ISHBEL   We won't ask for anything else.

NANA   I don't know. You all so young. Maybe you ain't even ready for that sort a thing yet.

MINDA   Oh please Nana.

SIS   We know you can help.

NANA   Well, if you sure, I might have a little something for you. Wait here. (*NANA exits inside house. Girls stand in silence looking at each other*)

SIS   Mama said to me the other day that if she did have her time over an' me father was proposin' to her by gully again, that instead a sayin' yes she woulda push him right down in a the water. (*NANA returns with a package wrapped in old newspapers*)

NANA   Unno sure about this?

MINDA   If we nuh sure what we doing here? Gimme nuh.

NANA   You Minda gyal, you want everything too quick. It going get you into trouble one day. This is unno life you playing wit. (*Gives package to SIS who takes it awkwardly, but proudly, aware of MINDA'S displeasure*) Inside is a powder. You got to burn it with something that belongs to him then say this three times. (*Whispers into SIS'S ear*)

ISHBEL   What she say?

NANA   Sis will tell you. Right then go. Unno madder mus' have plenty work fe unno do a yard.

MINDA   You sure it going work?

NANA   You don't trust me Minda? (*MINDA doesn't reply*)

ISHBEL   I trust you Nana.

NANA (*Cantankerous*) Right then go. Go! Before I tell unno madder what you up to.

The girls run off. NANA stands and watches them, shaking her head.

SCENE 2

A field near the Walker Estate. MINDA and ISHBEL sit on the ground, MINDA examining package. SIS appears carrying bamboo sticks which she puts on a fire.

ISHBEL   You going to have to tell me them words again. I forget already.

MINDA   You have the matches? *(SIS hands over matches and MINDA lights fire)* You first Sis.

SIS   Why me?

MINDA   Go on. *(SIS closes her eyes, mutters something under her breath and then lets something fall from her palm into the fire. She opens her eyes and sits back on her heels.)*

SIS   What if someone sees us?

MINDA   Who's going to see us stupid? Old woman Walker's shopping. You know what she's like. She won't be back for hours.

SIS   It seem a little strange.

MINDA   What?

SIS   Burning something so close to him like that.

ISHBEL   What did you burn?

MINDA   Why strange?

SIS   It just seem sort of... destructive.

MINDA   If Miss Nana say that this is what we must do, then this is what we must do.

SIS   I suppose you're right, but –

MINDA   What's wrong with you? Don't you want to get married girl?

ISHBEL   Why won't you tell us his name, Sis?

SIS   But if someone wants you he'll take you by himself. No matter what. It's nature. I don't want to force anybody to...

MINDA   Who's forcing anybody? We just helping nature out.

ISHBEL   Right or wrong. Left or right, I don't care as long as that Stanley gets what's coming to him – me.

MINDA   Your turn Ish. What you goin' to burn?

ISHBEL   I ain't got nothing.

MINDA *(Taking hold of ISHBEL'S arm)* What about this?

ISHBEL   Me bracelet?

MINDA   He bought it for you din he?

ISHBEL   Yes, but –

MINDA   Burn it.

ISHBEL   I can't.

MINDA   You want him or what? *(ISHBEL removes bracelet slowly, lets it fall into fire and sadly watches it burn)* Say the words. *(ISHBEL closes her eyes and mutters the words then opens them again.)*

ISHBEL *(Watching fire sadly)* The only thing he ever buy me.

MINDA   There'll be plenty more where that came from Ish. You just wait and see.

SIS   What you going to burn, Min? *(MINDA lifts her dress and takes something furry out of her knickers)* A dead rat?

MINDA   Don't be stupid. Is a wig.

SIS   A wig?

MINDA   Old Man Walker got hundreds a them. One for every single day of the year. That old man is so vain. *(She drops wig into the fire muttering)*

ISHBEL   It smells funny.

MINDA   Ssh! Remember what Nana said. Now, hold hands. Close your eyes. *(The girls close their eyes. MINDA looses her hands and takes out packet that NANA gave her from her breast. She dips into packet and sprinkles it over fire. MINDA inhales deeply over the fire. She begins to breathe heavily and shivers. Her shivers and muttering become more rapid. The others are still, eyes closed. Soon her shivers subside and she lowers her head. Silence. They open their eyes)*

ISHBEL   You sure this thing going work?

MINDA   Course it's going to work, Nana said din she?

ISHBEL   Well, I din feel nothing.

MINDA   You not supposed to stupid, is magic ennit?

SIS   I felt a tingling.

ISHBEL   Really? Where?

SIS   Well, sorta... all over, I suppose.

ISHBEL   Someone walking over your grave.

MINDA   That's the magic working.

ISHBEL   You sure? You sure it going work?

MINDA   Well, it won't if you don't believe in it, will it? Now shut up asking questions.

ISHBEL   I just hope you right, that's all. *(MINDA lies down, stretches out and look up at the sky.)*

MINDA   Have you ever laid down on Old Man Walker's bed? Soft. Like sinking into clouds.

SIS   *(Shocked)* You lie down on Old Man Walker's bed Min?

MINDA   Course. It's so soft.

SIS   Like your head. What if someone catches you?

MINDA   Them? They're too busy looking after their money to be bothered with what I'm getting up to in their bedroom.

SIS   You'd better not get it dirty, that's all.

MINDA   You could dream dreams in that bed.

ISHBEL   Stanley and me ain't never been together in a proper bed before. *(MINDA slowly lifts her skirt to reveal her stocking tops.)*

SIS　　　　Minda? Where you get those stockings from?

MINDA　　Woman Walker's dressing table.

SIS　　　　You're going to get into bad trouble one day Minda.

MINDA　　Why? She's got so much. She won't notice that one pair of stockings gone missing. Besides, she likes me.

SIS　　　　She wouldn't like you if she knew what you was up to.

MINDA　　He's a devil that man. Haven't you ever seen how he looks at us young girls? Imagine. If I played me cards right I could soon be dreaming right next to that ole man on that soft bed on a pillow full of crispy green dollars.

SIS　　　　Would you really take old Man Walker, Min?

MINDA　　I'm too poor to be choosy.

SIS　　　　I would starve to death before I let old Man Walker lay one finger on me.

ISHBEL　You're too damn picky girl.

MINDA　　Old Man Walker took me into the barn with him.

ISHBEL *(All ears)* You went to the barn with Mr. Walker? What for?

MINDA　　To show me something he said. He showed me something alright, and it wasn't no horse either.

SIS　　　　You're really nasty girl.

ISHBEL　What did he do?

SIS　　　　I woulda screamed.

MINDA　　I didn't scream.

SIS　　　　Just because you work for him. You wasn't employed for that sort of thing. You should tell him.

MINDA　　I ain't telling him nothin'. You see, Sis, that's the difference between you and me. One of us knows how to survive. And that's why you still wearing last year's rotten shoes while I picked up mine brand new from the market on Sunday.

ISHBEL　What if Walker really did take you Min. You would live like a queen.

SIS　　　　Mmm. *(Pause. Each girl is lost in her own dreams)*

ISHBEL　Stanley ain't never got any money.

MINDA *(Prodding fire)* That dying down now. *(Rising)* Come on, we better go home. They'll be wondering what happened to us.

SIS　　　　Do you think this thing is going to work?

ISHBEL　It's bound to work. Nana said it would.

SIS　　　　Yes, but –

MINDA　　Then it'll work. Come on.

MRS. WALKER *(Calling off)* Minda. Minda. *(The girls freeze then are galvanized into action)*
MINDA *(Stamping out fire)* Backside.

MRS WALKER, a quietly spoken fifty-five year old woman with a dignified air enters. She carries shopping bags.

MRS. WALKER Minda, you're here. I couldn't find you in the house.
MINDA *(Embarrassed)* No... My friends just stopped by for a few minutes.
MRS. WALKER I see. *(Slight pause)* How's your mother, Ishbel?
ISHBEL My mother? She's fine, Mrs Walker.
MRS. WALKER Tell her I asked for her.
ISHBEL Oh yes, Mrs Walker, I will.
MRS. WALKER You not at school today, Sis?
SIS Oh no. I give that up a long time ago. Mama needed me at home, you see, so I left.
MRS. WALKER What a pity. And you was doing so well. Imagine. I remember you all when you was so high. Them days Minda used to follow her mother to work. She was always shy of me. Wouldn't talk. And yet other times you'd hear her chattering all through the house. *(Slight pause)* You've all grown. *(Pause. Everyone except MRS. WALKER is embarrassed.)*
SIS I better be going back now Minda.
ISHBEL Me too. Bye Min. Mrs. Walker. *(They exit quickly.)*
MINDA I'm sorry Mrs. Walker, they just –
MRS. WALKER Shush girl. *(MRS. WALKER lets go of shopping and sits on stone. She stares straight ahead, preoccupied)*
MINDA You alright, Mrs. Walker?
MRS. WALKER *(Suddenly waking from reverie)* Yes, girl. Yes. A little tired that's all.
MINDA All that shopping. I could go for you.
MRS. WALKER A little girl like you? You wouldn't know how to deal wit that crook Smith. The man tried to charge me twice for one piece a soap. Is a good thing I see everything. People like Smith wouldn't dare to argue with me. You see Mr. Walker?
MINDA I think he did say he going to the harbour.
MRS. WALKER Of course. The man haunt that place. I wonder what him have there.

MINDA   He like to watch the boat them come in an' out. *(Catching herself up)* Maybe. *(MINDA doesn't know what to do with herself.)* I better go back in the house and put on the dinner.

MRS. WALKER Stay here girl. I want to talk to you.

MINDA   To me?

MRS. WALKER Sit down Minda. *(MINDA sits self-consciously on the ground, taking care not to reveal stocking tops.)* I can smell burning.

MINDA   Burning? Oh yes, that's Ishbel. Tobacco you know.

MRS. WALKER Tobacco? She's too poor to smoke.

MINDA   I keep telling her. She won't hear.

MRS. WALKER What do you expect from those people? *(Slight pause)* New shoes Minda?

MINDA *(Embarrassed)* Yes. *(Slight pause)* Me father sell a goat and bring them back as a present for me.

MRS. WALKER Nice. But you always look nice. Clean.

MINDA   Thank you Mrs. Walker.

MRS. WALKER I suppose you got plenty boyfriends, eh?

MINDA   I don't know, I suppose –

MRS. WALKER What about that soldier, the one with the limp?

MINDA *(Surprised)* Len?

MRS. WALKER He's a nice boy. I hear he have a little bit of money, his own land. He's doing well.

MINDA   He's not my type.

MRS. WALKER Still, I'm sure plenty men round here find you very attractive, Minda. I was the same. When I was your age *(Smiles)* I had to run away from them all. *(Slight pause, smiles)* And then Gregory came along. And I didn't run anymore. You understand?

MINDA *(A little unsure)* Yes'm.

MRS. WALKER He was so kind, so gentle and yet, I thought, so strong. I was just a child. Just a little bit younger than you. *(Slight pause)* I do understand you know.

MINDA   Understand?

MRS. WALKER Why a young girl would be attracted to a man like Gregory. These are hard times, Minda. I know that a girl would do nearly anything for a little bit of money. And Gregory, well, he's not a saint. He's mine though. He's all I have.

MINDA *(Frightened)* Mrs. Walker – I never...

MRS. WALKER I know that you're a good girl, Minda. *(MINDA reacts)* And that you would never say anything against a friend, but I need your help. *(Takes a deep breath)* I don't trust that Ruthie.

MINDA   Ruthie.

MRS. WALKER From the moment I set eyes on the girl. She look to me like a back-a-wall rat, stupid and dirty. If it wasn't for Gregory pleading on her behalf say how poor her family is, how they can do with the extra money, I would never have taken her on. But no, she's going too far. They think they so clever those kinda girls, but I know what she up to. *(Slight pause)* Is my fault I should take on people who use to a better kind a life. People like Ruthie grow up with them family in one room. When them come here them head turn. Them start to take advantage. You know, she even steal me underwear. Never marry, Minda. A married woman is a worried woman. *(Pause)* Minda?

MINDA   Yes'm.

MRS. WALKER I want you to – now this is a secret between me and you. Our secret. You understand? I want you to watch out for anything... strange that might happen. I'm not asking you to spy on your friends. I wouldn't do that. But if you see anything I want you to tell me straight away. You understand?

MINDA   Yes'm I understand.

MRS. WALKER *(Relieved)* Good. *(Sighs)* Now I feel like I got someone on my side. *(She rises and goes to take shopping.)*

MINDA   I'll take those.

MRS. WALKER No. You stay out here for a while and enjoy the sun. *(She starts to leave, then stops, she dips into shopping bag and takes out a bag of sweets. She hands them to MINDA.)* Here.

MINDA *(Taking sweets tentatively)* Thank you. *(Watches her go, puzzled, then roots about under a bush and takes out a brown paper package. She puts it on the ground, opens it carefully and takes out some silky underwear. She strokes it then puts on a half slip under her old dress, sits back, pops a sweet into her mouth and looks up at the sky. CHARLIE appears behind her. She doesn't see him. He takes a notebook and pencil out of his shirt pocket and scribbles notes. Lights down.)*

SCENE 3

Lights up outside LEN'S house. NANA is sitting outside. CHARLIE sits on a rock watching her closely and chipping at a block of wood with a pen knife.

NANA   You watching me boy? *(He doesn't reply.)* Did that Len set you to watch me? *(CHARLIE is silent.)* You're a strange little boy. *(Pause)* Guess what I did this morning Charlie? I made some lovely coconut drops. Not the nasty stuff you get these days, but just like they used to make in the old days – when I was your age. Why don't you go and get a piece, Charlie boy? *(Pause)* Did you hear what I said? It's rude not to answer an old woman when she talks to you.

CHARLIE You can't fool me, Miss Nana. As soon as I turn my back you're going to run away. Do you think I'm fool or something?

NANA You're not normal, boy. Any other little boy would jump at the chance. You sick or something?

CHARLIE It's just training, Nana.

NANA Training?

CHARLIE A soldier like me knows how to put his duty before his stomach.

NANA You a soldier boy?

CHARLIE British Intelligence really, but it's the same thing. It's a secret. Don't tell anybody.

NANA I won't tell a soul.

CHARLIE I trained myself.

NANA Yes?

CHARLIE With books. I know all about guns and things, unarmed combat, decoding. I could kill a tiger with me bare hands. I do my physical exercises every day. Like this, see. *(He lies down and executes some very rapid push ups.)*

NANA Take it easy boy before you damage something.

CHARLIE *(Sits up)* Every morning. I was too young for the last war but by God I'm going to be ready for the next one.

NANA There's going to be another one?

CHARLIE Course. *(NANA rises)* Where are you going?

NANA Inside. I'm tired. You young people make me very tired, Charlie boy.

CHARLIE But I'm supposed to be looking after you.

NANA I'm only going inside boy. I'm not running away. *(NANA goes inside. CHARLIE continues to sit chipping away at his block of wood, looking up every now and then. NANA re-enters holding a coconut drop.)* Here boy.

CHARLIE Thanks Nana. *(NANA sits in her chair. CHARLIE brings coconut drop to his mouth then stops himself and remembers to smell it first.)*

NANA It's all right boy, there ain't no poison in it. *(CHARLIE takes a small reluctant bite, swallows – finds he enjoys it and munches away quite happily)* Take it easy boy.

CHARLIE What do you do when you run away Nana?

NANA Is that any of your business?

CHARLIE I want to know.

NANA Commune.

CHARLIE What?

NANA   Nothing. Just feelings. Sensing things. Like talking with you mind.

CHARLIE Talking to who? Ghosts?

NANA   Something like that.

CHARLIE But why must you run away to do that. Plenty ghosts round here.

NANA   Since my Sam died there's been nothing to keep me here. You people don't seem to care what happens on this island any more. *(Pause. CHARLIE stares.)*

CHARLIE But what do you do?

NANA   You really want to know? I walk and walk. Seems like miles. By then I'm well into the bush. Right near the heart a things. I sit. I listen. Nuttin'. Then I close my eyes. And I remember. *(Smiling)* The Sat'day night dances. Me an' Sam was the best dancers in the whole distric'.

CHARLIE You used to dance?

NANA   All night. You should an' see how I could turn me foot so. I tell you child. You wouldn't believe it. Yes man, them were good days Charlie. Hard but good. *(Slight pause)* Sometimes when I'm out there I don't even think. I just sit and sit. You can smell the soil boy, an' the leaves an' the air. Sometimes it like as if I can feel Sam near by me.

CHARLIE A ghost?

NANA   I don't know. Maybe.

CHARLIE Kiss me beak. *(LEN enters holding fishing tackle. SIS follows carrying a bucket.)*

NANA   You shouldn't encourage that child, Len.

LEN   He's harmless.

NANA   That child's mind is disturbed.

LEN   He's a good boy. He keeps notes you know. Of everything that goes on here.

SIS   Look what we've brought back for you Nana.

NANA   I didn't know that you liked fishing Sis girl.

SIS   Oh, since I was a child. My father used to take me with him.

LEN   She's quieter than most women. She don't frighten the fish.

SIS   I'm used to going with me father. I'm used to the quiet, you see.

LEN   Let me put these things inside.

SIS   Do you need any help Len?

LEN   No. You stay and talk to Nana. *(He exits inside the house)*

NANA   Talk to me girl.

SIS   I ain't got anything to say.

NANA *(Not looking up)* How was the... *(Slyly)* fishing?

SIS *(Dreamy)* Wonderful Nana. *(Checking herself)* I mean, fishing is so
  peaceful.
NANA   Mmmmm? *(Pause)*
SIS   Miss Nana.
NANA   Yes girl.
SIS   Well...
NANA   What do you want girl?
SIS   Well, Nana, you know the thing that you gave us. To burn. That
  powder thing, you know.
NANA   Yes girl?
SIS   Well, how do you know if it's working?
NANA   You'll know girl. It'll be as plain as the pattern on the palm of
  your hand. *(Pause)*
SIS   Miss Nana?
NANA   Yes?
SIS   Can you read palms?
NANA   Girl, a word of advice. Some men ain't interested in nothing but
  what goes on in their own minds.
SIS   What you mean Nana?
NANA   Shell shock, they call it. They got explosions going on in them
  head all the time. Some men are just no good for a woman. Not for now
  anyway.
SIS *(Flustered)* I don't know what you mean.
NANA   I just don't want you to get hurt girl. *(LEN enters)*
LEN   Staying for dinner Sis?
SIS *(Embarrassed)* No. Er – I got to go. I've got lots of things to do. I'll see
  you tomorrow. *(She exits)*
LEN   What you say to her to make her run away like that?
NANA   Tomorrow? What happening tomorrow?
LEN   She helping me to chop wood.
NANA   Chopping wood? That girl spends a lot of time round here.
LEN   Perhaps she's lonely.
NANA   Her and that brother a hers. They both follow you around like
  little lovesick dogs.
LEN   I can talk to her Nana. She's got a mind.
NANA   You like her then?
LEN   Of course. She's like my little sister.
NANA   You mean you don't feel a fire in your loins every time you look
  at her?
LEN *(Laughs)* Nana.

NANA   I'm sure that her loin is like a furnace.

LEN   Nana, are you trying to say that that little girl...

NANA   She's not so little. Mind she don't chop off her hand tomorrow. She's so love stricken anything could happen.

LEN   You're wrong Nana. She sees me more like a big brother.

NANA   How you know? You can't see further than you own nose hole.

LEN   Besides, I ain't ready for marriage. I got a lot of things on me mind.

NANA   War. Is about time you put that behind you now boy.

LEN   When you see things like I saw, Nana, you never put them away, those sorta memories always with you. *(Pause)*

NANA   You know boy, since you come back it seem to me like you holding something back from me.

LEN   How you mean, Nana?

NANA   Is there something you ain't telling me, boy?

LEN   I ain't got no secrets, Nana.

NANA   I don't know but I can feel... Something. *(NANA looks at LEN.)* Well, whatever it is, I bound to find out sooner or later. Come, let's go eat.

SCENE 4

Lights up on an open field. Sound of crickets. STANLEY and MINDA sit on their heels facing each other. They're not touching, yet you can almost see the electricity between them as they both lean forward and peck each other's lips.

MINDA   Blue. *(Kiss)*

STANLEY What's your favourite food? *(Kiss)*

MINDA   Chicken. *(Kiss)* What's yours. *(Kiss)*

STANLEY You. *(Kiss)*

MINDA   Don't you feel guilty? *(Kiss)*

STANLEY Guilty? *(Kiss)*

MINDA   Ishbel. *(Kiss)* Your woman.

STANLEY Your friend. *(Kiss)* Minda I want you. *(STANLEY and MINDA hold each other. Soon they're lying on the ground. STANLEY on top of MINDA. He begins to move up and down. MINDA tries to push him away. To no avail. She scratches his cheek hard. He sits up quickly.)* Rarted!

MINDA   Get off me Stanley.

STANLEY What the hell you playing at?

MINDA   Did I tell you to do that?

STANLEY I'm bleeding.

MINDA Did I say I wanted that?

STANLEY Bitch.

MINDA You must think this is Ishbel Baker or something.

STANLEY Like a wild animal.

MINDA I'll scratch your eyes out next time, blind you.

STANLEY Leading me on.

MINDA Did I say I wanted that?

STANLEY So what you come out here for? What you think people does usually come out here for? To stare at the sky or something?

MINDA It'd make a change. That's all you think about. *(MINDA stands and rearranges herself.)*

STANLEY *(Nurses his cheek)* Damn bitch, you scar me for life.

MINDA *(Teasing)* Your cheek bleeding then? Poor baby.

STANLEY Get off me. Whore.

MINDA Now now Master Stanley.

STANLEY You say you want to come out with me, you get me heated then you turn into a block of ice.

MINDA Did you think it would be that easy, Stanley? Nothing comes so easy without you earn it.

STANLEY So what? You selling it now?

MINDA What give you the right to judge me? Least I don't steal, least I don't take other people's property.

STANLEY Mr. Walker ain't other people's property?

MINDA How you know? Ishbel got a big mouth. You wait till I see her.

STANLEY I bet he dribbles.

MINDA Leave it.

STANLEY All over you.

MINDA You disgust me. All of you. I hate this stinking rarted island.

STANLEY Calm down girl. I was only joking.

MINDA I'm not one of those fuck-a-bush girls, Stanley.

STANLEY I was only joking.

MINDA People here, they don't think about nothing. They just live from day to day, from hand to mouth.

STANLEY What more is there?

MINDA Some a these people think that this island is the centre of the universe. Imagine. They don't think that there's anything beyond that horizon. I want more than that. Stanley. Much more. *(Pause)*

STANLEY Come away with me, Minda.

MINDA   Don't make me laugh. You think I could live like a gypsy? *(STANLEY pulls money out of his pocket.)* Lord God. Where you get that from?

STANLEY Just say that I earned it.

MINDA   As if. You ain't ever done a day's work in your whole life, you thief you. It real?

STANLEY Smell it. *(She does. He dangles it in front of her nose, she follows the scent as he moves it around.)*

MINDA   Mmm. I could eat it.

STANLEY We'll go uptown. I'll buy you a new dress.

MINDA   A new dress?

STANLEY We'll eat till we belly burst and get drunk. I'll treat you like a queen tonight, Min.

MINDA   We're spending it all tonight?

STANLEY Course.

MINDA   Ent you good to me?

STANLEY You deserve it. *(Pause)*

MINDA   Stanley.

STANLEY What?

MINDA   Do you think I'll ever get off this island?

STANLEY Maybe. Maybe not.

MINDA   I can't stand to think that I'd stay here and rot till the day I died.

STANLEY You won't rot, Min, not you.

MINDA   First chance I get I'll be off.

STANLEY You move too fast.

MINDA   Not fast enough.

STANLEY You're a dreamer. How you going to get off this island? *(Pause)* How you know I won't be leaving before you?

MINDA   What?

STANLEY You think that I in love with this rarted place? This place too slow an' back-a-wall for me. Only time I really happy here is when I'm drunk.

MINDA   I would an' want to see the day when you go away. You won't never get enough money together. Soon as you have a few scraps a money it just slips through you fingers.

STANLEY We'll see eh?

MINDA   But if you do get the chance to go I'll kill you if you leave me behind.

STANLEY I won't leave you behind. I promise.

MINDA *(Touching his cheek)* Is a promise sealed in blood, remember. You better not forget.

STANLEY You coulda kill me you know, scratching me up like that I coulda bleed to death.

MINDA Thas' my mark. Jus' so that everybody know who you belong to.

STANLEY You crazy girl.

MINDA An' thas' exactly why you like me.

They kiss. Lights down.

SCENE 5
LEN and SIS enter laughing.

LEN This is the perfect spot.

SIS Yeah? *(LEN picks up fishing net and sits on the ground, mending it. SIS stares at him. He looks up, she looks away, picks up a machete and starts to chop at a lump of wood. LEN watches her, amused then puts down his net.)*

LEN Give me that.

SIS I can do it.

LEN You try too hard.

SIS That's how I'm ever going to get anywhere.

LEN Tell me, exactly where you going?

SIS *(Shrugs)* Somewhere.

LEN That's what's wrong with this place. Everybody wants to go somewhere else. Everybody running away without knowing that everything they want they can find here, right on this island.

SIS Oh, I wasn't thinking a running away. *(Slight pause)* Anyway, you left.

LEN That was different.

SIS Why?

LEN Because I always knew I was coming back.

SIS I thought you was never going to come back.

LEN Why?

SIS You was always talking about England an' thing. I thought you would prefer it to stay there.

LEN Oh no, Sis, this is my home. I couldn't ever leave this place no matter how tough it gets.

SIS *(Stops working)* I finish the book you did give me.

LEN You finish it? What you think?

SIS Is all right.

LEN   You follow it?

SIS   Well enough.

LEN   And?

SIS   Well it's just, it put me off because... How could anybody even dare to say that God is dead? Him no frighten a lightning bolt fall down lick him in him head?

LEN *(Smiling)* Oh Sis. I keep forgetting what a child you still are. He's dead.

SIS   You see. You can't say a thing like that an' get away with it.

LEN *(Smiling)* Despite all the books you still caught up in the old ways eh Sis?

SIS   Is just good sense.

LEN   Look, what he mean is that is *our* responsibility to change things, we can't put our faith in what we can't see or touch. Not in God, not in voodoo, not in America or England. Look, it's like those people who say that they leaving the island because they got the promise of a life a luxury an' glamour somewhere else. Is just illusion, Sis, a way a running away from the real job in hand. Our place is here, in the here and now an' because a that is our duty to stay an' build a better world. No matter how tough it gets we got to mek a go of it. *(Slight pause)* You understand?

SIS *(Nods)* Yes. *(Slight pause)* Is a big job. *(Slight pause)* You sound like a preacher.

LEN   You could shut me up.

SIS   I like listening to you.

LEN   The future's in your hands Sis.

SIS   Mine?

LEN   All young people. You just got to decide what you want.

SIS   I don't know.

LEN   You're still a child.

SIS   No I – You have any more books?

LEN   Yes. I bring you a –

MINDA *(Off)* Sis. Sis. *(MINDA runs on. She's out of breath)*

SIS   Minda? What's wrong?

MINDA   Oh Sis. Sis you got to help me.

SIS   Why? What's happened?

MINDA   I can't tell you.

LEN   What's wrong Minda?

SIS   Take it easy. Catch your breath. *(Pause as MINDA does so.)* What's wrong?

LEN   You seen a ghost or something? Nana says to spit three times and spin round anti-clockwise.

MINDA   I can't talk with him here.

SIS   You better go Len.

LEN   Why? All right, all right. Woman talk. I know. *(He goes)*

SIS   What's happened Minda? What's wrong?

MINDA   Old Man Walker.

SIS   What? He asked you to marry him?

MINDA   No.

SIS   Then what? Tell me.

MINDA   He's dead.

SIS   Dead?

MINDA   In the barn. Oh Sis, I didn't know what to do. I just left him and ran.

SIS   Jesus God Minda. Did you kill him?

MINDA   No. He just... died. Right in front of me. I've never seen a dead man before Sis. It was horrible. His eyes were wide open. He was staring hard at me as if to say that he was blaming me, as if I did it.

SIS   Oh God. You're sure he's dead?

MINDA   Yes.

SIS   How do you know?

MINDA   I just do.

SIS   How did it happen?

MINDA   I don't know. One minute the man was taking me into the barn. The next minute the man's eyes were popping out of his head and he was frothing at the mouth and clutching his chest. Meantime, I thought he was getting excited by the sight of a young girl's body so I just wiggled meself about a little more, the way I know he likes it. Next thing I know, the man's stretched out in the dirt, stone cold dead. It was horrible.

SIS   What are you going to do Min?

MINDA   Nothing.

SIS   Nothing?

MINDA   Someone's bound to find him soon.

SIS   You can't just leave him there like that.

MINDA   Why not? He's dead isn't he?

SIS   It just seems bad, that's all.

MINDA   So what do you want me to do? You want someone to see me moving him around? They're going to think that I did it. Worse, they're going to ask me what I was doing in the barn with the old man in the first place. If anyone found out I would be the dead one.

SIS   What a mess.
MINDA   You got to promise me you won't tell anybody. *(Slight pause)* Promise Sis.
SIS   *(Reluctantly)* All right, I promise.
MINDA   Who's going to marry me now? I was counting on that man. Blasted old fool.
SIS   How can you say something like that?
MINDA   I'm going to end up an old maid.
SIS   The man's dead.
MINDA   Shut up. I've got to think, clear my head. *(She starts to move off.)* Somewhere quiet. Where I can think. *(She exits. SIS stands looking after her then chases her.)*
SIS   Minda. Minda wait. *(She exits)*

SCENE 6
Lights up on the Walker Estate. MRS. WALKER sits upstage. She's dressed in black, gardening peacefully. MINDA, SIS and ISHBEL are downstage huddled together. MINDA wears a black dress and carries a bunch of flowers. CHARLIE sits a little apart from them, fiddling with a radio.

SIS   Go on Minda.
MINDA   Just a minute.
SIS   What's wrong? You scared or something?
MINDA   Course not. She just seems so private. I don't want to interfere.
ISHBEL   I think she's brave. Did you hear how they found him?
SIS   Yes Ishbel. Everybody heard.
ISHBEL   Stretched out in a barn, stone cold dead with his eyes wide open and his *(Looks at CHARLIE then whispers word)* penis hanging out.
SIS *(To CHARLIE)* Do you have to follow me everywhere?
CHARLIE Ssssh! I'm getting a signal.
ISHBEL   It musta happened right over there in that barn. *(Shivers)* This place gives me the spooks. I wonder how she can stay here all by herself. She's a brave woman all right.
CHARLIE Damn! The blasted thing's gone. How's a man supposed to do such important work if you women make up so much noise in his head?
SIS   Go on Min.
ISHBEL   It took them two days to find the body. Imagine. You start decaying from the minute you die, you know. Flies and maggots start to gorge on you seconds after you dead.
CHARLIE Sssssh! It's a special code.

MINDA   I don't know if this is a good idea Sis.
SIS   Course it is.
CHARLIE Blast! It's gone. Can't you women give a man a little peace when he's trying to work?
ISHBEL   I've never seen a dead man before. I've seen a dead pig and a dead –
SIS   For God's sake. Keep quiet Ish.
CHARLIE Damn. I'm going to find somewhere more peaceful to work.
MINDA   She might not want to see anyone.
SIS   Paying your respects.
ISHBEL   She's nice looking. Black suits her. *(MRS. WALKER rises)*
SIS   Oh look Min she's going. Run. *(MINDA dashes up to MRS. WALKER. From where they are SIS and ISHBEL endeavour to watch and listen to what takes place between the two women.)*
MINDA   Mrs. Walker. *(MRS. WALKER turns round. Seeing MINDA, she bristles.)*
MRS. WALKER You.
MINDA   Afternoon Mrs. Walker.
MRS. WALKER What you doing here girl?
MINDA   I come to pay my respects. I brought these for you. *(MINDA offers flowers. MRS. WALKER doesn't take them. MINDA stands awkwardly.)*
MRS. WALKER I thought I said you mustn't ever come round here again.
MINDA   Yes, my Mama say something to me about me job but it don't make no sense.
MRS. WALKER There's no job for you here Minda.
MINDA   But who's going to look after the house?
MRS. WALKER From now on I'm going to scrub my own floors.
MINDA   You can't do that.
MRS. WALKER Why not? You people can't be trusted. Why shouldn't I do everything myself.
MINDA   But Mrs. Walker, it's all I have. My family's poor. We'll go hungry.
MRS. WALKER The poor we will always have with us. What can I do? *(Slight pause. She smiles.)* That's all you people good at – begging.
MINDA   Please. I need that job.
MRS. WALKER I'm not going to stand here arguing with you Minda. I got things to do. Go home to your poor hungry family. *(MINDA turns to go)* Minda? *(MINDA stops)* I believe you got something for me.
MINDA   Yes. I brought you these flowers. Is not much but –

MRS. WALKER No not that. I mean, you got something else that belongs to me.

MINDA   What Mrs. Walker?

MRS. WALKER I'm missing a pair of stockings. I believe you was looking after them for me. *(Pause. MINDA puts down flowers. She hitches up her skirt. The stockings have now got ladders in them. MINDA takes off her shoes, unhooks the stockings from suspenders and starts to roll them down. Pause.)*

MINDA   He wanted to marry me, you know.

MRS. WALKER *(Slow, threatening)* How dare you?

MINDA   He loved me. He told me so himself.

MRS. WALKER Don't make me laugh girl.

MINDA   He love to touch me you know. His body might have been slow but he was fast with his hands you see. You couldn't stop him. *(Smiles)* The devil. *(She bares her shoulder and strokes it)* He used to touch me like this. And hold my breasts like this. And kiss me. All over.

MRS. WALKER Stop that girl.

MINDA   He told me once that every time he had to touch you, he closed his eyes an' imagined that it was my young body he was holding instead.

MRS. WALKER You little slut. *(She slaps MINDA hard)* If the old man did love you so much why he didn't leave you this place in the will? Eh? He knew you for the little whore you are. He would never have given me up for you. Never. Gregory could never have loved you. You people frightened him with your dirt and your ignorance. He spent his whole life running away from it.

MINDA   He said he loved me.

MRS. WALKER Grow up. What man doesn't say that sort a thing in the heat a the moment? He said the same thing to Ruthie, the same to the girl before her. Take a look at yourself girl. Take a long hard look, then ask yourself whether you really fit for a man like Gregory. Stick to your own kind.

MINDA   I'm as good as you are.

MRS. WALKER Yes? There were many girls like you in his life. There was only one woman like me. But you so different to the others, you want so much. The others settled for a new dress, a pair a shoes. They accepted the situation. But you, you want a ring on your finger. You want to be lady a the house. Why am I wasting my time talking to a little slut like you? You not even fit to lick my Gregory shoes. Go home girl. Where you belong. Because if I catch you even setting foot here again I swear I'll kill you. *(MINDA stands looking at her then throws stockings she's been holding at MRS. WALKER'S feet. She starts to walk away barefoot.)* Don't forget you shoes girl. *(Calling after her)* After all they were a gift from your father. *(She laughs bitterly. MINDA walks away.)*

SIS   What happened Min?

ISHBEL   We couldn't see much from here. Did she like the flowers?

SIS   Look at her face Ish. *(To MINDA)* What did she say?

MINDA *(Blankly)* Let's go.

SIS   Tell us what she said.

MINDA *(No reply)*

SIS   Oh God Min. Come, let's go, let's go.

MINDA   Just leave me! Leave me

SIS and ISHBEL look at one another then exit. MINDA collapses onto her knees and starts to sob, more out of anger and frustration than anything else. She picks up flowers and bangs them against the ground. She quietens down after a while and looks around her at the destroyed flowers. She starts to laugh quietly. She stands, hands on hips and laughs out loud.

SCENE 7
Lights up. In a clearing by a stream. The water reflects bright flickering light into LEN and SIS'S faces.

LEN   There it is. You see it?

SIS   No.

LEN   You're not looking. *(Takes her head in his hands and holds it steady)* There, can you see it now?

SIS   Yes. It's beautiful.

LEN   You like it?

SIS   Is it really a fish? It look like a tongue a fire, burning underwater.

LEN   Is a fish.

SIS   It's like magic.

LEN   It is magic Sis. All of it. All this.

SIS   Yes I can see it. When you show me these things I see them like as if for the first time.

LEN   It's all new to me too Sis. I never saw any of it before. *(Slight pause)* Maybe everyone should fight a war. *(He moves slowly)* Have you ever seen a dead man?

SIS   No. *(Shudders)* Horrible.

LEN   Have you ever seen a man blown to pieces?

SIS   Stop it Len. I don't want to hear these things.

LEN   No. I don't suppose you do. I suppose you just want me to show
you bright butterflies and flowers. You don't want to see dirt or ugliness.
Life for you is lovehearts and sugar sweeties. *(Pause)* Sometimes I just
want to get away from all this... all the greed and everything. I just want to
fly away sometimes, free as a bird. *(Pause. LEN has his back to SIS who
approaches him from behind as if to touch him tenderly. MINDA enters
and breaks mood.)*

MINDA   Sis.

LEN   Hello Min.

SIS   What do you want Minda?

MINDA   Your mother's looking for you.

SIS   What for?

MINDA   She says you'll know what for.

SIS   Tell her I'll come in a minute.

MINDA   She wants you now Sis. She said something about you not
finishing what you was doing.

SIS   Give me one minute.

MINDA   She's mad as hell.

SIS *(Hesitates then sighs. She's reluctant to leave)* All right. See you Len.

LEN   Bye Sis.

SIS   Coming Min?

MINDA   In a minute.

SIS *(Hesitates)* All right. *(She exits. Pause)*

MINDA   We ain't talked for a long time.

LEN   Wasn't so long I last see you.

MINDA   No I mean properly. We tease each other a lot and joke around
and things, but we never really talk.

LEN   What makes you think you can talk to me?

MINDA   Just a feeling.

LEN   Go ahead. *(Pause)*

MINDA   You look tired Len.

LEN   Yes.

MINDA   Thin too.

LEN   Uh-huh?

MINDA   You need looking after.

LEN   You think so?

MINDA   It's about time you was married.

LEN   So they keep telling me.

MINDA   Not to one of those wishy washy girls but a real tough woman.

LEN   You got someone in mind.

MINDA *(She smiles)* I've always liked you Len.

LEN   You've never even looked at me.

MINDA   Since I was a little girl. I used to watch you walk past the house on you way to work. You always looked so strong. And you always had a smile and a wave for me.

LEN   You were the cutest little girl for miles. And the naughtiest. *(They both laugh)* Some things never change.

MINDA   No. *(Pause)* You were the first person to ever break my heart.

LEN   Me?

MINDA   You forgot to smile and wave at me one day. And I was wearing my best Sunday outfit which I wasn't supposed to touch except for church.

LEN   Sorry. *(Slight pause)* You broke my heart too.

MINDA   When?

LEN   When I came home. They was all there to welcome me. Every single person from this district, cheering, waving banners. It was like a carnival. They made me feel like a hero. They was all there. Everybody except you Minda.

MINDA   I know but that was just –

LEN   What?

MINDA   I was frightened. I was glad you come back and everything but I didn't know what you'd think of me. I've done a lot of things over the years Len. Things I'm ashamed of.

LEN   What sort a things?

MINDA   I'm like a child. I know what I want – I want to be happy. I want people to respect me. I want to be somebody. But I don't know how to get what I want. They think I'm a piece of trash, nothing but a dirty little whore. You know Len, I lay under Old Man Walker a hundred times. A hundred times I felt that old man do what he could on top of me, felt him panting near my ear, while he dribbled on my neck. *(Slight pause)* I've worked as g'yal in lots of houses since I was thirteen. There was an old man Walker in every single one of them. *(She smiles wryly)* All I've got to show for it is a pair of plastic shoes.

LEN   Minda. *(LEN takes hold of her. She rests her head on his shoulder. He strokes her head.)*

MINDA   Does it disgust you?

LEN   You're honest. I respect you for it. *(Slight pause)* Where were you that day?

MINDA   What day?

LEN   The day I come back?

MINDA   Oh, I went off by meself. To think. *(Pause)*

LEN   A hero's welcome. I hated it.

MINDA   Why? You are a hero.

LEN   Most times I feel like a fake. I talk and talk about how happily we could live here on this island just as it is, but all the time I'm frightened of life.

MINDA   You? Frightened?

LEN   Yes.

MINDA   What of?

LEN   Of the future. Of what's going to happen.

MINDA   Yes. *(Slight pause)* I'm frightened too. *(SIS enters and watches them. MINDA kisses him. She stops. He kisses her. They hold each other. As they kiss lights go down slowly.)*

ACT TWO, SCENE 1

Outside LEN'S house. LEN and NANA on stage. CHARLIE enters wearing scouts uniform. He carries rolled up posters under his arm. He marches across stage and pins one up at one end of the stage then marches across stage and pins up another. They're recruitment to England posters. He marches towards LEN and NANA and sits and watches them.

NANA   I ain't happy Len.

LEN   Whas' wrong Nana?

NANA   That little girl. Ever since she came here she tek over the whole house.

LEN   Don't be silly.

NANA   This morning she throw me out, tell me to stay out here.

LEN   Only because she want to clean the place up.

NANA   The place clean already. Marriage gone to the girl head, I tell you. I thought she woulda calm down by now but she ain't tired a playing wife yet.

LEN   What's wrong with that? She's happy.

NANA   Happy? She? Thas' all you know boy.

LEN   What you saying Nana?

NANA   Nuttin'. I ain't saying nuttin'. She can't even do things properly. You ever taste food like she cook last night?

LEN   She's young. She'll learn. *(MINDA comes out holding a large basket full of clothes, she puts them down quickly, panting.)* You all right Min?

MINDA   All I've done since I came here is cook and wash clothes.

LEN   I help you don't I Min?

MINDA   You? You more get in the way than help me Len.

LEN   I try darling.

MINDA   Funny how you use to be able to do those things before an' now all of a sudden you all fingers and thumbs.

NANA   So what? You thought you were going to live like a queen here or something? We're simple people Minda.

MINDA   Simple not the word.

NANA   Slut.

MINDA   Are you going to let her talk to me like that?

LEN   Easy Nana. That's my wife you're talking to.

NANA   Now the two of you ganging up on me. Before was bad enough with that child standing guard over me all day. Now it's worse. You bring this slut into my house...

MINDA   You're lucky you've got me old woman. Damn lucky. See those hands? Nice and small, eh? Do these look like the kind of hands cut out for doing an old woman's dirty laundry? More like hands that a prince would kiss.

NANA   Stinking bitch.

LEN   Are you two going to fight all day?

NANA   No. Because I'm going inside. I know where I ain't wanted. *(She goes)*

MINDA   Damn old fool. Why doesn't she leave me alone?

LEN   She don't mean any harm.

MINDA   What did I ever do to her to make her hate me so much?

LEN   She'll get used to you.

MINDA   If she isn't used to me now she never will be.

LEN   Just give her time. She's an old woman.

MINDA   I suppose so.

LEN   I'm going. Look after her.

MINDA   Hey Len.

LEN   Yes?

MINDA   Ain't you forgotten something? *(He stands puzzled, then remembers. He kisses her hastily.)*

LEN   See you later.

MINDA   Remember, don't be late. *(He exits. Pause. MINDA sighs, bored. CHARLIE stares at her)* What you looking at?

CHARLIE Nothing much.

MINDA   It's rude to stare you know boy.

CHARLIE I don't care. *(MINDA reclines, holds her legs coquettishly.)*

MINDA   You like what you see?

CHARLIE You're nasty.

MINDA What would you do to me if you had the chance boy?

CHARLIE Nasty bitch.

MINDA *(Laughing)* As if boy. As if I would ever let you touch me with you little stick a liquorice.

CHARLIE Filthy bitch. I'm going to tell, you filthy bitch.

MINDA Tell who boy?

CHARLIE Len.

MINDA Tell him boy. That poor fool is too drunk with love. He's never had so much love in his whole life before. He's not going to give that up now is he?

CHARLIE Whore. *(STANLEY enters)*

STANLEY Hello Missus.

MINDA Stanley what you doing here?

STANLEY Just visitin'.

MINDA I thought we said you wouldn't come round here.

STANLEY So what? You think I'm one a those fuck-a-bush men?

MINDA Very funny Stanley.

STANLEY You ain't got a friendly kiss for a neighbour stop by to see you then?

MINDA The child.

STANLEY He doesn't mind. Do you Charlie boy eh?

CHARLIE I'm going to tell.

STANLEY Tell? You wouldn't do a thing like that now would you Charlie?

MINDA That child is weird.

STANLEY Shut up and kiss me.

MINDA The old woman's inside.

STANLEY So? They're all blind at that age.

MINDA Not this one. She got eyes like a hawk.

STANLEY She won't see anything. *(They kiss. STANLEY fondles her. She moves away.)*

MINDA Stanley.

STANLEY You wasn't always so fussy.

MINDA I wasn't always a respectable married woman.

STANLEY You're getting dull in your old age, Minda.

MINDA I feel like an old woman.

STANLEY Hard work suits you.

MINDA Like hell. Look at this figure. The body was destined for the best cut clothes and things.

STANLEY Let me take you away from all this.

MINDA   Where to?

STANLEY How you fancy England?

MINDA   England?

STANLEY That's why I stop by. To tell you.

MINDA   Tell me what?

STANLEY This is the chance we bin waiting for Min.

MINDA   What chance?

STANLEY All over the island them putting up posters: 'Come to England', 'Come find a job in England', 'The motherland needs you'. You musta seen them. But how am I going to get a place on that boat I ask myself. I'm just a poor country boy with nuttin' in his pockets but holes. But luck on my side Min. What happen to me last week?

MINDA   What?

STANLEY I go into town and, kiss me beak, if I don't win one hundred and fifty pounds.

MINDA   One hundred and fifty pounds?

STANLEY Enough for two tickets to London. *(He produces tickets)*

MINDA   Let me see. Is got my name on it.

STANLEY Course. Is yours ennit?

MINDA   Mine?

STANLEY Well I ain't going without you. I made a promise sealed wit blood, remember? So you better start packing.

CHARLIE I'm telling Len.

STANLEY You won't tell will you boy? Will you? *(STANLEY fishes for coins in his pocket.)* Here boy.

CHARLIE Thank you.

STANLEY You won't tell?

CHARLIE No one going hear a word from me Stan.

STANLEY Good boy.

MINDA   I can't come Stan.

STANLEY What you saying?

MINDA   I can't just leave like that.

STANLEY What? I can't believe you really saying this Min. Tell me you don't mean it.

MINDA   I mean it.

STANLEY You know the trouble I went to, to get these tickets?

MINDA   I'm a married woman.

STANLEY So what? You mean to tell me you want to stay here on this island and rot?

MINDA   No.

STANLEY I can just see you sitting in that chair covered in rolls of fat, your hair white like silver in the sun, an old woman nodding off to sleep an' mashing her gums.

MINDA   No.

STANLEY You bored already, else you wouldna start see me again. You can't stay here, there's nuttin' for you. You ain't got no choice Min.

MINDA   What you know?

STANLEY I know you Minda.

MINDA   What about Len?

STANLEY Is that you frightened of?

MINDA   Him have him ways but he's good to me, Stanley.

STANLEY Min if you leave him now you doing him a service. Like I said, I know you, you stay here you'll go crazy. How long before you tek up with someone else? How long before Len find out? Then what happen to you? What happen to Len?

MINDA   It don't have to be like that.

STANLEY Then how else would it be? Len ain't like me an' you Min. Look to me like Len a sit-down-in-one-place type a man.

MINDA   I don't know.

STANLEY You'll like England Min. They got cars as long as rivers, houses that touch the sky. And the people are so rich that gold and silver falls out of their pockets as they walk along the streets an' they don't even bother to run back an' pick it up.

MINDA   You're dreaming Stanley.

STANLEY What's wrong with dreams? Anyway, this one going come true. Mek up you mind Min.

MINDA   I was just getting settled. For the first time in me life I feel safe.

STANLEY Safe? Since when you want life to be safe Min? I thought you was a person really like to live.

MINDA   I am.

STANLEY Well then, come.

MINDA   It's not so easy to decide just like that, you know Stanley.

STANLEY It's what you always wanted.

MINDA   I need time.

STANLEY Two days. Thas' all I'm giving you.

MINDA   Why can't you just leave me alone, Stanley?

STANLEY Because I don't think that you want me to.

MINDA   Oh, just go Stanley.

STANLEY Two days.

MINDA   Just go away. *(NANA enters)*

NANA   What's going on here?

STANLEY Good day Nana. How you keeping?

NANA   You ain't finished hanging out those clothes yet girl?

STANLEY I was just going. See you soon Minda. *(He exits. Pause. NANA stands and watches MINDA.)*

NANA   What's going on?

MINDA   Nuttin'. *(MINDA smiles. She picks up laundry basket, hums quietly and start to hang clothes out.)*

NANA   You happy all on a sudden.

MINDA   You don't like to see me happy Nana?

NANA   What you got to be so happy about? You up to something I soon tell Len.

MINDA   Tell him what old woman?

NANA   That you... that you...

MINDA   Go tell tales you take youself make fool.

NANA   You feisty little –

MINDA   Watch youself Nana.

NANA   Charlie. You know what going on? *(CHARLIE lowers his head.)*

NANA   She cast some kinda spell over you too eh, Charlie?

MINDA   I ain't no witch.

NANA   Something bad's going to happen to you one day Minda.

MINDA   Like what? *(She giggles)* Nuttin' bad could ever happen to me Nana. I was born under a lucky star, me.

ACT TWO, SCENE 2

ISHBEL and SIS are on a hill overlooking the bay. It's nearly night time. From far away the sounds of drunken revelry can be heard. They sit hugging their knees. There's a bottle between them. MRS. WALKER enters dressed in black. She stares down into the bay, a half smile on her face. ISHBEL and SIS watch her closely. A boat in the bay emits a long, low mournful sound.

SIS   Here she is again. Same time same place.

ISHBEL   And still in widow's weeds. She musta really loved him.

SIS   Yes.

ISHBEL   S'funny. You never think of people their age being in love. Not really. Do you?

SIS   What d'you think she's thinking?

ISHBEL *(Thinking about herself)* The good times, the fun, the closeness. These sorta things.

SIS   Funny how things end.

ISHBEL   Eh?

SIS   I mean, how final things are sometimes. Everything ends some time. *(Slight pause)* Everything except this damn war business.

ISHBEL   But it's over now.

SIS   It's never over Ish. It won't be over in a hundred years.

ISHBEL   But it ain't our business.

SIS   It is Ish. It affects you don't it? Don't you family read the papers or something?

ISHBEL   You sound just like Len.

SIS *(Lowers her head)* Yes.

ISHBEL   We're just a small island Sis. Small island people. We just get on best we can.

SIS   That don't mean we can't think about things. If you think hard enough Ish things start to fall apart. Then they come together again and you see things clear.

ISHBEL   What?

SIS   Well, if you look at a flower, hard, soon you see all the tiny little details and it don't look like a flower no more. Then soon, as you look, it all comes together again. You see what a flower really looks like cos you looking at it, really looking at it for the first time.

ISHBEL *(Baffled)* I suppose.

SIS   It's the same with people, the world. If you look you see. *(Slight pause)* Don't you ever think?

ISHBEL   I'm always thinking.

SIS   I don't mean dreamin'. I mean thinking. Look, let's think about love – for a whole minute.

ISHBEL   A minute?

SIS   Yes. Start now. *(ISHBEL stares into space. SIS takes a swig from the bottle.)*

ISHBEL *(Coming to)* Finish.

SIS   That wasn't twenty seconds.

ISHBEL   I got bored. *(They laugh)* This is like before when it was... when it was the three of us.

SIS   Yes.

ISHBEL   When we worked that spell round the fire, remember?

SIS   Mmm.

ISHBEL   We musta done something wrong.

SIS   It worked for me.

ISHBEL   What did you wish for?

SIS   Nothing. That's what I got.

ISHBEL   Mine never worked. I think they made a mistake and mixed me up with someone else. *(MRS. WALKER goes)* What she see out there?

SIS   Maybe she wants to go with them. *(Pause)*

ISHBEL   It must be nice though.

SIS   What?

ISHBEL   To be out there. Right in the middle of the ocean. Right in the middle of nowhere. Nothing but sky nothing but sea. Freedom.

SIS   I'll never leave this island.

ISHBEL   I won't never have the chance.

SIS   It's my home. I'll grow old and die right here on this island, in this district. *(Pause)* Why can't you stay Ish?

ISHBEL   They won't let me. I don't blame them. It's not right. Anyway, I like me aunty a lot.

SIS   I'm going to miss you. You're my one real friend. Can I listen to it?

ISHBEL *(Reluctantly)* All right. But don't you make a habit of it girl. *(Sis puts her ear to stomach)* You won't hear nothing. Is too small.

SIS   I can you know. I can hear it moving around, sorta like underwater sounds.

ISHBEL   That's me dinner digesting.

SIS   I bet it's trying to tell us something.

ISHBEL   Quick. Get Charlie. He know all about secret code don't he?

SIS *(Laughing)* Fool.

ISHBEL   I'm gonna have to grow up now.

SIS   Why?

ISHBEL   Responsibilities.

SIS   Not you, you'll always be the same Ish, thank God. *(Slight pause)* You should tell Stanley you know Ish.

ISHBEL   I did.

SIS   Oh Ish.

ISHBEL   I only tell you he didn't know because I didn't want you to feel sorry for me. My life like a story book. *(Pause)* I wonder how Mrs. Walker manage on her own? I wonder if she don't get lonely.

SIS   Everybody's lonely Ish.

ISHBEL   You think?

SIS   Yes.

ISHBEL   What you going to do Sis?

SIS   I don't know. I really don't know.

ISHBEL   Time you was married. You could easy find someone.

SIS   I don't think I ever will marry Ish. Some people never do.
ISHBEL   So what? You going to live here by yourself till the day you die?
SIS   Why not? *(Sound of far away laughter, clinking glasses.)*
ISHBEL *(Into audience)* Oh. Take me with you. Please.
SIS   You got to have a ticket. *(Pause. Both girls look out into audience.)*
ISHBEL *(Laughing)* He got her legs.
SIS   An' that one coming up behind her. She ain't seen him yet. *(Calling out)* Watch out!
ISHBEL   Too late. In the water. *(They both laugh. Pause.)*
SIS *(Looking up)* Is the sky beautiful like this all over the world?
ISHBEL *(Looking up. Slight pause)* Look to me like it going rain.
SIS   Can I listen again?
ISHBEL   Oh girl can't you leave me alone? Every minute you want to listen to me belly.
SIS   Just this last time. Please.
ISHBEL *(Relenting)* All right. But this is the very last time y'hear?
SIS puts her ear to ISHBEL'S stomach. A loud bang, as from a gun is heard. A woman screams. SIS sits up quickly. Far off, laughter is heard - male and female, a woman screeching with laughter. SIS and ISHBEL look out into bay and laugh too. The long deep mournful hoot from the ship is heard again. Their laughter dies. They look out into the audience. Lights down.

ACT TWO, SCENE 3
Lights up outside LEN'S house. LEN is reading a book. MINDA watches him.

MINDA   What you reading? *(Shows her the cover. Pause)* Politics?
LEN   Uh-huh? *(Pause)*
MINDA   It interesting?
LEN   Mmmmmm.
MINDA   Let me see. *(LEN gives her the book. She reads)* You understand this?
LEN   Well enough.
MINDA   It look like English but it read like another language.
LEN *(Smiling)* Dialectics.
MINDA   Oh. I feel like taking a walk. You want to come?
LEN   I want to finish this, but you go ahead.
MINDA   You sure?
LEN   Yes. Don' mind me. You go.

MINDA   In a minute. *(Pause)* What it like in England Len?

LEN   Why you want to know?

MINDA *(Shrugs)* Just interested. *(Slight pause)* Eh?

LEN   What?

MINDA   What it like?

LEN   Oh. You know.

MINDA   It same way like they say it is?

LEN   Yes. I suppose.

MINDA   In what way?

LEN   Minda, I'm trying to read.

MINDA   Sorry. *(MINDA sighs and rests her head back on her hands.)* You lucky to have those books.

LEN   What?

MINDA   You lucky you got something to fill your life. I ain't got nuttin'.

LEN   Min.

MINDA   Take me to England, Len.

LEN   What?

MINDA   I want to see the place for meself.

LEN   You can't go to England just like that, just for a holiday. An' I certainly ain't going to live there.

MINDA   Why not? There must be plenty opportunities there, Len. They crying out for people. You see it all over the island now. You could get a good job. We'd live in a nice house an' have children. Two. A boy an' a girl.

LEN   We can do that here.

MINDA   No. No we can't. Is all the same here. I don't want to die without seeing the world Len.

LEN   England ain't the world Minda.

MINDA   Is part of it and I want to go there.

LEN   Minda, we ain't going nowhere. I don't want to talk about it.

(STANLEY enters)

STANLEY Hello Missus. *(Seeing LEN he stops)* Afternoon Len. How you keeping?

LEN   Fine. An' yourself?

STANLEY Oh. Same way as ever, you know. I see you still reading.

LEN   Yes, still reading man.

STANLEY *(To MINDA)* Your husband going die with a book in him hands, Minda. You must be proud a him. You married the brightest man on the island.

LEN   Just because I read books don't mean to say I'm bright, Stan.

STANLEY Brighter than me anyhow. I can't remember the last time I read a book.

LEN   Is good to see you Stan. Where you bin hiding? What you bin doing wit yourself?

STANLEY Oh. The usual you know. I ain't interrupting nuttin' am I?

MINDA   You ain't interrupting nuttin'.

STANLEY Well you see, the reason why I'm here is that I was passing by an' me auntie tell me to drop by an' deliver a message to Minda.

MINDA   You auntie?

STANLEY Yes. You know what the woman like, always organising something. Well, now she organising a picnic.

MINDA   A picnic?

STANLEY Right up Peggy Hill. She ask a whole heap a woman if them want to come. She say she would be pleased to see you there, Minda.

MINDA   You aunty ask me? On a picnic?

STANLEY Yes.

LEN   That's kind of her, to remember you Minda.

STANLEY Minda very popular wit me auntie. You comin' Minda?

MINDA   I don't know.

LEN   You see how women stay? Before you come by Stan, if the woman wasn' begging me say how we should get around, see more things. Now, when she got the chance she can't make up her mind. You know where she want me to take her Stan?

STANLEY Where?

LEN   England.

STANLEY England? You joking? *(To MINDA)* England a long way away you know Minda.

LEN   Is what I tell her.

STANLEY Well, if he won't give you Englan', why not take Peggy Hill?

LEN   Sounds like a good idea to me Min. *(STANLEY standing behind LEN holds tickets from previous scene up to MINDA.)*

STANLEY So. You make up you mind? You coming?

MINDA *(She hesitates, then)* Yes. *(MINDA and STANLEY look at each other. LEN doesn't notice.)*

LEN   There, you see, an outing. An' you don't even have to leave the island for it.

STANLEY Well I leave you two then. So I can tell me auntie that you coming?

LEN   She'll be there.

STANLEY And don't worry Len, they bring her back by evening.
LEN Take care Stanley. An' thanks. *(STANLEY exits)* That man certainly change a lot.
MINDA What?
LEN Him used to be something of a wild man. Cock-a-leg Stanley they used to call him. *(MINDA lowers her head.)*
MINDA I think I go inside Len.
LEN What about you walk.
MINDA I feel a little tired.
LEN You go inside then. Get some rest. *(She starts to move.)* Minda.
MINDA Yes.
LEN If you want a new frock for the outing we'll go into town an' get you one, all right?
MINDA All right. *(She exits. LEN, smiling, shakes his head, takes up book and continues to read. Lights down.)*

ACT TWO, SCENE 4

Lights up outside LEN'S house. Midnight. Owl hoots. CHARLIE sits outside dressed in night attire. He's totally absorbed in picking up signals on his radio. He hears a rustle. He stops, looks up, listens. Nothing. Rustle is heard again. STANLEY steps out of the shadows carrying an old suitcase.

STANLEY *(Whispering)* What the hell you doing here boy?
CHARLIE Picking up special codes on me radio.
STANLEY At this time a night? Boy you mad or something?
CHARLIE This is the best place. The signal's clearer here.
STANLEY You should be in bed.
CHARLIE So should you.
STANLEY Boy, somebody set you to spy on me or what?
CHARLIE I already tell you.
STANLEY Go home boy.
CHARLIE Why should I?
STANLEY *(Raising his hand to CHARLIE)* You cheek – *(An owl hoots. STANLEY stands still and places suitcase on ground. He cups his hands and blows into them. Nothing happens.)*
CHARLIE What you doing?
STANLEY Now look boy, you ain't seen nuttin' that happen tonight y'hear me?
CHARLIE Why should I keep your secrets?

STANLEY Because – oh look boy, here. *(Dips into his pocket and takes out coin.)* Take this. Now you keep you mouth shut, all right?

CHARLIE Yes sir, no one going hear anything from me.

STANLEY *(Marching up and down, agitated.)* What time is it?

CHARLIE How should I know?

STANLEY You in the scouts ain't you? Can't you tell by the stars or something? *(He stops and blows into his hands again. Nothing happens. An owl hoots.)* Listen, you're a clever little boy. Can you make that sound.

CHARLIE Which sound? *(Owl hoots again.)*

STANLEY That sound.

CHARLIE Oh that. That's easy.

STANLEY Well then do it. Three times. Quick. *(CHARLIE doesn't move.)* Go on boy. Three times. Now.

CHARLIE Why should I?

STANLEY Oh God, what the backside... Look boy. *(Fishes in his pockets. Takes out coin.)* Here.

CHARLIE Thank you Stanley. *(He cups his hands into his mouth)*

STANLEY Three times. *(CHARLIE hoots like an owl three times, pause. STANLEY watches house. Nothing)* Again boy.

CHARLIE I'm only a little boy. This sorta thing ain't no good for me health.

STANLEY *(Agitated)* Go on. Quick. *(CHARLIE hoots again. Pause)* What the backside going on? One more time boy. *(MINDA enters from the house. She's wearing her nightdress and carries suitcase.)* Where the hell you bin?

MINDA I was waiting for the signal. Three hoots you said. I heard about a hundred.

STANLEY Never mind. You here now, come on let's go.

MINDA Hold on, Stanley.

STANLEY What now?

MINDA *(Noticing CHARLIE who, as usual, is staring.)* What he doing here?

STANLEY Standing guard for us. Ain't that right Charlie boy?

MINDA What's wrong with you boy? Don't you even sleep?

STANLEY Don't mind him. Let's go.

MINDA Wait. I got to get dressed.

STANLEY Get dressed? We ain't got no time for that.

MINDA It won't take a minute.

STANLEY Backside.

MINDA You got the tickets?

STANLEY *(Pats his jacket pocket.)* Safe and sound.

MINDA   England here I come. Here, hold this. *(She hands a bag to STANLEY.)*

STANLEY What's this?

MINDA   Money.

STANLEY Money? Where you get it from?

MINDA   Twist foot thought he could hide it from me. Idiot. This could help us out when we arrive. Tell that boy to turn his head. He makes me nervous.

STANLEY Charlie. Hurry up Min. *(MINDA takes off her nightdress. Underneath she's dressed up to the nines.)*

MINDA   How do I look?

STANLEY Beautiful.

MINDA   You sure?

STANLEY You look like a queen already.

MINDA *(Putting on shoes.)* I don't want those English folk to think I'm any the worse.

STANLEY You look like the Queen a Sheba, don't she boy?

CHARLIE *(Turning round)* She look like a maypole.

MINDA   Stanley, I'm scared.

STANLEY What?

MINDA   I want to say goodbye.

STANLEY Goodbye? To who?

MINDA   I might never be coming back again.

STANLEY Quick. Time running out.

MINDA   Goodbye house. Goodbye Nana old woman. Goodbye Len.

STANLEY Goodbye Len. Let's go. *(Exit.)*

LEN *(Calling softly)* Minda. Minda is that you? *(To CHARLIE)* What's wrong? Can't you sleep Min? *(CHARLIE moves into the light.)* You!

CHARLIE Hello Len.

LEN   Boy, what you doing here this time a night?

CHARLIE The radio it –

LEN   You see Minda pass out here?

CHARLIE I ain't seen nuttin'.

LEN   Then where? How long you been out here? You sure you ain't seen anything.

CHARLIE Not a thing Len. *(NANA appears)*

NANA   What's going on out here?

CHARLIE Len looking for Minda.

LEN   I think she just gone out for a walk. You know how restless she was this evening. *(A clap of thunder is heard.)*

NANA   Come inside. It's going to rain.

LEN   What about Minda? She'll catch her death out here.

NANA   That girl will be all right. That sort always is. You sure she ain't inside or round the back?

LEN   Let me look. *(He exits)*

NANA   You staying out there all night?

CHARLIE I was listening for a signal.

NANA   What sort a signal?

CHARLIE An enemy signal. You never know when someone going to invade.

NANA   You think that anyone would want to invade this island?

CHARLIE Course.

NANA   You should be in bed.

CHARLIE So should you. *(SIS enters)*

SIS   Nana, have you seen my brother? I thought he might be –

NANA   See him there.

SIS   You little – wait till we get home Master Charlie. Boy sneak outa bed y' know Nana. This time a night.

CHARLIE I was only –

SIS   I don't want to hear anymore Charlie-tall-tales. Come on get you backside home. *(LEN enters)*

LEN   All her clothes are gone.

NANA   I knew it.

SIS   What's going on?

LEN   She's gone.

NANA   Good riddance.

LEN   Not a trace.

NANA   You better off without her.

SIS   Come on Charlie let's go.

LEN   Wait. The boy know something. You know where she is boy?

CHARLIE I don't know nothing.

LEN   Show me the notebook. You got something written down in there?

CHARLIE I don't know nothing.

LEN   Tell me boy.

SIS   Leave him. He's just a little boy.

LEN   He know something. *(He grabs hold of CHARLIE)* Tell me.

NANA   Take it easy boy.

SIS   Leave him alone. He doesn't know anything.

LEN *(He shakes CHARLIE.)* Tell me boy.

SIS *(Freeing her brother from LEN'S grasp)* Don't you touch him. You're mad. You should be ashamed of yourself roughing up a little boy like that. Y'all right, Charlie? *(CHARLIE nods)* Come on, let's go. *(LEN bows his head)*

SIS   If you really want to know, she's gone away to England.

LEN   England?

SIS   With Stanley.

NANA   Time you waste watching over me making sure I don't run away you shoulda been watching you own wife.

SIS   They be on their way by now.

NANA   What else you expect from a girl like that?

LEN   Why didn't you tell me?

SIS   You wouldna listened.

NANA   That girl really dumbfounded you with love nonsense Len. *(Sound of ship is heard. A farewell hoot, as it were. Silence. Lightning. A blast of thunder.)* You can't stay out here. Come inside.

SIS   In a minute. You go in Charlie.

CHARLIE I don't want to. I want to stay with you.

SIS   I said go in Charlie. Just do what I tell you. *(NANA and CHARLIE exit. Thunder blast.)* Why don't it rain? *(Pause)* You can cry if you want to.

LEN   What's the use in crying?

SIS   You're like the storm. I can feel that rain needs to fall but all it is is thunder and lightning. I can feel all the thunder inside but you won't let it out.

LEN   I loved her.

SIS   Did you?

LEN   She made me feel useful. She came to me. She asked me to look after her. She needed my protection. Mine. She made me feel special.

SIS   She was good at that. *(Sighs)* Maybe she'll come back. Maybe she'll get bored.

LEN   I'm done with dreams.

SIS   You always was a dreamer.

LEN   No more.

SIS   Sometimes it's good to make-believe. Then you don't expect too much. That way you hardly ever get disappointed.

LEN   You're a funny girl.

SIS   What will you do now?

LEN   Pick up the pieces. Carry on. What else can I do?

SIS   Cry.

LEN   No.

SIS   Why it don't rain?

LEN   She thought I was so strong. The conquering hero. And I tried so hard to live up to it for her. *(He laughs)* What a fool I musta looked to she. What a fake. I got something to tell you.

SIS   What?

LEN   I never involved in the war, you know. I mean, I never fought. The nearest I get to a gun was pushing bullets through a machine factory in Liverpool.

SIS   What?

LEN   I worked in a munitions factory.

SIS   A factory?

LEN   You shocked?

SIS   Now ain't the time for making jokes, Len.

LEN   I'm not joking Sis, is true.

SIS   Well, if it is true how you get you limp eh? Tell me that?

LEN   A piece a machinery fall on me foot.

SIS   No jerry gun shot.

LEN   No jerry.

SIS   Jesus God.

LEN   When I come back everybody was treating me like a hero. I couldn't disappoint them.

SIS   You mean to say you make up all them stories? *(LEN nods, CHARLIE enters.)*

CHARLIE I want to go home now Sis.

SIS   Well you can't. Get yourself inside. Poor Charlie.

LEN   He don't have to know.

SIS   No. *(Slight pause)* I'm glad in a way, you mighta get kill.

LEN   I was Sis. In a way.

SIS *(Reflectively)* I always liked listening to you.

LEN   They wouldn't work beside us, they didn't want to pay us what we were worth, they even went on strike to get rid of us. We forgot where the real war was because we were fighting one right there.

SIS   Len?

LEN   You ever been in a boat?

SIS   You know I never.

LEN   You get sick, I tell you. Not only because you can feel the sea moving in you belly but love sick with desire for the place you going to and heartbroken for the place you leave behind. I couldn't sleep I was so excited. Two a the other men force me to drink half a bottle a rum and I sleep for two whole days. When I wake up I couldn't hear a sound. Even the sea was quiet. I went up on deck an' everyone was there, jus' standing there looking out – an' there it was. A grey-blue sky wit a mass a pure white chalk stretch across it. Englan'.

SIS I woulda like to see that. *(Pause)*

LEN *(Quietly)* You see, Sis we got a duty to work, to make something of this world here by ourselves. It's true Sis. *(Pause)*

SIS Len, I got something to tell you too.

LEN What?

SIS I don't know how to say it... I'm going away.

LEN What?

SIS To study. Mrs. Walker give Momma a live-in job so I'm leaving.

LEN You Sis?

SIS I made up me mind. I can't change the world if I'm ignorant.

LEN Whas' happening tonight eh?

SIS You not dreaming Len.

LEN First Minda, now you. *(LEN sits awhile then laughs)*

SIS Don't laugh at me.

LEN I'm not laughing at you Sis. I'll miss you. *(CHARLIE has come out. He stands briskly and stiffly to attention. He carries a stick. He wheels around and marches sturdily across stage then back again. He repeats whole process. He stamps to attention again and brings the rifle down to waist level, changes sides then places rifle on the ground. standing easy. Another loud clap of thunder, a flash of lightning. It starts to pour with rain. SIS puts her cardigan over her head.)* Come, we better get inside.

SIS Why?

LEN It's raining.

SIS I want to stay out here. *(LEN turns to Charlie)*

LEN Attenshun! *(CHARLIE stands stiff, to SIS)* You'll get wet.

SIS I don't care. *(LEN shrugs and exits with CHARLIE. SIS alone on stage)* Let it rain, Len.

The End.

Monsoon

Monsoon started off as a poem called *Menstrual Monsoon*. The monsoon in India is associated with the colour red and I drew parallels with the cranky feeling everyone has in the summer heat waiting for the monsoon to change the climate and rejuvenate the earth, and the feeling of P.M.T., waiting for our blood to release us from the torment of our hormones and to begin the cycle of life again.

I decided to submit a play for the B B.C. Young Playwrights' Festival. Writing the play became a spiritual journey for me as I researched the spiritual cycles of life, weather, love and death. The poem expanded and became the narrative thread and spiritual journey of the play, a kind of thread of wisdom linking the themes of the play.

In *Monsoon,* I wanted to explore taboos, women's menstruation and sexuality. My inspiration came from my own life and other women's. Most of the things in the play really happened to us; some of it is based on my experiences of having my period in India. During the research I spent many days staring at a map of the onset of the South East Monsoon, looking for clues and insights. Some days I don't know where the writing came from. The ghosts of many women touched my pen.

Monsoon wouldn't have been possible without the producer/director Frances Ann Solomon, who put faith and hard work into making my drafts into a play. She supported and encouraged me to write beyond the boundaries – to be experimental and innovative in telling the story. On radio, it becomes a tapestry of sound, erotic and evocative. The finished play was all that I could have imagined and more.

The play has been played at Highways in Los Angeles and extracts read as part of my performance poetry. I have made an experimental film using the poem, discovering new images and ways of exploring our menstruation and sexuality.

Monsoon caused a storm with the establishment. *The Sunday Telegraph* responded with an article entitled *The Heavens Have Opened*. There appears to have been too much blood and lesbianism in the play. I hope so because there's not enough everywhere else.

Maya Chowdhry

MONSOON

Maya Chowdhry

CHARACTERS:

JALAARNAVA	Lolita Chakrabarti
NUSRAT	Shaheen Khan
MASSI/SAMEERAH/	
VOICE OF ALL WOMEN	Yasmin Sidhwa
KAVITAA/TANYA	Nina Wadia
YOUTH HOSTEL OWNER/	
PORTER/VENDORS	Neran Persaud
COMPOSER	Veyatummal Chandran
SINGER	Gopa Bose
MUSICIANS	Punita Gupta and
	Veyatummal Chandran

ACT ONE, SCENE 1

Woman's voice singing. Mix to –

POET *(Slow, loud and clear, with the emphasis of reciting a poem, slight reverb.)* The birth of Maya
the beginning of time
I cannot see my growing
the new moon in my eyes.

(Monsoon rain.)

Spring to summer
I shout and scream
can find no peace
everything is too big and small
all at once.

SCENE 2

Cut to Interior Indian train carriage, sound of others in carriage, mix to –

JALAARNAVA   I didn't imagine it like this.
KAVITAA   What, so crowded?

JALAARNAVA   No, I mean that it would be so, so beautiful, that one minute there'd be palm trees and rivers, and then flat, flat plains stretched so far into the shimmer of heat in the distance.

KAVITAA *(Laughs)* Shut up, you sound like something out of 'Heat and Dust'.

JALAARNAVA *(Laughs)*

KAVITAA   Yeah, it is amazing, better than Spain any day. I'm glad we didn't have to ride on the roof.

JALAARNAVA   Don't be so ignorant, you watch too much telly.

KAVITAA   No I don't.

JALAARNAVA   There's no comparison Kavitaa. Oh! Station coming up, you run out and get the water this time, here's the bottle.

KAVITAA   Oh no, you go, I'm too young, they'll shove me out of the way and we'll end up with no water.

JALAARNAVA   They won't, go, go!

(Train pulling into station, noise of station platform grows louder. Voices shouting, people chattering.)

CHAI WALLAH *(Crying)* Chai, chai, chai.

KHAANAA WALLAH *(Crying)* Chaat, pakori, samosi.

JALAARNAVA *(Shouting)* Kavitaa, get some chaat.

SCENE 3

Ext. Chandigarh railway station. Sound of people and trains. Sound of a bag being pulled from carriage and landing with a thud on concrete platform. Music - Shelia Chandra.

KAVITAA *(Singing)* You must by my lucky star... Where's auntie? Late like her birthday cards. I'm boiling, it's so hot. No more drizzly London rain for three months.

JALAARNAVA   Not 'til the monsoon and then you'll wish you were back in London.

KAVITAA   We can go home before then.

JALAARNAVA   It depends, I like the idea of the monsoon, I might want to stay for it.

KAVITAA   Well you're mad, I'm not...

PORTER *(Interrupting)* Madam, one rupee carry your bag?

JALAARNAVA   No thanks. *(Under her breath)* Where is she?

KAVITAA *(Excitedly shouting)* Auntie, auntie, over here.

MASSI *(Shouting)* Jalaamava, Kavitaa. *(Walks towards them and hugs them.)* Beti.

JALAARNAVA   Namaste Chandaa Massi.
KAVITAA Hello auntie Chandaa.
MASSI   How was the journey? Chalo, let's go. You must be tired.

SCENE 4
*Int. room of Indian concrete house, facing onto front yard. with shutters
closed. Sound of fan whirring. Intermittent sounds of unpacking of luggage.*

KAVITAA What's this, your diary?
JALAARNAVA   No, it's my menstrual diary.
KAVITAA *(Giggles)* What does E and I mean?
JALAARNAVA   I plot how I'm feeling, my menstrual cycle, E is for days of
   high energy level, and I for days of irritability.
KAVITAA *(Exclaims)* Irritability, that's today.
JALAARNAVA   Very funny.
KAVITAA Anyway, what do you want to know all that for?
JALAARNAVA   So I know when to stay away from everyone. *(Laughs)* No,
   really, it's just to help predict things, so I know good times to do things.
KAVITAA Like what?
JALAARNAVA   Well, travelling for a start, the hot season and periods
   don't mix.
KAVITAA Why, cause you've got to take the bucket with you?
JALAARNAVA   What bucket?
KAVITAA You know, the bucket.
JALAARNAVA   Kavitaa, what are you talking about?
KAVITAA The bucket for the blood.
JALAARNAVA   You wear a towel, what do you mean the bucket for the
   blood?
KAVITAA Meera told me, she said, when you sit on the toilet it overflows,
   so you have to sit over a bucket to catch the blood.
JALAARNAVA *(Laughing)* It's only a little blood, how do you imagine you
   could produce so much blood for a bucket?
KAVITAA *(Indignantly)* I don't know, that's what she told me.

SCENE 5
*Ext. Market. Sound of town traffic, rickshaws, cars, hooters blowing, bicycle
bells ringing, people chatting, vendors shouting.*

MASSI   This is the old market, anything you want you can get here.
KAVITAA Anything, even Madonna tapes?

MASSI *(Laughs)* You want a drink.

JALAARNAVA   Yeah, I'm so hot and thirsty.

(Int. small on-street cafe, street sounds outside. Sound of fan whirring.)

VENDOR   Han ji.

MASSI   Teen nimbo pani.

KAVITAA   What's that?

MASSI   Wait and see.

(Glasses on formica table and water from jug being poured.)

KAVITAA *(Chanting quietly)* nimbo, nimbo, nimbo pani.

JALAARNAVA *(Smacks lips and sighs)* Sugary lemon, is that what it is?

MASSI   I shouldn't really let you drink the water, it's been such a dry spring, when water's scarce you don't know where they got it from, it's dry from here to Kashmir.

JALAARNAVA   I'd like to go to Kashmir.

MASSI   Well, maybe we could all go for a week next month.

JALAARNAVA   I mean on my own.

MASSI   It's not possible, you can't go alone.

JALAARNAVA   Why not? Mum would let me.

MASSI   It's not safe, you can't go and that's it.

SCENE 6

Int. room of Indian concrete house, facing onto front yard, with shutters closed. Sound of fan whirring.

KAVITAA   It's not fair, I'm going to be really bored here on my own.

JALAARNAVA   Well you can't come and that's it. Anyway, Massi won't let you, and I can't be responsible for you.

KAVITAA   Massi says you can't go either.

JALAARNAVA   Well she won't know, will she?

KAVITAA   She'll find out.

JALAARNAVA   No she won't, unless you tell her.

KAVITAA   Well, what's it worth?

JALAARNAVA   Get lost, I'm the reason you're here in the first place, I persuaded mum to let you come. Come on, don't fall out now, I'm about to leave.

KAVITAA   Huh, *(Tuts)* well you better write.

ACT TWO, SCENE 1

Montage S.F.X. of JAL leaving, train pulling out of station, whizzing through landscape. Then steady hum of travel by bus and arrival in the busy Srinagar bus station. These effects develop under JAL'S voice over.

JALAARNAVA   Dear Kavitaa *(Deep exhalation)* it's much, much cooler here, though I thought I was going to cook on the train for the first part of the journey from Chandigarh to Jammu. Actually I felt like a toasted sandwich, it was so crammed full, so much for the seat reservation on the Tourist Quota. Kashmir is more beautiful than I imagined – so wild and green, the mountains encircling the vale and rising up further than I can imagine. I'm writing this from the roof of the Youth Hostel. It's 5 o'clock and there's a gentle breeze nuzzling my paper so it flutters while I'm writing.

(Mix to Ext. Roof of youth hostel in quiet area of town, intermittent sounds of fountain pen scratching on paper, writing quickly throughout next section. Music – light tapping of tabla to sound chatty.)

JALAARNAVA   I haven't done any exploring yet but I will tomorrow, my period's here and I've got cramps, so I'll go now. Say hello to everyone. Sending my love. Jal, kiss, kiss, kiss.
(Piece of paper being folded and put into an envelope. Atmos. continues then fades out. Mix to tabla playing a rhythm denoting a build up of tension. Fade out.)

ACT TWO, SCENE 2

Int. room of youth hostel. Sound of pages of a notebook being turned over. Intermittent scribbling sounds of a pen writing in a notebook. Music – flute opens out to reflect her emotional inner life.

JALAARNAVA *(Groaning with period pain)* April 3rd. I have exchanged the dry city dust of Chandigarh for the cool mountain breeze of Kashmir. This is the real beginning of my journey. Today my period is heavy, I feel under a great weight.

(Transition to poem. Mix to sound of the tabla. Faint, light rhythm, sound increases. Mix to –)

POET   I feel wet and heavy
          I feel bloated
          and weak

I sense gravity
claiming my ocean of blood,
stained sheets
menstrual madness
bringing me closer
to the earth.
(Fade out music)

ACT TWO, SCENE 3
Int. corridor in youth hostel. Sound of feet in chappals on stone floor clicking.

JALAARNAVA *(Hindi, approaching)* Pani daido?
WARDEN *(Hindi)* Pani pina?
JALAARNAVA   Nahin: pani daido, er, not drinking, washing, samajh, understand?
WARDEN*(Hindi)* Pani pina?
JALAARNAVA   Oh never mind, dhanyavaad, thanks. *(Sighs deeply and groans)* Ooh.
(Feet in chappals clicking on stone floor moving off along corridor.)

ACT TWO, SCENE 4
Int. room in youth hostel. Intermittent sounds of fountain pen scratching on paper, writing quickly throughout next section. Music – light tap of letter writing tabla.

JALAARNAVA   P.S. I arrived at the Youth Hostel and found there was no water 'til evening. I sat on the edge of the bed, blood dry and crusted between my thighs. In my menstrual diary I wrote 'heavy period'.
(Pages of a notebook being turned over. Music – flute opens out into menstrual diary.)
April 4th: I've got a bag full of tampons and towels and my blood dried out, wrapped in newspaper and brown paper bags. I heard a story about a woman from England who just threw them on the rubbish tip each day, only when she came back one day she saw a pig grunting and chewing with a small blood-stained string hanging from its mouth. I sneak out in the afternoon when everyone is asleep and go down a back lane to make a small fire, throwing them on one by one – a ceremony of blood to ashes.

ACT TWO, SCENE 5
Int. room in youth hostel. Sound of footsteps approaching on wooden floor.

TANYA   Hello, I'm Tanya.
JALAARNAVA   I'm Jal.
TANYA   You on holiday?
JALAARNAVA   Yeah, sort of, are you?
TANYA   Well I'm on another of my expeditions.
JALAARNAVA   Oh. You on your own?
TANYA   Yes, are you?
JALAARNAVA   Sort of. Have you travelled alone before?
TANYA   Oh yeah, all the time.
JALAARNAVA   Oh.
TANYA   You're Indian aren't you? I didn't think Indians stayed here.
JALAARNAVA   What do you mean?
TANYA   Well, it's a bit basic isn't it.
JALAARNAVA   What do you expect for seven rupees?
TANYA   This I suppose. Er, do you want to go and eat?
JALAARNAVA   Okay, where shall we go?
TANYA   Oh, I thought you'd know.
JALAARNAVA   Why, I've never been here before.
TANYA *(Surprised)* You've never been to India?
JALAARNAVA   No, I've never been to Kashmir.

ACT TWO, SCENE 6
Cut to exterior. Market sound, faint traffic noises, bicycles going past, rickshaws and cars, voices near and far chattering in Kashmiri.

TANYA   What about here? It smells nice.
JALAARNAVA   No, the food doesn't look that good, let's try somewhere else.
TANYA   Oh really, I think this is fine and it'll suit my budget, I'm trying to last as long as I can before asking for some more money to be telexed out. My mother's made an arrangement with Lloyds.
JALAARNAVA   Well, it's best not to eat at the very cheapest place, you have to be used to it. I'm not.
YOUNG WOMAN *(Begging/whining)* Behn, Behn...
TANYA   Go away. *(Pauses)* Well I've hardened myself, I can eat anywhere, this isn't the cheapest anyhow. Let's have those triangular pastries with spicy vegetables in.

JALAARNAVA *(Tuts)* Oh, all right.

MAN   Han ji?

JALAARNAVA   Do, dena, *(Pauses)* dhanyavaad.

(Sound of paper wrapping food and it being handed to someone, then unwrapping noises and eating noises of someone crunching a snack, sound of market and street in background. Voices begin to fade out.)

TANYA   Mmm, really hot.

JALAARNAVA   Let's go back this way.

TANYA   O.K.

ACT TWO, SCENE 7

Int. room in youth hostel. Sound of pen writing on paper. Music – light tabla imitating writing.

JALAARNAVA   Dear Kavitaa, I'm writing this from the prison cell, oh I mean, my room in the Youth Hostel. I can't stand it much longer, I'm going to go and look for somewhere else tomorrow. There's this English tourist who gives me the third degree all the time. I mean I don't mind having someone to go out and eat with, but I get indigestion listening to her going on all the time about how amazing this is, how wonderful the people are and so colourful, such interesting habits... you can imagine... *(Groan)*

(Paper falling on the floor and footsteps running across floor and out of door.)

ACT TWO, SCENE 8

Int. toilet in youth hostel. Sound of person being sick down toilet. Toilet flushes, sound of tap running, washing face. Footsteps approaching. Knock on door.

TANYA *(Through door)* Jal, are you all right?

JALAARNAVA *(Groaning, weakly)* No, go away.

(Tabla music. Mix to Poet)

POET   From the darkness of this cave
               I wait noon to noon
               for the moon-dew
               under a lowering monsoon sky.

ACT THREE, SCENE 1

Ext. boulevard of lake. Sound of water lapping the side of the lake wall. Faint traffic noises in the distance, sounds of people out and about.

MEN'S VOICES Madam, come with me. Madam I have best price. Madam, come for ride with me.

JALAARNAVA No, no, go away.

NUSRAT Jao, jao, jao! Are you okay?

JALAARNAVA Yes. *(Under breath)* Bloody men.

NUSRAT Are you lost?

JALAARNAVA No, I was just wondering what to do next, I'm looking for somewhere to stay, I've been staying at this Youth Hostel, it was really bad.

NUSRAT *(Laughs)* Well you won't find it by staring into the lake.

JALAARNAVA Very funny, do you have a better idea?

NUSRAT You're looking at one – have you thought about staying on a houseboat?

JALAARNAVA Sounds like a great idea, how do I find out about it?

NUSRAT We have one, want to come and see it? I'll take you there. Come, I have a boat.

(Distant women's voices getting onto boat. Sound of feet stepping into rowing boat. NUSRAT shouts 'Give me your hand', JAL goes 'Aaahhh' as she almost tips overboard, then sound of boat moving out into lake, and oars.)

NUSRAT Sit up there, it's safer.

(Women's voices receding. Music – lake music, beginning of relationship. Waves on boat and sound of oars in water.)

ACT THREE, SCENE 2

Cut to ext. boat on lake. Sound of water on side of rowing boat and splashing sound of oars pushing in water throughout next section. Music – lake music weaves in and out.

NUSRAT Have you come here alone?

JALAARNAVA Yes.

NUSRAT *(Surprised)* Come to India alone?

JALAARNAVA No, with my sister, she's in Chandigarh. It's beautiful here, I love the mountains all around. What a place to live.

NUSRAT It's not safe to travel alone here you know.

JALAARNAVA   Yeah, my massi said that too. It was okay, I don't mind, people were really friendly.

NUSRAT   Not married?

JALAARNAVA   No.

NUSRAT   Me neither.

JALAARNAVA   The lake is like something from a picture book, with the rushes and all these lilies.

NUSRAT   How old are you?

JALAARNAVA   Nineteen.

NUSRAT   I thought so, me too.

ACT THREE, SCENE 3
Small boat hitting the side of houseboat. Sound of a rope being thrown onto the boat and the two women stepping out.

NUSRAT   This is it, you better give me your hand. Ummi, *(Shouting)* Ummi.

TWINS *(Laughing)* Nusrat aaai, Nusrat aaai.

SAMEERAH   Choph rho.

NUSRAT   Ummi, visitor aaai hai. This is my mother and these are the twins.

TWINS   Hello *(Giggle)*

JALAARNAVA   Hello, nice to meet you.

SAMEERAH   Yes hello, come, look, tea.

NUSRAT   Neh, phela kamre dekona. Come I'll show you the room.
   (Footsteps along wooden corridor of houseboat to room. Door to room opening. The women go inside.)

JALAARNAVA   Oh. *(Appreciation)*

NUSRAT   It's really quiet, the twins sleep up in the back. Do you like it?

JALAARNAVA   Yes, really nice, how much?

NUSRAT   Not much. *(Shouting)* Ummi, kitna paisa hai?

SAMEERAH *(Shouting)* Bis rupee.

NUSRAT *(Laughs)* Come on, come and have some tea.
   (Sound of tea being poured into a cup.)

ACT THREE, SCENE 4
Int. room in houseboat. S.F.X. writing. Music – tabla imitating writing.

JALAARNAVA   Dear Kavitaa, you'll never guess where I am now. In the middle of the lake staying on a houseboat. It's beautiful here. I met a woman at the lakeside, and she must have needed the money, there's just her and her mother and her two sisters, they live in the back part of the boat and rent out the room at the front. It's like a floating hotel. Her name's Nusrat.

(Sound of writing and paper being folded. Footsteps along wooden corridor outside the door. Knock on door.)

JALAARNAVA *(Shouting)* Oh, Nusrat, is that you?

(Sound of door opening. NUSRAT looks in.)

NUSRAT Hi, how are you?

JALAARNAVA Are you going into town? Would you mind getting me some stamps and posting this? Could you also get me some more writing paper too, here's the money. *(Pause, NUSRAT doesn't respond, then takes money and letter.)* Is that O.K?

NUSRAT Fine.

(Sound of door closing. Writing resumes. Music – tabla imitating writing.)

JALAARNAVA She's the same age as me, she seems really nice, but I think she thinks I'm very westemised and naive about India, which is true. Her mother Sameerah (it means story-teller) spoke to me in English and I answered in Hindi, I think she was really confused. I'm not English, I don't know why everyone keeps thinking I am...

(City. Sound of people shouting market sounds. Mix to mountain bird-song, sound of JAL alone walking in mountains. Music – tabla, chatty writing sounds building up through letter.)

JALAARNAVA P.S. I'm sorry you felt so pissed off with me about coming here alone. I needed time, it's not that easy to forget Tony. It's been hard keeping it all in and not being able to tell anyone. I didn't want to say anything before, in case you told mum. I know by the time you get this letter you'll understand. Sending my love, Jal, kiss, kiss, kiss.

(Lake, sound of houseboat rocking and scribbling on paper. Music – diary music, inner thoughts, flute building and falling.)

April 11. I'm floating, living in a place of water and dreams, I am living with silence and coldness. The April sun cannot penetrate.

(Footsteps. Writing sound stops.)

SAMEERAH *(Approaching)* Chai pina?

JALAARNAVA Ji nehin.

SAMEERAH Chai lao, hot tea make you cool.

JALAARNAVA O.K. *(Tea being poured)* I can pour.

SAMEERAH   Nehin: pardeshi nehin: kardhi.
   *(Tea being drunk. Music – diary music, inner thoughts, flute building
   and falling.)*

JALAARNAVA   April 12. I am being fed and nurtured by women. My
   solitude is disallowed, frowned upon. I want to be alone. April 19. It is not
   a secret that I am lost. I am not keeping it from myself. The lake and
   mountains enclose me, are silent, do not answer my questions.

ACT THREE, SCENE 5
Int. room on houseboat. Sound of sewing-machine.

JALAARNAVA *(Shouting from outside room)* Is Nusrat here?
SAMEERAH   She's working.
JALAARNAVA   Oh, what you sewing?
SAMEERAH   For shop.
JALAARNAVA   Shop?
SAMEERAH   Meena's Designs.
JALAARNAVA   On the Broadway, I know it. *(Pauses)* I thought this was
   your business, this houseboat?
SAMEERAH   Yes, not much money, repairs, repairs, then only summer
tourist come. *(Machine stops)* Come look, you like? **JALAARNAVA**   Oh,
they're really beautiful.
SAMEERAH   You want? They will look nice. See nice colours suit
   England. Suit your lovely fair skin.
JALAARNAVA   Yes, I'll take one for Kavitaa too.
SAMEERAH   60 rupees is price.
JALAARNAVA *(Surprised)* Oh... yes, of course, alright... *(Rustle of
   notes in hand. Machine starts again.)*
SAMEERAH   Women work hard. It same if daughter, if wife, if mother.

ACT THREE, SCENE 6
*Int. room in houseboat. Writing resumes, a fountain pen scratching paper,
writing quickly. Music – tabla rhythm of writing building with tension.*

JALAARNAVA   May 25. P.M.T. It's like waiting for the monsoon. I'm tired
   and cranky waiting to bleed, there's a war brewing up in my belly. It can
   make you go mad waiting for the monsoon.
   *(JAL in bath washing, splash of water, and satisfied gasp as cold water
   hits skin. Music – tabla imitating monsoon.)*

And it's so hot, I want the rain washing my hair. Headlines today say 'Floods in Bangladesh'.

ACT THREE, SCENE 7

Int. Bathroom on houseboat. Sound of water running and clothes being rinsed. Door is opened and NUSRAT looks around door.

NUSRAT   Sorry.

JALAARNAVA *(Startled)* Oh. *(Pauses)* Urn, I'm glad you're here, I was just corning to ask if you had any washing powder I could use, I've forgotten mine.

NUSRAT   Yes, I'll get some.

JALAARNAVA   Thanks, you don't have to go right now.

NUSRAT   It's O.K.

(Sound of footsteps walking away up corridor of houseboat. Cut to sound of clothes being scrubbed and splashed into a bucket of water.)

NUSRAT   What do you do?

JALAARNAVA   I'm going to University when I get back, to study medicine.

NUSRAT   Oh. *(Pauses)* Why do you wash your clothes like that?

JALAARNAVA   Like what?

NUSRAT   Leaving them in the dirty water like that.

JALAARNAVA   I'm soaking them, they're dusty from the bus last week.

NUSRAT *(Exclaims)* You've not washed clothes since you came?

JALAARNAVA   No, I couldn't, there was no water at the Youth Hostel *(Pauses)* and...

NUSRAT   Oh, what?

JALAARNAVA   Nothing. *(Pauses)* You don't like me do you?

NUSRAT   That's not true. I'm just fed up with tourists that's all.

JALAARNAVA   I'm not a tourist.

NUSRAT   Yes you are.

JALAARNAVA   I'm not like them though.

NUSRAT *(Laughing)* No, except for washing your clothes. Why don't you have a bath in that water while you're at it. Here's the soap.

(Sound of a bar of soap being thrown in the bucket with a splash.)

JALAARNAVA *(Laughing)* I'm soaked.

NUSRAT   Well you need a bath. Here, rinse off...

(Jug of water being thrown over JAL and splashing on wooden bathroom floor. JAL screams and laughs and splutters then tries to do the same back to NUSRAT.)

NUSRAT *(Laughing)* Missed. Jal, here, catch.
(Bucket of water being thrown over someone with a loud splash. Laughing and screaming.)
JALAARNAVA *(Breathlessly)* Are we even now?
NUSRAT *(Breathlessly)* Yeah, I suppose so. I have to go and work now, I better change first.
JALAARNAVA Well, *(Sighs)* do you want to drop in my room later?
NUSRAT Maybe.

ACT THREE, SCENE 8
Int. room on houseboat. Sound of writing on paper. Music – tabla imitating chatty letter writing.

JALAARNAVA Dear Kavitaa, I got your letter, just about the only excursion I've made recently was to collect it. I've recovered from the depression of last week, don't know why I felt so low, I'm okay now. Yesterday Nusrat skipped college and we rowed around the lake chatting. Her mum blew up at her, but she's really tough and wasn't bothered. I like Nusrat, she's really clear about things and makes me think. You'll like her too.

ACT THREE, SCENE 9
Writing in diary. Music – flute denoting inner thoughts and emotions.

JALAARNAVA June 1st. Heavy flow. I lie in agony, tossing from side to side, front to back. I keep getting up to go to the toilet, thinking I'm leaking but I'm not. I wake up at 4 a.m, my belly feels like lead, pinning me down on the bed. I feel a wetness and know I've spilled out onto the sheets. I stagger to my feet, cup my hand between my legs and tiptoe to the toilet. I bend over the sink with a jug of cold water and the soap and start scrubbing.

(Music – woman's voice and tabla symbolising the POET)

POET The heavens have opened
and my womb has shed her lining
and flows endlessly
for days.
The flesh of Durga
fighting for change
the hungry red earth heaving

and growing.
I cannot look at the sun,
or swim in the seas,
or speak,
or behold the altar fire
in the Temple of Durga
my womb sanctuary.

ACT THREE, SCENE 10

Ext. river bank. Dream sequence: slight reverb. throughout. Sound of rushing water, heavy monsoon rain, footsteps running in rain through deep puddles, heavy splashing. Music – lake music denoting change in relationship, imitating sound of monsoon. Cut to heavy sound of panting from woman running in rain.

JALAARNAVA *(Shouting)* Where are you, where are you? *(Landslide, earth falling into water, loud splashing sound of a woman falling into water, loud scream, splashing sounds of woman struggling in water, sound of woman rising and sinking in river, heavy rain and rushing of river.)*
(Shrieking) Help! Someone, help!
(Woman rising and sinking in river, sound of gasping and spluttering, heavy rain and rushing of river.)
JALAARNAVA *(Struggling)* Tony, Tony, it's me, help me...
(Woman rising and sinking in river, sound of gasping and spluttering, heavy rain and rushing of river.)
JALAARNAVA *(Weakly)* Tony, help me...
(River roaring, heavy sound of monsoon rain. Cut to. Int. room in houseboat. Sound of crickets.)
NUSRAT *(Loud whisper)* Jal, Jal, wake up, Jal.
JALAARNAVA   Oh, where am I, *(Pauses)* Nusrat?
NUSRAT   It's O.K. I'm here. What happened? You were shouting out.
JALAARNAVA   I'm so cold and wet.
NUSRAT   You're just sweating, it's so hot in here. There wrap yourself up. Come here, you're okay now.
JALAARNAVA   He let me drown.
NUSRAT   Who, who did?
JALAARNAVA   Oh. *(Pause)* No one, it was a dream.
NUSRAT   My grandmother always said that dreams were gifts to take us beyond our fears and show us the way.

ACT THREE, SCENE 11

Night crickets. Music – tabla imitating chatty letter writing.

JALAARNAVA Dear Kavitaa, it's 2 a.m. I couldn't sleep, so I just got up in the end. There's a fine mist across the lake, the water is still and flat, it makes you feel like you could just roll over it. Nusrat says the moon is Kali rising over the mountain and her fire lifts the mist...

ACT THREE, SCENE 12

Int. room on houseboat. Music – lake music denoting relationship changing. Sound of bare feet walking on wooden floor of houseboat. Door of room opens. Sound of writing stops.

JALAARNAVA Oh Nusrat I didn't think you were in, I thought you had lessons at the Mosque today?

NUSRAT No, not today. *(Pause)* There were floods today in Bangladesh.

JALAARNAVA Why?

NUSRAT Because of deforestation, I suppose.

JALAARNAVA No, I mean why can't you go to the Mosque?

NUSRAT You know.

JALAARNAVA What's wrong, are you tired?

NUSRAT No.

JALAARNAVA Who's prepared all the food already?

NUSRAT My sister.

JALAARNAVA Oh, I thought you always did it.

NUSRAT Not today.

JALAARNAVA Oh, were you too busy?

NUSRAT Sort of, *(Whispered)* it's my unclean day.

JALAARNAVA What, do you mean your period, why can't you cook?

NUSRAT It's not allowed.

JALAARNAVA I thought you didn't believe in all of that.

NUSRAT I've just been brought up like it, I can't help it.

JALAARNAVA That's rubbish.

NUSRAT Jal, shut up, someone might hear. Anyway, I don't mind, I like the rest and having some time to myself.

JALAARNAVA *(Pause)* Here, put your feet up, let me make you some tea.

NUSRAT Ummi wouldn't like it, she says visitors shouldn't.

JALAARNAVA Well don't tell her.

NUSRAT *(Giggles)* O.K.

JALAARNAVA Come on, have you got cramps? Let me rub your back.

NUSRAT   Yeah, that feels better.

ACT THREE, SCENE 13
Music – flute denoting inner thoughts.

JALAARNAVA   June 3rd. My dreams are of her blood, thick ruby red, it is flowing fast and heavy into the lake. I am swimming in the lake, I lift my hands from the water, they are stained in her blood, I cup them and drink deeply.
(Ext. top deck of boat. Sound of crickets. Close Up of intimate voices of two women. Music – lake music denoting intimacy in relationship)

JALAARNAVA   You know my Mum said I was special when my period started, that I was a woman now. I was shocked at the blood, but I liked being special. I started telling everyone I had my period, but mum told me to be quiet.

NUSRAT   I didn't think it was like that in Britain, I thought everyone was so liberal.

JALAARNAVA   Well, not my mum.

NUSRAT   I was never allowed to talk about it either. I told my mum I was bleeding, I thought I was going to die. She just said I was a woman now and not to tell anyone.

JALAARNAVA   Your hair's really soft, do you put oil in it?

NUSRAT   Mmmmm.

ACT THREE, SCENE 14
Writing in diary. Music – flute denoting inner thoughts.

JALAARNAVA   June 4th. Floating I dream of her. June 5th. Waking I dream of her. June 6th. I have no place for the feelings you generate in me. I want to tell you of my dreams but they are your taboos, my silence will not lift. I pull the petals from lilies and scatter them at your feet.

ACT THREE, SCENE 15
Int. JAL'S room in houseboat.

NUSRAT   Jal, Jal, wake up, wake up!

JALAARNAVA *(Groaning)* Nusrat, what's up, what time is it?

NUSRAT   Come on, wake up, let's go swimming.

JALAARNAVA   You're mad, go away, it's 5 a.m.

NUSRAT   Come on, the sun's up, it's beautiful out, just the right time for swimming.

JALAARNAVA *(Laughs)* O.K., O.K., I'm coming, pass my shalwaar kameez.

NUSRAT   Come on sleepy head. *(Scuffling and giggling)*

JALAARNAVA *(Laughing)* Dal Lake, here I come.

ACT THREE, SCENE 16

Ext. boat on lake. Sound of water lapping side of boat. Music – lake music denoting growth of relationship.

NUSRAT   Welcome to the floating gardens of Dal Lake.

JALAARNAVA   It's beautiful, Nusrat. Can you walk on it?

NUSRAT   Yeah, it's solid, the roots of the garden reach down into the lake.

JALAARNAVA   I never came across places like this when I was roaming around being a tourist.

NUSRAT   Where else do you want to go, ruins, temples, Mogul Gardens? *(Laughs)* Roll up, roll up for Nusrat's tours.

JALAARNAVA *(Laughs)* What next?

NUSRAT   How about a swim?

JALAARNAVA *(Shouts)* Nusrat! Aagh! *(JAL is thrown in water. NUSRAT laughing JAL splashing in water.)* Oh, it's lovely, come on in.

NUSRAT   O.K. *(NUSRAT dives into water. Sound of women swimming in lake, laughing and splashing.)*

JALAARNAVA   What are you going to do when you leave college?

NUSRAT   I'm going to marry a tailor, that way I can carry on with my designing and support my Ummi.

JALAARNAVA   You don't have to get married, follow Islam, stuff like that.

NUSRAT   It's fine. At least I don't have to get very involved with the man I marry, except to have children.

JALAARNAVA   Don't you like him?

NUSRAT   He's O.K., better than some, most men are bastards, they're just rude.

JALAARNAVA   I know. *(Pause)* I'm getting cold...

NUSRAT   I'll race you back.

(Splashing in water as they swim back.)

ACT THREE, SCENE 17

Ext. floating garden. Sound of water lapping. Close Up of Women lying down. Music –lake music denoting turn in relationship.

NUSRAT   Do you think you'd ever want to live here?

JALAARNAVA   I don't think I could. I would get really frustrated with the way women have to live, and with the levels of poverty.

NUSRAT   But what about you, what about what you really want?

JALAARNAVA *(Pause)* India's special to me, I love being here, but... I don't think it's enough.

NUSRAT   When are you leaving?

JALAARNAVA   I don't know. Soon. I wanted to leave before the monsoon.

NUSRAT   You could change your mind.

JALAARNAVA   I can't think about it now. *(Close Up sound)* Look, your fingers are all wrinkled from the water.

NUSRAT   Yes, come here.

JALAARNAVA   Nusrat...

NUSRAT   Mmm?

JALAARNAVA   ... I want to kiss you.

NUSRAT   I know.

(Music – lake music denoting climax in relationship. Sound of bodies moving together and slow passionate kiss. Music – woman singing.)

JALAARNAVA   She rose from
my fingers dipped into
her lips on
soft sweet brown skin
the taste of gujerella.

ACT FOUR, SCENE 1
Int. room on houseboat. Sound of stainless steel plates being stacked on wooden table.

SAMEERAH   Ek minute, shsh.

NUSRAT   Ummi, randho mai karthi hun:.

JALAARNAVA   I'll help clear up.

SAMEERAH   Neh, Nusrat turn karo.

JALAARNAVA   But...

NUSRAT   No, mum says no, I'll manage.

JALAARNAVA   But I want to.

NUSRAT   Jal, no.

JALAARNAVA   Fine then, I'm going to bed. Good night.

(Sound of stainless steel plates, cups and dishes being collected from table. Door slams.)

ACT FOUR, SCENE 2
Int. JAL'S room on houseboat. Door opens.

NUSRAT *(Whispers)* Jal.
JALAARNAVA   I'm tired Nusrat, I'm going to sleep.
NUSRAT *(Comes in and lies on JAL'S bed.)* Can I get in?
JALAARNAVA   What? Here?
NUSRAT   Yeah, why not? *(Moving about and giggling.)*
    It's really hot.
JALAARNAVA   Take off your kameez then. Here, let me. You're
    beautiful Nusrat. Your skin is like almond butter, mmmm.
NUSRAT   I feel really good.
JALAARNAVA   *(Whispers)* I'm so scared, I care about you so much.
NUSRAT   It's O.K., lie here, let's sleep.

(Music – lake music denoting a passionate relationship.)

JALAARNAVA   By candle light
             I moved on her
             through her
             into her body
             bells on ribbons
             of bangles
             and janjura
             ankles curved like.

NUSRAT   Red blood mendhi
         on palms soft and
         sweat sweet
         licking taste of
         chilli and masala
         touch of silk on
         my skin, thighs
         arch of my movement
         up and into
         earth, water, blood.

ACT FOUR, SCENE 3
Ext. floating garden. Sound of water lapping and two bodies moving in the water. Sound of women breathing and kissing. Music – lake music denoting passion in relationship.

JALAARNAVA *(Breathlessly)* I want to, I really want to, I want you before I lose you, I want to remember that we shared everything.
NUSRAT *(Whispers)* My body aches for you. For your touch, your kisses, your skin on mine. *(Movement in water increases, heavier breathing, light moaning sounds.)*
JALAARNAVA *(Breathlessly)* I want to give myself to you.
NUSRAT *(Breathlessly)* I want you so much.
JALAARNAVA   Nusrat, I love you. I need you.

(Music – woman singing and tabla denoting the POET)

POET   The heavens have opened
             The soul of Uma
             Flying free
             Himalaya, Heaven, and mountain.
             Before death,
             Kali devouring time
             And after...

ACT FOUR, SCENE 4
Ext. verandah of houseboat, faint sound of water gently lapping.

TWINS   Ummi...
SAMEERAH   You going where?
JALAARNAVA   Umm, to the market, do you want anything?
SAMEERAH   Thank you, no. It will rain, take umbrella. Nusrat, Kehaa jelee? Kam kamla piar.
NUSRAT   To the market with Jal Ummi. I'll do my work when I get back.
             (Sound of feet hurriedly stepping into rowing boat and boat gliding through water, oars splashing in the water.)
SAMEERAH *(Shouting)* Nusrat aa ja. *(Louder)* Nusrat.
             (Thunder and rain.)

ACT FOUR, SCENE 5
Music – woman singing and tabla imitating the monsoon.

POET   The heavens have opened
        first drops fall
        heavy and full
        absorbing the dry air.
        From a steady trickle
        to a torrent
        the roads are awash
        rivers cascading
        and overflowing
        the dust of the earth
        is reborn
        the water giving life.

ACT FOUR, SCENE 6

Ext. quiet town street. Crows croaking, circling above. Sudden sound of monsoon rain, water rushing. Footsteps running and splashing through puddles. Mix to tabla imitating the monsoon rain. Mix to –

JALAARNAVA *(Breathless)* Nusrat, hurry, we'll get soaked.
NUSRAT *(Giggling, screams)* Aah, right in a puddle, Jal, you're splashing me.
JALAARNAVA *(Laughing breathlessly then shivering)* Oh I'm soaked through, wow, look at the rain.
NUSRAT *(Laughs)* We're used to it.
JALAARNAVA   Let's go along the river, it'll be shorter.
NUSRAT   Are you mad, look how fast it is, it might flood anytime, the banks are really soft. *(Shouts)* Careful Jal!
JALAARNAVA *(Scream)* Jesus Christ!

ACT FOUR, SCENE 7

Persistent drumming sound of monsoon rain. Water rushing, footsteps running andsplashing through puddles. Mix to –

JALAARNAVA   We're standing outside the temple, reading a sign which says *(Sighs deeply)* 'Women with period not to enter'.
NUSRAT   No, I'm not coming, I'll wait for you here.
    (Ext. entrance to Mosque. Faint sounds of Qaawali music, harmonium and woman's voice chanting faintly. Chanting continues throughout piece.)

JALAARNAVA   Once inside I wonder who made up this rule, that the very blood which creates life is banned from places of worship of life. Maybe they don't worship life, maybe men made up the rules, cause they're jealous that life doesn't abound from deep within the warm flesh of their womb.
(Faint sounds of woman chanting. Music – harmonium and chanting faintly. Sound of women gasping.)

CHANTING
> Inside this room, womb, sanctuary
> I discover a taste for myself
> dipping into hot wet flesh
> into taste on tongue sucking.

(Faint sounds of woman chanting. Music – harmonium and chanting, faintly.)

CHANTING
> Outside this womb, room sanctuary
> I discover a taste for women
> Dipping into hot wet flesh
> Into taste on tongue sucking.

ACT FIVE, SCENE 1
Ext. boat on lake. Sound of water lapping against boat and oars pulling through water.

JALAARNAVA   Do you think we'll get across before the next downpour?
NUSRAT   Yeah, the clouds are far off. Do you have to go now?
JALAARNAVA   Yes, I want to go before the landslides come, my flight's next week. Maybe I can get a later flight.
NUSRAT   I think you should go. *(Pause)* Oh no, here it comes again. Delaying won't make a difference. It'll just make it harder to leave in the end.
(Thunder and lightning and sudden sound of monsoon rain falling heavily on lake.)
JALAARNAVA *(Softly)* I'm going to miss you.
NUSRAT   Yes.
JALAARNAVA   Will you write?
NUSRAT   Of course I will.

ACT FIVE, SCENE 2
*Int. room on houseboat. S.F.X. Writing in diary. Diary music – flute
denoting inner thoughts.*

JALAARNAVA   July 3rd. I have passion and it blinds me. I am
growing and changing before you, with you.

ACT FIVE, SCENE 3
*Thunder and lightning and sudden sound of monsoon rain falling heavily on
lake.*

NUSRAT   Here, get under this.
*(Sound of movement in boat floating on lake. Rain falling heavily. Music
to end –Shelia Chandra 'Fly to me'.)*
JALAARNAVA   July 5th. I arrived in spring, scoured the country in the
summer heat of May and June. July leaves me waiting. I'll be leaving in
August, after the monsoon.
POET   The heavens have opened. A gift from the Goddess to be able to
create life.

The End.

Leonora's Dance

For a long time now I've been trying to find a word which describes the way I like to write — that is, the integrating of the naturalistic with the non-naturalistic, but I had been unable to find such a word. Since *Leonora's Dance* I've heard a few people describe it as magic realism. Although I'm wary of such terms, I'd like to think that my writing does take you into a world that is both magical and real — and certainly spiritual.

The play was first written as a TV script, during a Screenwriters' Workshop, but I'd conceived it as a theatre piece. After the success of my first play *Paper and Stone* (1990) I decided to rewrite it for the stage. I was able to work on it as part of The Black Theatre Forum's Writer/Director project. It also received a public reading at the Wordplay Festival (1992).

The character of Leonora had been with me for some while. I knew everything about her, her mannerisms, delusions of grandeur, that she was ill, that she was trapped both physically and mentally — although I wasn't quite clear if it was eccentricity or madness. The play traces the pattern of Leonora's illness from agoraphobia through to final mental breakdown — where her negativity takes on a life of its own in the shape of the spirit Medusa.

I knew that Leonora could not have just any ordinary career and I'd read about the 'Black Swan/White Swan' syndrome. So I chose to make her a ballerina to highlight the issue of the stereotyping of Black people in certain jobs, careers, artforms while others remain European-preserved.

The issue of illiteracy as examined through the character Daphine came about because I'd worked in a Literacy Project and was intrigued by how people were able to disguise their reading ability and compensate for this problem. I view all my characters as important and tend to have a very packed script. Although juggling so many stories can be tough at times, the process of seeing it through onto the page and finally onto the stage is fulfilling and worthwhile in the end.

Zindika

LEONORA'S DANCE

Zindika

First performed at the Cockpit theatre February 9th 1993, produced by Black Theatre Co-operative. Directed by Joan-Ann Maynard and designed by Zara Conway.

CHARACTERS:

LEONORA	Judith Hepburn
DAPHINE	Doreen Blackstock
MELISA CHUNG	Toshie Ogura
FRIEDA	Ellen Thomas
MEDUSA	Glenna Forster-Jones

Notes:
All scenes take place in the house. There is no clear indication of day or night. Each character will occupy a different space on stage. There is a communal space where they always meet. The communal space is dominated and controlled by Leonora. The other two lodgers must go through the communal space always to get to their own space. Each character controls their own space, they never invade each other's space uninvited. Whenever they do, something dramatic happens.

ACT ONE, SCENE 1
Dark stage. Cacophony of noise – music, LEONORA appears on stage dancing. She is a young middle-aged woman, dressed very smartly with a little make-up. There is confusion and panic in her movements. MEDUSA, a militant spirit, almost like her shadow, teases her in movement. She is a threat to LEONORA'S sanity and LEONORA'S loss of contact with the outside world.

LEONORA   Deterioration. Deterioration all round. Who wants to be out there? Out there where they snatch away every last bit of dignity you got. *(Recovering slightly. She sits in a chair)* The last time I was out there I nearly got run over, on purpose too. There I was taking my own sweet time to cross the road – built like a desert. Next thing I know it's like hell break loose. The horns are blowing. The people are shouting, eating fast food like cannibals. The hooligans are swearing. Dizziness. *(She holds her head)* You wanna die old lady, he shouted abuse from the car window and swerve round me. Vroom. Vroom. Such abusive language. I don't even care to repeat it. I felt like a thousand volts of electricity building up inside me. I was so angry. The sweat was racing down my back cold and clammy. That was when I saw it trickling down my brand new winter coat. *(She brushes off her clothes)* The rotten egg the boy had thrown from the window on me. *(She makes a face of disgust. She goes over to her plants which she begins to talk to. She has names for all of them)* Aida... Giselle... it's time for your feed. *(She stops momentarily)* I could have danced Giselle more beautiful than any other. *(She polishes and sprays the plants)*

MEDUSA *(Sneering – she tells us what she thinks of LEONORA)* She could dance Giselle more beautiful than any other. *(Laughter)* She skinny foot Lou... they called her. Anorexia Nervosa Lil. *(She puts her finger to her throat)* She little black sambo... She couldn't even make it into the Black and White Minstrel show. She, who couldn't even charm her way into the heart of a Grenadian man. She little Miss so and so, Miss high brown and mighty, who found love only in vanity. *(She points at LEONORA who continues to mutter to her plants)* People like her we can do without. *(MEDUSA steps forward, centre stage. Spotlight)* I know what you're thinking, that I'm weird, strange. But, I'm quite ordinary really. I like to sing and dance, throw cartwheels, talk French in Spanish style. Wiggle my body like the liquid swim of the Limpopo river. *(She wiggles)* I'll walk with you, talk with you, linger at your door. Listen to you – an agony aunt for comfort. I dress like you, I eat like you, plantains and fried rice – that's my favourite. I'm sensitive, shy. Tell me a courageous story and I'll cry. Where I come from there are good and bad spirits, spirits full of wisdom and wit. Ordinary spirits like you or I. I'm no fairy tale or fable. I like hanging out, looking mean and moody – spirits come in all colours and guises, male spirits, female spirits with all the qualities of the universe. *(She steps back and points)* This is the house. Let me show you around courtesy of Medusa tours. This is the window. This is the door. There are no children or apple trees in sight, no scuff marks on the landing – just chiselled faces, sparse lives. A house built on cracks, fissures I mean. I landed here like a meteorite. Right here *(She points)* where I'm standing... in perfect bliss blurred in time. This is the house that Jerry built, Jack built, Jill built, Hyacinth built, I built, a garden on the window sill... the house where ivy climbs the inside wall, and stains of insanity leak through the cracks. Two up two down floor of misery. This is my castle. I protect it with infra red sensor, I guard it with barbed wire fencing and armoured knights. This is the house... some come to cower, some come to hide... built on stilts, shifting sands. Make sure you believe me. Make sure you believe what I believe. Make sure you see what I see. Make sure you hear what I hear. This is the house...a sanctuary full of refugees. Come... come in. This is my house. Medusa that's me – welcomes you in.

(She beckons us in, walking backwards. As she leaves there is a noise. LEONORA hears the noise of the front door and stops her activity. Enter MELISA. She is wrapped up in a winter coat. She begins to take off her outdoor clothes slowly. Hat. Scarf. Gloves. Boots. LEONORA goes to investigate and sneaks up on her in the dark.)

LEONORA *(From the dark)* Jezebel... Jezebel... you Jezebel you... *(MELISA looks around and is startled by LEONORA)* Oh Miss Chung it's you. I'm sorry I didn't know it was you. I thought it was that good fe nuttin' girl Daphine. You know she comes in all hours.

MELISA *(Embarrassed)* No, it's only me. I'm sorry.

LEONORA   No need to be sorry my dear. I should be the one apologising after giving you such a scare. *(She looks at the books MELISA is carrying and she shifts them from her gaze. LEONORA scrutinizes MELISA.)* Still not use to our English weather yet I see.

MELISA   No, not quite.

LEONORA   I bet it never gets this cold in Hong Kong.

MELISA   No.

LEONORA   Still nothing like a bit of cold weather to kill off all the germs and calm the temperament. You'll soon get use to it like us English. *(MELISA smiles)* Anyway, it's all worth it in the long run – just think one day you'll be a doctor, make you family proud.

MELISA   I hope so.

LEONORA   Of course you will. I know a bit about medicine myself. *(Looks bashful)* I wasn't exactly qualified, but as a trained ballerina and teacher, I had to treat many sprained ankles and broken bones... and you know you have to treat young bones right. So first aid became my forte.

MELISA *(Looking at her)* Is that why you retired?

LEONORA   No... No dear. I was much too careful for all that. These limbs were my fortune. They have served me well. No my dear. It's my illness. *(Smiles and waits for sympathy)*

MELISA   Your illness... *(Looks perplexed)* Oh, your illness. *(Smiling)* Well, you're looking much better.

LEONORA   It comes and goes Miss Chung, you know these symptoms comes and goes.

MELISA   Well you should try and get out a bit more. A little fresh air is perhaps all you need – but if there is anything I can do...

LEONORA   Oh no, there's nothing you can do. Old age that is all. Science can cure everything except old age. You know I was only reading the other day in this month's medical journal –

MELISA   Oh... *(Advancing away suddenly)* I must go now. I have studies. *(In her hurry a book falls and LEONORA goes to pick it up.)*

LEONORA   New books, they are so expensive nowadays. I don't know how you students cope.

MELISA *(Grabbing the book from her)* Yes, my new anatomy manual... lab practice tomorrow.

LEONORA   Well I mustn't keep you from your studies. *(MELISA leaves and LEONORA mutters)*... even test tube babies.

MELISA   I beg your pardon.

LEONORA *(Shouting to her)* Test tube babies Miss Chung and heart transplant. Science is such a wonderful thing. Just think one day you'll be part of all that.

MELISA   Oh yes... Bye Miss Leonora.

LEONORA   ... and remember my dear, if you ever want anything, I'm just down the stairs. Don't be afraid to ask.

(MELISA leaves and LEONORA returns to her room. MEDUSA awaits her.)

My therapist Mrs. Brown, she says I have such green fingers. I tell her, plants are like people. If you treat them right, they will treat you right. *(She sighs deeply)* It's not safe out there. It's not safe out there for anyone... man, woman, animal... especially the plants... We must all do our bit in the race to save the planet. Acid rain... pollution. It was prophesy that there would be a hole in the sky through which the sun would pour down one day like volcanic larva... Brimstone and fire... Noah he had the ark... and Cleopatra she had her tomb, and what did they find when they opened it years later... she was there preserved, refined in all her glorious beauty – the years had not touched her. You see... I must save the plants, stamen and roots, every species.

(Dim light on MELISA in her room. We see her preparing for her ritual. She lights a candle, and some incense. She reads from a book very reverently. Then she puts on a ritual cloak. She does her ritual and offers sacrifice in four directions, east, west, heaven and earth – to evoke the spirit. LEONORA continues to speak.)

I Leonora Lavender being of sound mind and body do declare that on this day 1992 – after a premonition of the world's deterioration – will resign to a place of safety. *(She holds up a container)* This room is my capsule. In it I will preserve my memories. Here, I will preserve my grand dance... *(She holds each invisible item up slowly and then lays it carefully into container.)* my grandmother's song which she taught me at her knees. *(She sings briefly)* My mother's warning – all about men – *(She laughs)* What to preserve. *(She leaps up and moves around collecting things.)* Here, Vivaldi's *Four Seasons*, Beethoven's concerto – what are they going to think? Leonora Lavender... Heroine. Prima Donna, diva, opera queen, as predictable as the monsoon rain.

MEDUSA   This is the house... *(Refrain)* One woman's crusade – it will cost her dearly.

LEONORA   I'll preserve the smell of rain on parched earth, children's voice full of glee... I'll preserve it all...

MEDUSA *(Seeming pleased with herself)* Tomorrow they'll come in their contamination suits, like bailiffs, anonymous callers, to her door. *(Whispers)* They'll dissect her mind, tell her she's disturbed, demented, not all there. *(She picks up a bottle in the room)* Here take your pills Leonora – you know they're good for you.

(She hands LEONORA the pills. She takes them. We hear music – which suggests the appearance of the diviner whom MELISA is trying to summon. It disturbs MEDUSA. She is angry and she storms out of the room to MELISA'S room to confront her.)

MELISA *(Looking round the room for signs of the diviner)* Where are you? I know you're here somewhere. Stop playing games. I need your help. Why won't you answer me. *(There's no answer)* I know you're here. I can sense you. *(She backs into MEDUSA who stands looking furious at her)*... Oh, my god, you're here, you're real flesh and blood... *(She touches MEDUSA)*... you even breathe. Where did you come from? Are you from Shanghai? You don't even look Chinese, that is brilliant. No-one will ever guess who you are. Sit down, you're making me nervous, can I get you a drink? What do spirits drink – spirits I guess – sorry, bad joke? How did you get here? I was only playing, well what I mean is... I didn't think it was possible. I followed all the instructions in the book. *(She shows book to MEDUSA)* And bingo... I can't believe it. *(MELISA goes to touch her again and she moves away)* Anyway, now that you're here, you've got to help me. It's my father, you have to get rid of him. I don't care how drastic it is – but, just don't let him find me.

Exit MEDUSA. Lights fade.

SCENE 2
Enter DAPHINE.

LEONORA *(Sneaks up on her)* You Jezebel...

DAPHINE *(Startled)* Miss Leonora!

LEONORA   You know the rules of this house Daphine. In by ten and no men.

DAPHINE   In by ten... it's only...

LEONORA *(Firmly)* You know the rules Daphine. I don't make rules for fun.

DAPHINE   I wish I knew what you was talking about.

LEONORA   I heard you last night, there was a man in your room.

DAPHINE   There was no man in my room. It must be your imagination, Miss Leonora.

LEONORA   Next thing I know you breeding.

DAPHINE   Oh, I don't have to listen to this.

LEONORA   I promised your mother.

DAPHINE   You promised my mother to give me a roof over my head, she didn't ask you to chaperone me or spy on me.

LEONORA   This is London girl, not Liverpool. London is a big city full of strange people with evil intent. You know what happens to girls like you, they get chopped up into little pieces and end up floating down there in the river Thames.

DAPHINE   Oh, you're sick. *(Goes to leave)*

LEONORA   ... and by the way, where is my rent?

DAPHINE   Rent, huh, ask the Social.

LEONORA   The Social... when are you going to find work?

DAPHINE   I'm looking for a job, you know that. I wrote to the gas board, the electricity board, Telecom and they all turned me down. What do you want me to do, sell my body?

LEONORA   I wouldn't put it past you. *(DAPHINE looks exasperated)* Miss Chung always manages to pay her rent on time and she's a poor student.

DAPHINE   Miss Chung is rich. Don't be fooled by her Oxfam look. Her father owns factories all over Hong Kong. My father is unemployed and so am I. If only you understood that.

LEONORA   You've got G.C.S.E., why can't you find a job? You just not trying.

DAPHINE   It's not as simple as that, is it? I'm what they call part of the Thatcher legacy... if you ain't up then you're down, if you black, get back... if you ain't in the city... it's a pity. If you can't cope, there's always dope. This is the age of bottles and bricks. Violence is the only thing that talks. Fight the power. *(Fist up)*

LEONORA   Is that what they teach you at school? Rebelliousness.

DAPHINE   They didn't teach me anything at school. Well, nothing worth learning anyway... like who gave science and mathematics to the Greeks? It was us Africans. Everything in the West originated from Africa.

LEONORA *(Shocked)* Africa.

DAPHINE   Yes, Miss Leonora. We're Africans... you and me.

LEONORA   Don't tar me with the same brush.

DAPHINE   It's nothing to be ashamed of...

LEONORA   You don't see it on the television? They digging in the earth, fighting over a mouthful of grain. Africa is one dry up piece of land.

DAPHINE   No, it's not. You don't know what you're talking about.

LEONORA   Daphine you are young... *(She sighs hopelessly)* Oh, what's the point?... look at Miss Chung upstairs.

DAPHINE   Miss Chung. Miss Chung... I am not Miss Chung.

LEONORA   You may sneer my girl... but one thing I know. The black race will never prosper – not with people like you bringing us down.

DAPHINE   You cow.

LEONORA *(Shocked)* What did you call me? I'll pack you off back to your mother favour or no favour.

DAPHINE   Look, I don't have to stay here. There are lots of people out there who would put me up. I just have to say the word and I could live like a queen compared to here.

LEONORA   I suppose a cardboard box and soup kitchen is a lot cheaper than proper roof over you head... you'll thank me one day.

DAPHINE   I'm leaving.

LEONORA   Good riddance.

(DAPHINE storms away upstairs and bangs on MELISA'S door. MELISA in her room jumps up and speedily puts away her ritual tools and takes off robe.)

DAPHINE   Melisa... open the door... Melisa. *(MELISA composes herself and goes to door)* Didn't you hear me calling?

MELISA   Sorry...

DAPHINE   Did you hear what she called me? *(MELISA looks lost)* God, Melisa sometimes I think you're deaf, dumb and blind. She hates me, she really does.

MELISA   Who?

DAPHINE   Leonora, who else? Well you better talk to her before I lick her down.

MELISA   I'm sure she didn't mean anything by it...

DAPHINE   I'm not going to let her push me out onto the streets.

MELISA   I'm sure she wouldn't do something like that.

DAPHINE   She would. She called me a slag and she locked me out again the other night. Didn't you hear me calling you? *(MELISA shrugs shoulders)* God, you better clean the wax out guy. You know something, she's worse than my dad. I've had six boyfriends in three months.

MELISA   Six...

DAPHINE *(Feeling the need to explain)* I wasn't sleeping with them all – it's her, she drove them away. I'll never keep a man as long as I'm living here.

MELISA   Ignore her. She's very old and very sick.

DAPHINE   Sick in the head more like it. And she ain't that old.

MELISA   She's retired.

DAPHINE   Not cos' of her age. She was jilted.

MELISA   Jilted?

DAPHINE   Shhh... yes, left at the altar. Her husband *(Snigger)*... or her husband-to-be saw sense at the last minute. It was like being caught between the devil and the deep blue sea – he said. He chose the deep blue sea, can't say I blame him.

MELISA   Who told you all that?

DAPHINE   My mother.

MELISA   You sure you not making it all up?

DAPHINE   I swear. I use to admire her once. She was independent. A free-thinking career woman. So beautiful. My mother talked about her like she was a film star. Now look at her - she's wasted. I was so glad when you moved in Melisa. I don't think I could have gone on living here much longer with just her for company. You know I used to have these horrible dreams – that I was trapped in this house with her and her plants – they were sucking all the oxygen out of the house – they were growing big and fat – with long arms, *(Demonstrates)* – like *The Day of theTriffids* and they crept into my room one night and strangled me... eeugh.

MELISA *(Worried look)* Do you still have those dreams?

DAPHINE   No, thank god. Well not since you moved in. Anyway, who was that you was talking to? You haven't got a visitor have you? *(Concerned)* First time innit? Is it a man? *(She tries to see into MELISA'S room but she blocks her view.)*

MELISA   There's no-one...

DAPHINE   But I could have sworn...

MELISA   You must be hearing things.

DAPHINE   At least I can hear. *(We hear a shouting and laughter from LEONORA'S room.)* See what I mean? She's as mad as a bat. I wish I knew what her problem was. I mean what would make somebody like her throwaway their life?

MELISA   She wants to have a baby.

DAPHINE   What! Well I've heard of immaculate conceptions, but this one is impossible conception. I mean she's fifty if not more. She never goes out and she's got no man.

MELISA   She doesn't need a man. She told me she's donated her eggs to science and genetic engineering. Didn't she tell you? She said something about saving the planet and preserving her genes – I don't know what she was going on about.

DAPHINE   She must be desperate... electric engineering my foot...

MELISA   Genetic...

DAPHINE   Well – whatever. You've told her she's been stupid.

MELISA   How could I?

DAPHINE   You feel so sorry for her don't you?

MELISA   You know there's nothing really wrong with her. She's just lonely that's all. I don't know why you dislike her so... after all... *(She hesitates)*

DAPHINE   What?

MELISA   ... you both black.

DAPHINE   What's that got to do with anything?

MELISA   I mean you should unite and be strong – not always at each other's throat.

DAPHINE   In case you hadn't noticed Melisa, I don't dislike her. She dislikes me.

MELISA   And you are her next of kin. You should try to be nice to her for a change.

DAPHINE   Next of kin? Distant relative... very distant.

MELISA   Well if anything should happen to her, you could be –

DAPHINE   What?

MELISA   Well, think about it. People like her always have it stashed away somewhere and who else she got to leave her fortune to?

DAPHINE   What fortune?

MELISA   Well, what is it you would like most in the world?

DAPHINE *(Thoughtful)* A job... a flat... a car... new shoes. A life.

MELISA   Well you could have all that and more, holiday of a lifetime – Bermuda, Barbados, safari in Kenya – all you have to do is be nice to her.

DAPHINE   Gosh, you're sly, Melisa – underneath that shy, innocent exterior lurks a demon.

Lights change.

SCENE 3
LEONORA catches MELISA in the hallway.

LEONORA   Oh Miss Chung. *(She beckons her)* Have you seen this month's medical journal? There is an article on those two eminent specialists – you know the ones I was telling you about. They can fertilise the egg outside the woman's body – freeze it; replant it days even years later and it will grow in the womb as surely as if nature had taken its natural course. *(She hands MELISA the magazine.)* Frozen eggs hey... what a revolution. You scientists have the future in your hands.

MELISA   Well I'm...

LEONORA   You know a woman's body is so intricate. You will specialise won't you Miss Chung?

MELISA   Surgery perhaps, or tropical medicine.

LEONORA *(Surprised)* Oh no, that's not for you, my dear. You are much too delicate for that field, and you don't want to end up in some fly-infested place where they don't even have running water; and those uncivilised pit latrines. *(She makes a face)* No, you're a scientist my dear – maybe a paediatrician. You have a gentle way about you. I can tell you'll get on well with children.

MELISA   Miss Leonora. Why didn't you have any children?
(LEONORA does not answer – but looks embarrassed) Well, what I mean is...

LEONORA   Oh, I know what you mean Miss Chung. It's just that no-one has been that direct before.

MELISA   Sorry, I didn't mean to pry... it's just that. Well don't get me wrong, I'm on your side, not all women are programmed for marriage and reproduction.

LEONORA *(Ecstatic)* Oh, Miss Chung – a woman after my own heart. You know from the moment I saw you, I knew you were suited for occupying that room upstairs, I just had a feeling, kindred spirits *(winks at her)* call it what you will. *(MELISA smiles nervously)* Here, come inside, I have something to show you.

MELISA   Well... I eerr... *(Tries to make excuses but LEONORA ushers her in.)* I was going out to make a phone call. It's my mother's birthday. I have to call her or she will get very upset. *(MEDUSA looks awe-struck as if it's the first time she's been in LEONORA'S room.)*

LEONORA   Yes, a girl must do her duty by her mother. I know the meaning of duty only too well, at least I used to. She's passed on some years now, but I never forget her. Dear mama... *(LEONORA searches through container in which she had placed things. She finds what she is looking for. She holds up some ballerina shoes and other things.)* Dancing was my life Miss Chung, I've been dancing since the age of four. I was the first little girl back home with a tutu. All crinoline with a silk bodice – pristine in pink. I read Diagliev memoirs when I was twelve.

MELISA   Dia... who?

LEONORA   Diagliev... Miss Chung, shame on you. Diagliev was only one of the greatest Russians that ever lived. *(Excited)* I haven't seen the contents of this box for years. *(She shows MELISA a scrapbook on her life and other things.)* I remember the first time I danced for the public. It was at the colonial club – an exclusive joint. I was fifteen, long-limbed, brown and thin, all the young men were staring at me as if they hadn't seen a woman before. Anyway, I didn't even notice them. All I wanted to do was dance. I toe and spin. Toe and spinned. Pavlova was my arms. Nijinsky my legs. It was exhilarating. I remember the feeling to this day. *(She clasps her hands – ecstatic)* They loved me. They had never experienced anything like it before. I took them – like a storm. They reported it in the newspaper–that I should be sent abroad to dance. *(Shows her press cuttings)* So I came to England on my scholarship. I haven't been back to the island since. Yes, dancing was my life... Pasuka. *(Holds up photograph)* He was hailed as the first black ballet dancer. He paved the way for a lot of us. He gave me my first break, when I auditioned for him at the playhouse, watched by the great Russians. They were intrigued – Negro ballet was unheard of before him. I would have had a great future had I been Russian. *(Thoughtful)* You know everybody in Russia gets a house from the state.

MELISA   So what happened when you danced at the playhouse? Were you a success?

LEONORA   Of course.

MELISA   I can imagine. I've never wanted to be a dancer myself but I do remember once seeing Dame Margot Fonteyn dance. She was so graceful.

LEONORA   I spent three years trying to get into the Royal Ballet. Never made it of course. *(Thoughtful)* I regret to inform you... plenty of those kinds of letters. I regret to inform you.

MELISA   Well perhaps you would have been more suited to modern dance. African. Jazz. Calypso... oh I love calypso. I wanted to go to the Carnival, but I was scared in case I got mugged, so I watched it on the telly.

LEONORA *(Not hearing her)* Oh a black dancer could make it to the top of course. There were reasonable cabarets around. I could paint my face white. *(Chuckle)* I thought I was white enough. But one per cent black can ruin your life.

MELISA   Perhaps we could go together. *(LEONORA looks at her. She hadn't been listening)*... to the Carnival I mean. You could teach me how to calypso. *(MELISA dances calypso)*

LEONORA   Miss Chung, do I look like the sort of person who jump up in the street whining my bottom? I was talking about the classic... Giselle, pas de deux in Swan Lake. *(Thoughtful)* I wanted to tour Japan, Copenhagen, USA, Australia, places where I'd never been before. I would be the toast of London. They would throw roses at my feet, play music on my entrance – I wanted to be at the top of every millionaire's guest list. Dancing was my life. Dancing was my life.

MELISA   You could dance again.

LEONORA *(Excited)* You really think so?

MELISA   I don't see why not. You're still young.

LEONORA   Oh, you're too kind, my dear Miss Chung. *(Swaying to the music)* They said that I had an exquisite neck – long arms. I would go far. *(We hear the music that signifies the appearance of MEDUSA. She takes on the stem mocking voice of LEONORA'S mother.)*

MEDUSA   Leonora, stop that dancing girl. I've told you already, you too fat. If the Lord had made black people to dance, their arms wouldn't be so strong, they back so broad.

LEONORA *(As MEDUSA speaks, LEONORA becomes more agitated and tries to shut her out.)* They said that I had poise and posture and a good sense of rhythm. I would make a great dancer.

MEDUSA   You too black and you hair don't even tie back in a bun. *(Mocking laughter)*

LEONORA   I'm not black, I'm brown. I have beautiful hair – just like my daddy.

MELISA   Miss Leonora, you all right?

MEDUSA   If you tink those white people going to let you into their ting, you got another ting coming. They have their ting and we have our ting... that's the way it was meant to be. Puss and rat can't live together – Leonora, don't worry. One day you'll be a famous Dibi woman like you granny.

LEONORA   She's got brown teeth, her house is dark and smells of tobacco... and she makes me drink nasty medicine. I think she's trying to poison me... really mama, you have to believe me.

MEDUSA   If you not careful I'll take you round to Granny's and I'll lock you in the dark, dark house... all by yourself.

LEONORA   I hate you.

MEDUSA   What did I do to deserve you chile?

LEONORA   I'm going to live with my daddy. My daddy lives in a big house.

MELISA   Miss Leonora... you alright? What is it?

LEONORA   Oh, Miss Chung. Sorry I didn't mean to frighten you. *(MELISA helps her to a chair)* Mama was right, there are no doors to be opened here. Just closed ones. I should have gone to America with George.

MELISA   George?

LEONORA   My ex-husband. Come to America – he said. America is the future. But I was too stubborn.

MELISA   There's always choreography. Perhaps even set up your own exclusive dance school.

LEONORA   Miss Leonora – Dance Academy – yes, I can see it.

MELISA   Dancers never retire. Isn't that right?

LEONORA   Oh, I'm too old to be bothering with all that now. *(She holds MELISA'S hands)* You must be a scientist. You must make great discovery – to save mankind. Let the future be you only concern. The future is not for mere mortals Miss Chung – it's for people like you and I. *(MEDUSA appears to be handing LEONORA her pills)*

MELISA   Well, I really must go now. *(MEDUSA begins to leave. LEONORA follows her into the hallway. She puts on her coat and wraps up well.)*

MEDUSA   Deterioration...

LEONORA   That's it, wrap up well my dear, after all you can't be too careful. These days, you can't eat the food, breathe the air or drink the water. What's the point of taking unnecessary risk? I'll stay in here.

MELISA   The phone booth is just on the corner. I won't be long. *(Enter DAPHINE who bursts through the door and passes them - crying. She exits to the top of the stage.)*

MELISA *(Reaching Daphine who moves away from her sulkily.)* You're shaking. Are you cold? Tell me – it can't be that bad. What's the matter?

DAPHINE   Nothing.

MELISA *(Insistent)* Tell me.

DAPHINE   Why should I tell you anything? You only take it back to her. I thought you were meant to be my friend.

MELISA *(Snobbishly)* I'm nobody's friend.

DAPHINE   It's O. K. for you, you don't have to stay here.

MELISA   That's not true. I'm here because I've got nowhere else to go.

DAPHINE   Liar!

MELISA *(Worried)* Look – I'm nothing to Leonora. I've got nothing to gain from all this. All she does is talk and I listen – I'm your friend.

DAPHINE   I don't need your friendship.

MEDUSA   I was only trying to smooth things between you. I thought I was doing you a big favour.

DAPHINE   I don't need your favours either.

MELISA   Oh sod you... *(Apologetic hands to mouth)* Anyway, it can't be Leonora making you feel this bad. I thought you'd be used to her by now.

DAPHINE *(Alarmed)* Used to her. If you think I'm going to sit around here for her to drive me loopy as well. I'm going back to Liverpool where I belong. *(She awaits MELISA'S reaction)* I'm going to see my child. *(MELISA looks surprised)* My daughter Daryl. I haven't seen her in over a year. I missed her last two birthdays.

MELISA   You have a child? Where is she?

DAPHINE   At home.

MELISA   In a home?

DAPHINE   No. At home. My mother looks after her.

MELISA   I'm sorry. I didn't know.

DAPHINE   Why should you? I keep it to myself. I don't want Leonora knowing. She hates children.

MELISA   She doesn't.

DAPHINE   Well, she hasn't got any.

MELISA   But she donated her eggs.

DAPHINE   That sort of thing is unnatural... on the other hand I don't blame her. Motherhood is scary.

MELISA   How old is your daughter?

DAPHINE   Three. Before Daryl was born, I thought I wouldn't be able to cope. I was only fifteen. I thought she would take all my energy and I wouldn't have any left for raving or going out with me mates. Then I saw her. She was so cute – I didn't want to give her up. That's why I can't wait to get her back. My mum is doing her bit – but she's mine. *(Deep sigh)* Something has to change soon. Something has to change.

Lights change.

SCENE 4

LEONORA'S room. She sits in a chair. MEDUSA is with her.

MEDUSA *(Walking around her)* Something has to change soon Leonora. Something has to change. Are you listening to me Leonora? I've never failed to conquer before and I refuse to start now. Soon. Soon, all will be mine. Are you listening? *(LEONORA stirs)* Listen to 'em. I want you to take a walk – outside.

LEONORA   ... outside.

MEDUSA   To the end of the road.

LEONORA   ... to the end of the road...

MEDUSA   You remember that little exercise – we tried it before – it won't take long and you'll feel much better afterwards.

LEONORA *(Getting up as if in a trance)* I haven't been out for ages.

MEDUSA   That's right. Gentle does it.

LEONORA   I'll walk to the big house. It's my daddy's house. I want to see my daddy dance.

MEDUSA   Yes, we can go dancing if you like... where we're going you can dance all day.

LEONORA   I want to dance.

MEDUSA *(Imitating LEONORA'S mother)* Come Leonora, I'll fix up your hair with some hibiscus flowers, you look so pretty, just like when you was a girl. Here, splash on some lavender water... take my hands, let's walk.

LEONORA   Mama, Mama, where are you taking me?

MEDUSA   To see your daddy of course.

LEONORA   No I don't want to go, not with you.

MEDUSA   Why not, you ungrateful girl – sometimes...

LEONORA   You wished I'd never been born.

MEDUSA   Why do you have to say a thing like that?

LEONORA   Why not, it's what you were thinking. That I make you unhappy, that I ruined your life. Why do I have to suffer for your mistakes?

MEDUSA   Just one more step Leonora.

LEONORA   It's not easy... *(Begins to walk towards the door.)*

MEDUSA   I know you can make it. It's only the front door. Your front door. Look at it. Touch it. You see it every day *(She pushes LEONORA)* You can touch it... it's not going to bite. *(LEONORA reaches out to touch)* It's harmless. *(LEONORA pulls back. MEDUSA loses temper)* You're not trying. Look at the door, it's wide open, there's fresh air outside.

LEONORA *(Sniffing the air begins to choke.)* I can't breathe... *(She panics and rushes back to the chair for safety.)*

MEDUSA *(Mocking laughter)* Oh so near and yet so far. *(Calms down)* Don't you miss anything on the outside?

LEONORA   No.

MEDUSA   Not even the trees? There are guava trees and mango trees. People going by.

LEONORA   The greenhouse effect. I've read about it.

MEDUSA   No. It's a lovely day... the breeze is cool.

LEONORA   Pesticides and pollution.

MEDUSA   There's the sky. You miss the sky don't you? There are birds in the sky...

LEONORA   Nuclear fallout. Oh yes, I've heard about it all. *(LEONORA becomes frightened and gulps down a glass of water. MEDUSA tries another tactic.)*

MEDUSA   You know what they say about you, don't you Leonora? That you're unable to cope with life. Know what I mean?

LEONORA *(In a dream)* They'll try and taint me with lunacy.

MEDUSA   That's right.

LEONORA   Well, I'm not ready for the loony bin yet and anyway, there's no history of that kind of thing in my family. My lineage goes way back – I might even be related to royalty.

MEDUSA   You want to be well again don't you, Leonora?

LEONORA   Yes.

MEDUSA   Then we must prepare you for the way ahead.

LEONORA   The way ahead...

MEDUSA   The future. You want to be part of the future don't you? *(LEONORA nods)* Then you had better pull yourself together. Have you ever seen a bird trapped in a room? Beating its wings hard, flying from wall to wall – just looking for a way out. Well that's you. One day your wings will break and it will be too late. Come on Leonora let's open the door – come on Leonora let's fly away, let's be free. *(She holds her and tries to pull her out of the door – LEONORA pulls back.)*

LEONORA   I can't.

MEDUSA *(Consoles her)* Don't worry. I'm here, I'll look after you.

LEONORA   I do miss the children.

MEDUSA   ... the glow in their eyes, their happy smiling faces.

LEONORA   Yes, I used to watch them a lot, the mothers-to-be. I miss that. I watched them at the park, on picnics. The school outings. The seaside. Summer is the best time. They come out laughing, playing like carefree birds. Sometimes I get real close to them. I feel part of it all. Then I think they get scared when they seeme watching. They think I'm a nosey old woman or something.

MEDUSA   Come on let's pretend we're with the children... see them jump skipping rope, play hopscotch in the rain, play tag and clap hands. *(They skip and play children's games as she speaks.)*

LEONORA *(Enjoying herself)* Yes, this one here is Tyrone and he's going to be a real live footballer one day. I can tell Natasha is a tomboy. She thinks she can move mountains, and little Gemma is a dancer if I ever did see one.

MEDUSA   How do you feel Leonora, do you feel good? You can trust me. You can tell me your deepest fears.

LEONORA   I feel elated. I've never felt so happy in all me life. To tell you the truth I could dance with joy. Then it happen... Boom... Boom *(She panics and rushes back grabbing her chest)* Boom... Boom. Like a thousand and one army marching onwards. It seems forever. First it starts here in my ovaries, then it works its way up to my stomach and settles there like indigestion... *(She clutches stomach)* Then it's my heart – it burns. There's fire in my throat. Choking, the blood rushing to my head. Soon everything is going round and round, the noise... it's unbearable... somebody help me. *(MEDUSA watches with satisfaction as she breaks* *down. Leonora crawls back to her chair.)* I wonder if I'll ever experience summers again.

Lights change.

SCENE 5
Lights on DAPHINE and MELISA. Landing.

DAPHINE   I was only fourteen when I met him. He was twenty-four. I didn't think about any birth control plans. It was my first time – a one night stand, there was no wedding band. I made up this poem about him. Do you want to hear it? *(MELISA nods. DAPHINE stands up and begins her rap poem.)*

> Now listen girls. I want to warn you about this facety boy.
> I'll call him Stingray to protect his identity.
> Now he go bout wearing him gold chain and ting.
> Him smile is gleaming – is what him scheming.
> With him Reebok and ting. And him hard boy chat
> I tink he's trying to impress me, with him seductive glance.
> But girls listen to me – don't be no pushover,
> cos he'll leave you when its over
> Listen to me when I chat, cos' of the experience I got.
> My name is queen Daphine with a regal and mean personality.
> I'm gonna rock you... shock you.

MELISA *(Clapping)* That's brilliant.
DAPHINE *(Sitting down)* You like it?
MELISA   Yeh, you should write it down before you forget it.
DAPHINE   Naw... I never write anything down. You never know who might see it. I've got a computer brain. I keep it all up there. *(She taps her head)*
MELISA   Really, I've never met anyone with a computer brain.
DAPHINE   Yeh, I can memorise anything. I memorise menus, bus routes, street names... songs I hear on the radio. That's how I use to while away my time at Fastburgers composing lyric in my head.
MELISA   So, why did they sack you?
DAPHINE *(Insulted)* They didn't sack me. I resigned. *(MELISA looks at her with disbelief DAPHINE begins to mimic working at Fastburgers.)* Fries, large, regular, medium. Large, extra large, huge, colossal, with relish,

topping. *(MELISA watches her and laughs.)* One large milkshake coming up. Pig yourself and get out – *Fastburgers*. Anything else sir? Yes. Big smile. Madam – can I help you? *(Smile)* I hate this place. *(Smile)* I wish I was someplace else. Milk with shakes... choco, vanilla. Help me. I am out of control. I cannot respond. *(Grimace like a robot – then back to normal.)* They said that I day-dreamed too much. Well, how else was I suppose to keep sane? You don't know what it's like working in a place like that. So I told them to stuff their job where it hurts. At least in my dreams there were no chip fat, greasy burgers and certainly no time management. In fact I was thinking of starting me own business. What do you think? They're always encouraging you to start you own business down at the job club.

MELISA *(Uncertain false smile)* That's a good idea.

DAPHINE   Something practical. I'm good with me hands. My art teacher said so at school. Daphine is a crafty girl she wrote on my report.

MELISA *(Chuckle)* I wonder what she meant.

DAPHINE   I'll open a craft shop, get into the tourist trade...Perhaps we could go into business together. With your brains and my craftiness, we could go far.

MELISA   No thanks. I'm not interested in ripping people off.

DAPHINE   Well it's O.K. for you to turn you nose up at money... you've got it.

MELISA *(Interrupting angrily)* I haven't. *(Calms down)* Well... well... what I mean is I won't have it for much longer. My father is going to stop my allowance soon. I don't know how I'm going to survive. I've never been without money. I've never been without my family. I've never been alone.

DAPHINE   Why would he do a thing like that? *(Pause)* Oh come on Melisa spill the beans.

MELISA   Well... *(Shy pause)* I was promised to wed since the age of four.

DAPHINE *(Shocked)* What? To some old dick with a fat wallet?

MELISA   Exactly... and my father is a man of honour, he never goes back on his promise. He's not concerned about my happiness – just more business contracts. I feel as if I'm being sold off to the highest bidder. You know the saying – money doesn't make you happy. It's true. I've had everything money could buy, yet I've never been happy.

DAPHINE *(Angry defence)* Oh, my heart bleeds for you. Do you know what it's like to see love turn to hate without money? I do. Take my dad, the day he lost his job he lost his mind... and my mum. She lost three fingers you know under that bloody steam machine she works with. She can't get compensation, she's tired of fighting and shit scared of losing her job. Why do you think I'm stuck here Melisa, cos' I can't go back to Liverpool empty-handed... cos' the only thing my parents respect is money.

MELISA   I'm sorry. I... I... think you misunderstood me... I...

DAPHINE   I understand alright... people like you, telling people like me we should be grateful we've got nothing, cos' we'd only be unhappy with something.

MELISA   That's not what I meant... Daphine if only you'd listen...

DAPHINE   ... anyway you don't have to worry, you'll finish University soon, then you'll be out of here – earning mega dosh as a doctor so you won't even need your daddy's money.

MELISA *(Insulted)* I don't want to be a doctor to get rich.

DAPHINE   Pull the other one.

MELISA   I never wanted to be a doctor. It was my father's idea. That I should be an educated little wife, who could make polite conversation with rich men. Look, I'm not trying to put you off.

DAPHINE   Don't worry, you haven't... I've made me mind up already... I ain't slaving no more for nobody. I'm going to be me own boss. There are plenty of women heading big companies... and you're wrong – money does make you happy.

MELISA   Well, look if you're really serious about starting your own business...

DAPHINE   Of course I'm serious, if only for Daryl's sake. I'll have to secure a better future for her than I ever had.

MELISA   Well... if you're really serious, you should do it properly – get qualified. I could help you.

DAPHINE *(Sudden loss of enthusiasm)* Qualified? But I've got O' levels, I told you.

MELISA   I mean a professional qualification. Business Studies or something. I've got some U.C.C.A. forms we can fill them out together.

DAPHINE   U.C.C.A. forms... *(Unsure of what it is)*

MELISA   University... I know lots of people if you want advice.

DAPHINE *(Panicking)* Well... err... hold you horses. I wasn't thinking of anything straight away. There's plenty of time. I have to think of practical things first. Like getting a flat... a job, earning some money so I can have me daughter with me. I would have to do all that before I could even think about studying.

Lights dim – change.

SCENE 6

LEONORA'S room. There is music playing. LEONORA mimes along to the music and appears to be lost in the enjoyment of it. MEDUSA watches her intensely and with relish. She imitates LEONORA'S movements. There is a knock at the door, which interrupts LEONORA – she stops. Enter DAPHINE.

DAPHINE *(Hands rent book to LEONORA.)* I've come to pay my rent.

LEONORA *(Glares rudely at DAPHINE – snatches the rent book from her. Examines it.)* That only leaves sixty-five pounds in arrears. *(She closes the rent book.)* Make sure you pay it in two weeks time.

DAPHINE   Two weeks? Where am I going to get that kind of money in two weeks?

LEONORA   Don't ask me.

DAPHINE   Can't I pay it off in kind?

LEONORA   No Daphine. In this world you must learn to accept your responsibility. I learnt that from an early age. I was only sixteen when I came to England. I had no mother or father to look after me. I was vulnerable. I lived in a cramped bedsit over a fish and chip shop for years. The air vent came right out underneath my window. You can imagine the smell. I couldn't make friends.

DAPHINE   I'm not surprised.

LEONORA *(She looks at DAPHINE sternly.)* One thing I learnt and that was how to be thrifty. I could make a packet of *Uncle Ben* rice last me for weeks. Ask me how I keep butter fresh without a refrigerator?

DAPHINE   I don't know. How do you keep butter fresh without a refrigerator Miss Leonora?

LEONORA   Well I put it in a little Tupperware container, then I put it in a bucket of cold water and I hang it outside the window. The temperature was lethal in those days. But despite the hardship, I still made it to the height of my career.

DAPHINE   So what's the moral of this little tale?

LEONORA   It means you must try harder. Get that chip off your shoulder.

DAPHINE   This ain't no chip – it feels like a huge great log. Look there are loads of white people out there with degrees and they can't even find jobs, so what chance I got?

LEONORA   It means you must try harder.

DAPHINE   Oh, so I end up trying ten times as hard. That's not equality.

LEONORA   Who's talking about equality? You have to prove yourself.

DAPHINE   Why should I – because I'm black? I've been in this country all me life and I still feel like an alien.

LEONORA   Well, if that is your attitude, I'm not surprised. Look at you, you squander your money on trashy clothes – and then you say you have no rent. Tell me how you can afford new clothes so often. I hope you not shoplifting.

DAPHINE   I wait for the sales, it's no secret. Plus I've got me *Freeman's* catalogue.

LEONORA   Common credit. There are some golden rules in life Daphine and the first one you should learn, is how to live within your means. What are you going to do when I sell the house?

DAPHINE *(Flabbergasted)* Sell the house.

LEONORA   Yes, I've been thinking I need a smaller place.

DAPHINE   But you can't sell.

LEONORA   They say it's a seller's market at the moment.

DAPHINE   You'll need lawyers, surveyors... all that...

LEONORA *(Calmly)* I'll manage.

DAPHINE   How? This place sweats like the tropics and smells like a swamp. It's all them plants. You should get rid of them.

LEONORA   Never.

DAPHINE   It's not healthy. You'll never sell the house like this.

LEONORA   I knew a woman years ago. She increase the value of her house by thirty thousand over night.

DAPHINE How?

LEONORA   The Queen Mother, during the war – had to make an emergency stop. She stayed for tea. She had a plaque outside. The Queen Mother stayed there. Everyone wanted to buy it then.

DAPHINE   So how you gonna get the Queen Mother to come to tea?

LEONORA   Where there's a will, there's a way.

DAPHINE   You've got no right to sell this house. Not without discussing it with me and Melisa first.

LEONORA   I didn't realise I had a joint mortgage.

DAPHINE   It's our home.

LEONORA   I always thought you was too proud to live here. You had so many friends you said.

DAPHINE   I have no friends.

LEONORA   So you're a liar as well.

DAPHINE   Only, Melisa... you won't let my boyfriends near this house. How do you expect my life to improve if my friends can't come and go?

LEONORA   It's for your own good that I keep young men out. I can't have looseness under my roof. I'm a respectable woman. Remember – it's you who end up with the baby.

DAPHINE   What baby?

LEONORA   I don't understand you young people these days, you throw
away your freedom for one night of pleasure.

DAPHINE   What you talking about? *(Suspicious)* Has Melisa been
blabbing to you?

LEONORA   I'm talking about respect. At least in my days the men had
respect for the women. We didn't have much freedom then, but at least we
had respect. Nowadays women got all the freedomthey want – but what is
the price of that freedom? Danger. Sometimes I think you young girls
bring it on yourselves. You know another get attack on Blackheath
Common the other day. She was wearing a dress similar to yours. He crept
up behind her. They could hardly recognise the body. *(MEDUSA appears
silently behind LEONORA.)*

DAPHINE   Why do you have to be so morbid?

LEONORA   All I'm saying is be careful, there are lunatics out there.
They'll come bearing gifts and promises like snake charmers. Before you
know it, you guard is down, and they mutate before you very eyes. I've
seen it.

DAPHINE   What could you have seen? What keeps you in here? Are you
afraid of something... someone... *(She approaches LEONORA
sympathetically)* Look, I know we don't get on – but sometimes we have
to forget your pride Miss Leonora. Why won't you let me help you?

LEONORA   I don't need your help. The world might be sliding into
anarchy and decay, but it doesn't mean that I have to be part of it.

DAPHINE   You shouldn't think like that. It doesn't matter what   you
wear, what time of night you're out, or how many locks you got on the
door, somebody could still break in an' murder you in bed. *(Sighs heavily)*
Oh look, I'm beginning to sound like you now. *(Turns to leave, as she does
so MEDUSA appears silently)* Anyway, if it puts you mind at ease, I'm
only going down the job centre, not hitch-hiking across Broadmoor.

MEDUSA   Deterioration.

(LEONORA sees MEDUSA and begins to have a panic attack)

DAPHINE   Miss Leonora you alright... you O.K.?

LEONORA   Help me... Help me...

DAPHINE   What is it? What's wrong?

LEONORA   Get me my pills. I can't breathe. *(DAPHINE helps her to a
chair.)*

DAPHINE   What pills?

LEONORA *(Points to drawer where pills are kept)* It's in the drawer...
fetch them... Diazepan.

DAPHINE   What?...

LEONORA   Diazepan... Diazepan.

DAPHINE   Dia... Dia... I don't know it. What does it look like?

LEONORA   DIAZEPAN.

DAPHINE *(Panicking as she searches through drawer full of pills.)* What colour is it?... Oh, god Miss Leonora don't die. Don't die on me. This is my worst fear. *(She grabs up a handful of pills and takes them to LEONORA.)* This one? *(LEONORA shakes head)* This one? *(DAPHINE chucks the bottle onto the floor.)*

LEONORA   No... No... No... *(Agitated)*

DAPHINE   This one? Oh look, I'll have to get Melisa. She's the doctor... Melisa. *(She calls out)*

LEONORA *(The last bottle and LEONORA grabs it and begins to stuff the pills into her mouth. Then she looks at the bottle label and screams. She spits out the pills.)* You stupid girl. What you trying to do – poison me?

DAPHINE No.

LEONORA   I said Diazepan. This isn't Diazepan. What's the matter with you? You can't read. *(She grabs DAPHINE and shows her the label)* You can't read.

DAPHINE *(Begins to break down and cry, kneeling beside LEONORA.)* No. No I can't read... not properly. I've had this problem ever since I was a kid. I can't even get a job. People judge you, don't they? They think you're mentally retarded. They think you should be locked away in a dungeon or hidden away in the attic with embarrassment. *(In the meantime LEONORA has found the right pills and is beginning to recover. MEDUSA watches.)*

LEONORA   You should be ashamed of yourself.

DAPHINE   I am. I am.

LEONORA   All these years in the education system and you can't read.

DAPHINE   It's not my fault. The teachers were on strike.

LEONORA   Teachers on strike for fourteen years. You know something girl, you are worthless, nothing but worthless. If you was my daughter...

DAPHINE   Well, I'm not your daughter.

LEONORA   I dread to think what will happen to you. *(Sees MEDUSA smile)* You have no aim, no ambition. *(MEDUSA appears but they don't see her. MELISA sees MEDUSA and is shocked by her blatant appearance.)* You try to poison me. It's just as well I had a little strength left in me body to reach these pills. I could be dead by now, all because you didn't see fit to attend school and learn a basic thing like reading. All you do is backchat. You're no good girl... you hear me... no good.

MEDUSA chuckles with satisfaction – exit. Lights down.

ACT TWO, SCENE 1

DAPHINE   What do you want? Come to gloat?

MELISA   No. I want to help you.

DAPHINE *(Sucks teeth. MELISA turns to leave but DAPHINE goes after her.)* You better not tell anyone I feel so ashamed.

MELISA   It's nothing to be ashamed of. Thousands of people can't read or write.

DAPHINE   Yeh, but they got reasons for it – like they didn't go to school. I did and I still can't read.

MELISA   Dyslexia. *(DAPHINE looks at her)* There's a condition called Dyslexia. Perhaps that's what you've got.

DAPHINE   You mean there's a name for it, I'm not just stupid?

MELISA   There are plenty of evening classes you can go to.

DAPHINE   Me, walk into one of them places? You must think I got a screw loose.

MELISA   Everyone there will be in the same position.

DAPHINE   I hated school, I really did. The teachers, they didn't give a shit. They thought all the girls were going to end up as baby machine, so what was the point – and there was always shelf-filling at *Tesco's*. Trouble is you need a damn degree even for that these days.

MELISA   You have to make the first move. No-one can force you to go and get help.

DAPHINE   He made me read the Bible you know, me dad – backwards. Revelation... John... Peter... James... Hebrew... He'd hit me every time I got it wrong. Titus... Timothy... Thessalonian... Even now I wet myself thinking about it. I was only five. Colossians... Phillipian... Corinthians... He just didn't want me to end up like him that's all.

MELISA   You know these classes, the teachers there, it won't be like school. They'll be quite sympathetic. Go on give it a try. You've got nothing to lose.

DAPHINE   Oh sure, just me pride. *(MELISA looks exasperated and turns away)*

MELISA   Look, just because you can't read or write, it doesn't mean everyone has it in for you. There are plenty of people on your side.

DAPHINE   Oh yeh... name me one.

MELISA   I am for a start.

DAPHINE   Oh good. Does that mean you'll teach me? I'd be a good pupil. I just don't think I could face talking to a stranger.

MELISA   I didn't mean it that way. You'd be much better off in a proper literacy class with trained professionals.

DAPHINE   I'm not illiterate. I'm just a bit slow. That's all.

MELISA   Whatever it is, they will sort you out.

DAPHINE *(Snapping)* Alright. Thanks. What you're really trying to say is you don't want to help me. I get the message. You know something Melisa, I've always wondered what you were doing round here – slumming it. I thought people like you always stuck to your own kind.

MELISA *(Offended)* My kind...

DAPHINE   ... or perhaps you think you're black as well.

MELISA   It's a free country – I can live where I like. I'm not a racist. Unlike some people I know. *(She looks at DAPHINE accusingly.)*

DAPHINE   You think you're so damn clever don't you – coming round here, pulling your poor little rich girl stunt, getting everybody on your side. Well I know what you're up to. *(MELISA looks at her then walks away. DAPHINE blocks her way.)* Studious little Doctor Melisa. I've seen the kind of books you read.

MELISA   What do you mean?

DAPHINE   I've heard you chanting in your room.

MELISA   I have to say my mantra every day.

DAPHINE   And you wait till Miss Leonora finds out that her sweet little, butter wouldn't melt in her mouth Melisa sleeps with another woman's picture underneath her pillow.

MELISA *(Alarmed)* What? That's a damn lie and you know it. *(DAPHINE runs towards LEONORA'S room. MELISA goes after her.)*

DAPHINE *(Calling)* Miss Leonora...

MELISA   Daphine... I'm warning you. Don't start.

DAPHINE   I ain't starting anything. I just don't like two-faced people that's all. *(Holds up picture which MELISA tries to snatch.)* Who is it?

MELISA   Where did you get that? Have you been in my room?

DAPHINE   Who is she? Tell me? Miss Leonora...

MELISA   ... all right.

DAPHINE   I'm waiting. *(Draws her own conclusion)* You're a lesbian aren't you?

MELISA   How dare you. How dare you suggest such a thing.

DAPHINE   It's O.K. I don't have nothing against people like that... as long as they stay away from me... I'm not like that. I've got me daughter – she's living proof.

MELISA   I refuse to discuss this. It's none of your business and you should never have gone into my room.

DAPHINE   Look what's your problem?

MELISA   I'm not the one with the problem. I'm not the one who steals other people's property.

DAPHINE *(Rubbing it in)* You know I've often wondered, what would the world be like without men. *(MELISA turns away furiously)* Oh, come off it Melisa... it's never going to happen... *(Goes up to console her)* Look, I'm sorry I took your picture. I'm sorry for teasing you. Here *(She hands her the picture and MELISA takes it and examines it.)...* Forgive me. *(MELISA smiles at the picture.)* Who is she? Go on you can tell Aunty Daph... she's pretty. Where's she from?

MELISA   Her name is Mioshan. She's a Taoist princess. A woman of great insight and powers. One of the few women who surpasses men in greatness. I'm going to find her. We'll live together at the foot of the Himalayas. I'll specialise in homeopathy and acupuncture – and treat the local peasants and mountain people free of charge. We'll be unconventional wanderers. We'll wear disguises like Tibetan nomads, play sword-fights and wrestlings. No-one will find us there. Not even my father.

DAPHINE   That sounds kinda crazy.

MELISA   That's what they said about Mioshan – but she wasn't crazy. She just refused to get married that was all. One day her father tried to cajole her into marrying the local tax collector and she stabbed him to death.

DAPHINE   The tax collector?

MELISA   No. Her father. She was found guilty and sentenced to face the firing squad. The day came and Mioshan stood waiting – she was brave and calm. They took aim and fired. There was a cloud of smoke – when it cleared they went up to check the body but she had disappeared. The only thing that remained was her shoes with a handful of ashes in them. No-one knew the secret of her disappearance – but it is believed that she roams the earth constantly as a peasant woman, a herbalist – all kinds of disguises looking for lost souls to guide and protect...There's a place where women like Mioshan go – an immortal place, I want to go there. That's why she visits me. You could say I'm her apprentice. *(An old woman enters. She is unseen.)*

DAPHINE   How do you get to this place then?

MELISA   First you have to relinquish all material bondage to this world. Then you have to roam the earth for forty days and forty nights doing virtuous deeds.

DAPHINE *(Flippant)* Oh, it's that easy then?

MELISA   You don't believe me do you? Well I can sense her presence in this house even now. She's always with me.

DAPHINE *(Notices woman)* Melisa... what does this Mioshan look like?

MELISA   Difficult to say. She takes many forms as I said.

DAPHINE *(Tapping MELISA)* Melisa... look round now and tell me I'm not seeing things.

MELISA *(Looks round)* My god – she's never taken this form before. *(Old woman moves forward and scrutinises the two girls.)*

FRIEDA   Is this Leonora Lavender's residence?

Lights dim.

ACT TWO, SCENE 2
LEONORA'S room. FRIEDA is sitting down. LEONORA paces around nervously.

LEONORA   Why didn't you tell me you was coming?

FRIEDA   I thought you'd be glad to see me.

LEONORA   I am.

FRIEDA   You could have fooled me. I haven't heard from you in over a year. What happened to all my letters? You didn't get them? *(LEONORA remains suspiciously silent.)* Too busy to write then? *(Loudly)*

LEONORA   Shhh... keep your voice down.

FRIEDA   Why? You shame of me.

LEONORA   No... You look tired, perhaps you should take a nap... Jetlag can be –

FRIEDA   I'm fine.

LEONORA *(Allowing her anger to surface)* What possessed you to fly all this way at your age... are you crazy? How on earth did you get across London at this time?

FRIEDA   I took a taxi. I gave the nice man your address and he got me here. No trouble.

LEONORA   But I still think you took a bit of a risk coming across London on your own... It's like a war-zone out there. The last time I was out there...

FRIEDA   I didn't notice anything unusual. Anyway, if Mohammed won't come to the mountain... then –

LEONORA   It's not like that – believe me.

FRIEDA   I don't know what to believe. I come all this way to see my favourite daughter and this is the reception I get. I'm beginning to think –

LEONORA   Don't start all that.

FRIEDA   All what?

LEONORA   Making me feel guilty for staying in England.

FRIEDA   That's all long forgotten. *(Looks around the room dismally.)* So it look like you done well in England. A dream come true.

LEONORA *(Changing the subject)* Would you like a cup of tea?

FRIEDA   You don't have anything stronger? *(LEONORA looks at her)* Like whisky.

LEONORA   Oh, no I never keep liquor in the house.

FRIEDA   O.K. if tea is all you have. *(LEONORA leaves to make the tea. FRIEDA calls her back and searches for something in her large bag. She hands her a sprig of bush.)*

LEONORA   What is it?

FRIEDA   Cerusi... mek a strong cup of tea and mek one fe yourself. *(LEONORA takes it scornfully)* It purifies the blood. Just boil it in some hot water and put plenty of sugar in it. *(FRIEDA examines things in the room as LEONORA returns with tea.)* Oh... by the way, everyone sends their love, even your father's family. They asked about you.

LEONORA *(Nearly spilling tea)* My father's family...? But you never talk about my father – much less his family. So does that mean they know about me?

FRIEDA   Of course they know about you. They always knew about you.

LEONORA   Well, what am I to think mother? You always told me I never had a father. You made up all sorts of stories about him when I was young. I was so confused.

FRIEDA   It's not that I didn't want you to know your father, or benefit from his success. It's just that I thought once you got to know him, you wouldn't want to know me, and I was right. The minute you set foot into that posh school. You changed.

LEONORA   So why did you keep me there so long?

FRIEDA   Because, I had nine children. I was looking for a way out for all of you.

LEONORA   But I always knew who he was. He had ginger hair.

FRIEDA   Did he?

LEONORA   He used to come to the house.

FRIEDA   Did he?

LEONORA *(FRIEDA occupies herself)* He used to carry a shooting stick and two fierce dogs by his side. The first time I saw him, I ran. He came up onto the verandah. It was raining. I remember every spot he touched because I touched them too... He was wearing a green rainmac and tall Wellington boots. He bent down to kiss me on the cheek. It was warm. *(She touches her cheek.)* He gave me chocolate from England – that's how I knew I was special to him. I was seven, mother – don't you remember?

FRIEDA   Well, as they say, blood is thicker than water – because your name was the last word on his lips when he died. You remember?

LEONORA   Remember. What?

FRIEDA   How could you forget such a thing?

LEONORA   My memory is sometimes a little fuzzy. He was a good man...
wasn't he?

FRIEDA   Is there such a thing?

LEONORA   Why didn't he marry you?

FRIEDA *(Begins to laugh)* Marry me? Him with his big white house... his
grand piano and huge ballroom, crystal chandelier – the Colonel, lord and
mighty – marry me, a field hand – who cut cane under the burning sun?
(She laughs louder.) His money may have sent you to school, but it was
only because he didn't want to face the shame of your conception.

LEONORA   I'm sorry mama, I'm sorry you never found happiness.

FRIEDA   Not many do. Anyway, enough about me. What about you,
how long you been cooped up here in this house? Living on dreams. Is this
all you got to show for your years in England?

LEONORA   This is my house. I bought it.

FRIEDA *(She walks around the room)* Where's your husband? Where's
your children? Where is your ever so fabulous dancing career? *(She
goes over to the curtains.)* It's so dark in here... let in some daylight.

LEONORA *(Runs to stop her)* No. It's the plants, they're very sensitive...
they'll die.

FRIEDA   You're a strange one. *(FRIEDA sits down again)* Lies... Lies...
all these years... *(She takes out some letters and begins to read.)* Dear
mother. I am well. I am married now. He has money... *(She looks at
LEONORA. Takes out another letter.)* Dear mother. I am well. I have a
little girl now. She beautiful... she look like you. *(Another letter)* Dear
mother. I am well. Good news. I am going to dance in front of the Queen.
Stops reading – puts down letters.) Then all of a sudden the letters
stopped coming... why? Everybody in the village was obsessed with you
life. How is Leonora getting on in England now? They always wanted to
know about you and I would read your letter in the square to everyone.
You was our ambassador. So tell me girl. What happened?

LEONORA   Nothing. I met a man. Satisfied?

FRIEDA *(Tutting)* Same old story.

LEONORA   George wasn't just any kind of man. He had hands like a
piano player and he was in the airforce – a real catch. He knew how to
treat a lady right. Together we was a real swinging couple. I was the
dancer but he could show me a step or two... to waltz. To tango. Rock and
Roll. We were going to America. That was my only regret. Things are
better there – more opportunities. I could have made it in America.

FRIEDA   You should have come to me if you wanted to keep a man.
There are potions a woman can take. Just sprinkle a little in his tea and

he's yours forever. Anyway, that's all water under the bridge now. Come back home with me – now. Come back and tek you rightful place as eldest daughter.

LEONORA What would I do in the bush? You're living in the modern world now mama. One man's heart beats within another – genetic engineering...

FRIEDA It's not right all this tampering with nature. If the Lord –

LEONORA Miss Chung is going to be a doctor of science.

FRIEDA What I know you can't learn from a book. My mother passed it on at her deathbed.

LEONORA It's different nowadays, Miss Chung –

FRIEDA How you let that little girl pull the wool over your eyes?

LEONORA What do you mean?

FRIEDA I mean she's not what she seem.

LEONORA Oh mama, you've only just met her.

FRIEDA Yes, but I'm a good judge of character. I know evil when I see it. Do you know what she really studies? *(LEONORA looks at her.)* Witchcraft.

LEONORA Don't be stupid mama. What would Miss Chung know about witchcraft? She's never said a bad word against anyone. That girl know only how to help people.

FRIEDA Go to her room and find out.

LEONORA I can't go into her room.

FRIEDA Why no? It's your house. Perhaps you fraid fe her.

LEONORA Course not. It's just so ridiculous.

FRIEDA Well, if you won't sort this thing out. I will.

Lights change.

ACT TWO, SCENE 3
MELISA'S room.

DAPHINE *(Reading from a book)* Early in the spring of 1750, in the vi... vi...

MELISA Village of Juffure.

DAPHINE ... village of Juffure. Four days up river from the coast of Gambia. West Africa. A child is born to Om... Om...

MELISA Omora and Kunta Kinte.

DAPHINE *(Smiles widely)* I'm so pleased you're helping me with this. I know quite a lot of words really so you see I'm not that bad. It's my confidence that's lacking that's all. *(She starts to read again. MELISA* *looks preoccupied.)* The names which were great and many... went back more than two hundred rains. Out under the moon that night Omora completed the naming ritual. Fend killing... doro... doro... what's this?

MELISA *(Takes a look)* It's African. Oh for godsakes, how you going to read African if you can't even read English. Ohhh sorry Daphine... I didn't mean...

DAPHINE *(Hurt)* It's O.K. I'll never go to that job centre again. They made me fill out forms.

MELISA   What did you do?

DAPHINE   I ran. When I got here I saw you and Leonora in the hall. I freaked. I thought you knew.

MELISA   You can't keep running.

DAPHINE   I know that. It's my problem. I have to face up to it. *(Suddenly full of enthusiasm)* You know what I'm going to do? I'll go out tomorrow and join a class. Maybe there's a cure for it – dyslexia – that's what I've got isn't it?

MELISA   Well, I don't know for certain, and you won't know either till you go and see them – they'll do tests...

DAPHINE   You know I never thought I'd be grateful to Leonora, but I am. Thanks to her, it's all out in the open. I don't have to hide it any more.

MELISA   Look, Daphine I hope you didn't think anything of it. I mean the way I snapped at you just now. I seem to be losing my cool ever so easily lately. Sometimes words just seem to fly out of my mouth and I can't stop them. It's as if... as if...

DAPHINE *(Gets up to go)* Oh I wouldn't worry about it if I was you. My mother always said I had a thick skin.

MELISA   Not just that, but I can't seem to get any answers any more. *(DAPHINE stops and appears interested.)* I feel so lost without her.

DAPHINE   Who?

MELISA   Mioshan – my mentor. You know she has always been here when I needed her. Perhaps I'm losing my touch. *(Moves to sit down)* She told me to come here you know. Go to a house of women she said. There you will find the energy of the sacred pearl. It was in this house that she first appeared to me. She is the pearl.

DAPHINE   Maybe she's given up on you.

MELISA   You're right, perhaps she's found someone more deserving of her time. After all I haven't been very nice to people lately.

DAPHINE   How do you get in touch with her anyway – perhaps I should have a go?

MELISA   No, she doesn't work for just anyone – you know.

DAPHINE *(Taking insult)* What's that supposed to mean?

MELISA   I mean... I mean you've got to have the gift.
DAPHINE   My mother sees spirits.
MELISA   Oh really – O.K. then go on. I'll try anything.
DAPHINE *(Rubbing hands with glee)* Oh great. What have I got to do?
MELISA   Sit down and close your eyes. *(MELISA lights candle, leads DAPHINE in ritual.)* Now concentrate.
DAPHINE   I am.
MELISA   Now cleanse the space around you – it's all done in the mind. Prepare the space, only then will the spirits come gladly.
DAPHINE   What happens now? What does she do when she arrives?
MELISA   She guides and protects. You can ask her anything you want. She knows everything.
DAPHINE *(After some thought)* Does she know when I'll get a job?
MELISA   No! You have to ask her something more profound. More deep.
DAPHINE   That is deep. *(After a while begins to lose concentration.)* Melisa...
MELISA *(Snapping)* Concentrate.
DAPHINE   I'm trying to, but I keep thinking Leonora is going to sell this house. What's going to happen to us? I reckon that's why her mother is here. Leonora must have sent for her. They're going to sell up and move back home. She's got 'nuff land back home you know... big house... swimming pool... My mum told me. What have I got? We have to fight. It's not just me I'm concerned about. What about you?
MELISA   I'll find somewhere.
DAPHINE   Nowhere as safe as this.
MELISA   It's a chance I have to take.
DAPHINE   Look, she's not throwing me out onto the street. I'll fight her. You either with me or against me.
MELISA   Don't worry she's not going to sell.
DAPHINE   How do you know?
MELISA   I just know. *(Snapping impatiently)* Now concentrate. *(They close eyes and there is silence.)* Oh great sage. Forces that guide me and my ancestors. Grant me the power to the universe. Grant me the power to see through darkness and evilness. Lead me to the truth. Guide me to the path of immortality – to the path of the mysterious females. *(MEDUSA appears. This time MELISA does not see her as she is too busy.)* Something is happening.
DAPHINE   What's happening?
MELISA   It's Mioshan. Her spirit is here. I don't believe it, she's come back. I can sense change. *(Appears confused)* I see two women, dancing or

fighting. I can't tell. One woman is in white. She's being pulled by the other woman towards the sun – or something. A very bright light. I can't see their faces. One is old – the other young. Oh, I don't know, it's not clear, perhaps they're both young or both old... it's difficult.

DAPHINE *(Sniggering)* Perhaps it's you and Mioshan – two old maids growing old together.

MELISA   Very funny. You've interrupted the energy flow.

DAPHINE   Sorry.

(LEONORA'S room. FRIEDA is cradling the large bag to her chest.)

FRIEDA   There I was sitting by rock on water, when suddenly a great cloud came down over the sun like a shroud. I tell you it came right down and sat on the water. The moon followed behind it. The moon was my mother's face – round and bright. She was calling to me. *(She beckons)* When you get the calling Leonora you just can't ignore it. It was a great responsibility for me to take on the role which my mother had left me – but I was proud to do it. It is a powerful gift I'm telling you. I haven't studied any books or science – but send me anyone with any ailment and mother Frieda will cure it. I am a servant of the spirit guided by water and light. There is only one successor Leonora. You – eldest daughter – you don't know how lucky you are. *(She walks over and hands her the bag.)* Take it.

LEONORA   I don't want it.

FRIEDA   You just can't refuse like that.

LEONORA   Why not? It's my life.

FRIEDA   It's not just your life – what about those who will come after you? What about history and tradition? You forget where you come from.

LEONORA *(Screaming)* I don't want it!

FRIEDA *(Turning away as if distracted)* There is something not quite right here... something not quite right.

LEONORA   What you talking about mama?

FRIEDA   That girl, she too meddlesome.

LEONORA   Daphine?

FRIEDA   No, the other one. I told you what I saw in her room. She's trouble. I'll fix her, interfering wretch.

LEONORA   She's only a chile mama. She don't mean any harm.

FRIEDA *(Losing temper)* I can't believe you is my flesh and blood, talking like that. You have no backbone. There's evil in this house.

LEONORA   What you going to do? Can't you see I'm past saving.

FRIEDA   If you think I'm going to sit here and watch this house crumble on your head...
LEONORA   It's too late. Save yourself. Go home.

(MELISA'S room)

MELISA *(Stands shivering)* It's cold.
DAPHINE   You're always cold.
MELISA   No. I mean I'm freezing. I'm beginning to hate this house. It's always so cold lately.
DAPHINE   I'm hot. In fact very hot.
MELISA   Something has gone wrong. I don't know what but...
DAPHINE *(Plays along with MELISA. Pretends to be possessed.)* It's hot. *(She pulls at her clothes)* Oh my throat.
MELISA   What is it?
DAPHINE   It's burning... like fire... Melisa help me...
    (DAPHINE grabs her throat and falls to the ground. MELISA grabs her as she falls.)
MELISA *(Whispering out of breath)* Daphine... you alright?
DAPHINE *(Raises head and speaks in strange voice)* They'll come like soldiers in the night. Like bloodhounds to your door.
MELISA   Who? What are you talking about?
DAPHINE   Your father's men...
MELISA   My father's men. *(Alarm)* My father's men! You saw him? My father.
DAPHINE   A woman in a wedding dress.
MELISA   It's me, isn't it?
DAPHINE   He wants you to get married. You have to do as he says. He'll take you back to Hong Kong. It's all arranged. I saw them signing the contract. They drank cognac and shook hands. The bride price is set. You'll be alright. He'll look after you. I see the house. It's built like a palace... I see it on an island, surrounded by water. There's no escape. I see five children.
MELISA *(Shocked)* Five children.
DAPHINE   Yes, there's nothing to be afraid of – you'll get used to it.
MELISA   I'll send a thousand plagues to wipe him out, him and his companies – everything he stands for. I despise him.
DAPHINE *(Urgently)* He's near. You better not go out. He'll find you.
MELISA   How near?

DAPHINE   I don't know. *(Confused)* Girl I don't know but he's near...
Knightsbridge perhaps.

MELISA *(Panicking)* Knightsbridge... my god. *(She starts to pack up some
of her things frantically.)* What else did you see? *(She shakes DAPHINE.)*
Tell me.

DAPHINE   I don't know. I'm... I... I'm not feeling so good. I feel dizzy.
Perhaps I should go to my room and lie down.

MELISA   Once a policeman in Trafalgar Square grabbed me by the
shoulder. I thought it was my father. I turned around and kicked him and
ran. He's looking for me. Oh Daphine I'm so scared. Every sound is him.
Every voice is him. Every siren, every footstep. I'm trapped. *(FRIEDA
bursts in without knocking.)*

FRIEDA *(To MELISA)* I want you to leave this house.

MELISA *(Recovering suddenly)* Why?

FRIEDA   Because I said so. You've cause enough trouble here.

MELISA   I'm not aware of any trouble I've caused, isn't that right
Daphine? Tell her.

FRIEDA *(To DAPHINE, as she hesitates)* You stay out of this.

MELISA   Did Leonora send you? You can't take any notice of her. She's
cracked.

DAPHINE *(Shocked)* Melisa...

MELISA   It's true and you hate her as much as I do. How can she throw
me out after what I've done for her? I'm the only one that talks to her.

FRIEDA   This is nothing to do with my daughter. I'm in charge now.

MELISA   You have to give me a month's notice. I know my rights.

FRIEDA   Well I'm giving you the two minute warning girl. Out or else.

MELISA   You don't scare me.

FRIEDA   You don't know what you messing with. *(She grabs MELISA)*
Who you in touch with? Tell me...

MELISA   I don't know what you're talking about. I only meditate.
Meditation is not a crime.

FRIEDA   You had better get out of this house while you can. People like
you think bad is good and good is bad, before you know it, you end up in
disaster.

MELISA   Well, you know what they say – you have to be evil to
recognise evil.

FRIEDA   I warned you. *(She walks around and begins to smash things
in MELISA'S room, her ritual items.)*

MELISA   My things. My beautiful things. *(She tries to stop FRIEDA
and as she moves towards her, MEDUSA appears and trips her to the
floor.)* My shoulder... my shoulder... She's done something to my

shoulder... help me Daphine... *(FRIEDA leaves MELISA lying in agony –
MEDUSA disappears with satisfaction on her face.)*

DAPHINE *(At last rushing to MELISA'S aid)* Why did you have to
antagonise her?

MELISA   She's just like my father. *(As DAPHINE helps her up)* Oh
Mioshan where are you when I need you?

DAPHINE   Forget Mioshan – I'm here. We have to think of some
strategies now. We should become sitting-tenants, they won't be able to
budge us then. Then we have to deal with your father.

MELISA *(Feeling defeated)* Oh, I don't know, maybe she's right. It's all in
my head. I have no powers. Perhaps I'll just do the normal thing and settle
down, have a few children, take my father's trust fund and run.

DAPHINE   You can't do that. I don't see what right your father has to tell
you who to get married to anyway. What about love?

MELISA   Marriage is a punishment Daphine. I'll end up like my
mother. First I'll lose my body then my mind. Don't tell anyone, but she
drank, you know. She had to. That was how she stayed married to my
father for thirty years. It's no use I'll just have to keep moving.

DAPHINE   But, he'll find you if you leave...

MELISA   He'll find me anyway. You heard the message – Mioshan, she
spoke to you.

DAPHINE   But that wasn't for real. It was just a game – right.

MELISA   Mioshan never lie.

DAPHINE   But I did. I made it all up. I thought you knew that.

MELISA   Mioshan never lie. You have a rare gift.

DAPHINE   Me. I'm nothing. I don't believe in them kind of things. I
don't even read my horoscope. Look, you can't leave me here on my own
with them.

MELISA   Perhaps you should think about moving as well.

DAPHINE   Where would I go? It's alright for you. At least you can go
back to Hong Kong. *(Urgently)* Take me with you. Have they got black
people there?

MELISA   I don't know. I've never been to Hong Kong in my life.

DAPHINE   But I thought...

MELISA   You're not the only one with skeletons in the cupboard.

DAPHINE   So where are you from then?

MELISA   Haywards Heath.

DAPHINE   Where the hell is that?

MELISA   Who knows? Somewhere. Nowhere. A place full of dusty old
cobwebs – my family. I'm not going back there.

DAPHINE   Well perhaps you should take your own advice. Stop running. Anyway, I don't think you're running from your father, I think you're running from yourself.

ACT TWO, SCENE 4
LEONORA paces in the hallway impatiently. Enter FRIEDA.

FRIEDA   What's going on?
LEONORA *(Looks surprised and acts guilty)* Oh nothing. I thought you were asleep.
FRIEDA   How you expect me to sleep? There's work to do.
LEONORA   You should relax more, you're on holiday. I couldn't possibly let you work.
FRIEDA   I meant spiritual work. You have the gift too. You just need to know how to make it work for you.
LEONORA   You still going on – and how do I know you not talking a lot of rubbish?
FRIEDA   Because... *(Enter DAPHINE)*
LEONORA *(Turns and pounces on her)* Have you got my prescription, girl?
DAPHINE   Yes, here it is – *(About to take pills out of her pocket)* I feel like a bleeding chemist shop.
FRIEDA *(Appearing suddenly behind LEONORA)* What's going on?
DAPHINE *(To FRIEDA)* She needs her pills.
FRIEDA *(Storms forward)* Give them to me.
LEONORA *(Rushes forward also – they both try to wrestle the pills from DAPHINE.)* No, they're mine... They're mine. *(FRIEDA wins the struggle.)* Why can't you stop interfering in my life? *(LEONORA retreats back to her room.)*
DAPHINE *(To FRIEDA)* She needs her pills. She goes crazy without them.
FRIEDA   She's crazy with them. You really must stop running errands for her. She has to snap out of this behaviour. *(FRIEDA puts the pills in a bag she always carries with her.)* Tell me what's been going on in this house.
DAPHINE   What do you mean?
FRIEDA   How long she been behaving like this?
DAPHINE   You mean the pills?
FRIEDA   Yes. What else she been doing? *(DAPHINE looks hesitant.)* Tell me.
DAPHINE   She talks to herself a lot. She has these attacks and sometimes she's up all night... Sometimes she plays her classical music real loud – I've to wear earplugs.

FRIEDA   She got any friends?

DAPHINE   I've never seen any. What's wrong with her?

FRIEDA   Never you mind. I'll sort it out. What about the girl upstairs?

DAPHINE   Melisa?

FRIEDA   What's her business here?

DAPHINE   She's alright.

FRIEDA   I said what's her business here?

DAPHINE   She's a student. That's all I know.

FRIEDA   Why you protecting her?

DAPHINE   I'm not protecting her. Both she and Leonora has got it in for me. They've been scheming to get me out of this house. Look at me. *(Seeking sympathy)* I wouldn't survive on the street. I've got no bottle.

FRIEDA *(Thoughtful)* So this girl has a lot of influence over Leonora?

DAPHINE   Perhaps. Or Leonora influence her. I'm not sure. I try to mind me own business Mrs...

FRIEDA   Call me Frieda.

DAPHINE   Mrs. Frieda... I just want a quiet life. I deserve that.

FRIEDA   I knew there was something wrong the moment I stepped into this house. I knew it had to be something bad to have kept my daughter from writing to me all these years. You must help me deal with her.

DAPHINE   Melisa's got a good heart really. She's just the kind of do-gooder who let her heart rule her head. That's why you can't trust her.

FRIEDA   Keep an eye on her, make sure she stays in her room. Tell me if you see or hear anything strange happening.

DAPHINE   How strange?

FRIEDA   Anything at all. I have to get my daughter back to the Caribbean and no-one is going to stand in my way.

DAPHINE   The Caribbean? It sounds so heavenly. All that sun, sea and open skies. That's what I call real freedom. Not like here where we live on top of each other.

FRIEDA   If only I could get Leonora to see that. But there's something more powerful here...

DAPHINE   You're talking about spirits aren't you?

FRIEDA   Never you mind.

DAPHINE   You think Melisa might have something to do with this? You think she, may have brought them here unintentionally?

FRIEDA   Never you mind.

DAPHINE   My mother sees spirits. She says that one day I'll see spirits too... and my daughter Daryl she'll see spirits too – when she's older. She says it generic – but I don't know whether to believe her though.

FRIEDA *(Showing sudden interest in DAPHINE)* You have a daughter?

DAPHINE   Yes, Daryl.

FRIEDA   But you look so young.

DAPHINE   She's nearly three. She's staying with my mother – till I can find a place.

FRIEDA   Who's your Mother?

DAPHINE   Esther Smith.

FRIEDA   Esther Smith. I used to know a little girl back home ... but her name wasn't Smith. Esther... Esther Thompson.

DAPHINE *(Excited)* That's my mother's maiden name.

FRIEDA   She came to England... nineteen sixty... sixty... you know I can't remember. She was my cousin's daughter. *(Approaches her)* So you must be my cousin's daughter, daughter. And you know Leonora never told me.

DAPHINE   Well, she wouldn't, would she? She's not exactly proud to be related to me.

FRIEDA   Your grandmother was a very calm... woman. Very adventurous.

DAPHINE   Not like me, heh? I never go anywhere. I never go anywhere. Sometimes, I wonder if I'll ever get out of here. That's why I'm doing literacy classes. Gosh! I don't know why I told you that. I don't normally. *(FRIEDA looks patient. DAPHINE chatters on covering her embarrassment.)* They said I was sub-normal, they gave me electric shock treatment. It didn't make me better. It made meworse.

FRIEDA   This could only happen in England.

DAPHINE   They just didn't recognise my talent. Did I tell you I have a computer brain? I can memorise anything you tell me. Go on try me.

FRIEDA   No time for that. Run along now.

DAPHINE   You know something Mrs. Frieda. I really like you. You're the first person I've met whom I can really talk to.

FRIEDA *(Warmly)* Mmmm. Run along now. *(Exit DAPHINE. FRIEDA lays down some candles and a bowl of water. Stands up and   admires her creation.)* If she comes along. She'll step right here and I'll trap her. Then I'll wrap her up and sling her out, as far away from my daughter as possible.

(As she goes about her preparations, MEDUSA appears looking smug. She looks at the trap FRIEDA has laid and laughs.)

MEDUSA   She thinks she can work miracles. She thinks she can curtail my influence here, cast me out. She's audacious, I'll give her that – but we'll see.

FRIEDA   I shall have to call them all – no matter how far away they are; Ivory Coast, New Guinea, Benin, Bermuda, and Burundi. I shall go way back, past the middle passage, to the old world, to Africa. This is one battle I cannot afford to lose. I shall call them all to this house.

MEDUSA *(Sneers)* This is the house.

FRIEDA   Come griots, come. Come marabouts and kings. Come sprinkle Sam-Sam for your followers. *(Sprinkle water)* Sing Tai-nai your warrior songs.

MEDUSA *(She walks around and begins to pick each candle up.)* This is the house. They say if you stay here too long you take on the idiosyncrasies of the occupants. Senile dementia. Psychosis. Persecution complex.

FRIEDA   Come mediators, convenors of life and rituals. Come overseers of the past. Come voice of the people. Come myals, speakers of parables, come sisters of the spirit.

MEDUSA   This is the house. This is the house that Jack built. Jill built. Hyacinth built a garden on the window-sill. A house built on unstable ground... distorted dreams, stagnant lives... a house where souls compete.

FRIEDA   Come bring us wisdom and love in all its potency. Come like the rhythm of the drum. Come if you are able *(Makes drum noises – whilst moving forward as if to stop MEDUSA. She appears to freeze.)*

MEDUSA *(Looks at Frieda. Walks around her)* This is my house. My name is Medusa – the name that launched a thousand spells. *(Defiant)* Come on move me if you dare. You'll wish you'd never heard my name. Wish you'd never seen my face. *(Walks away. Turns)* This is my house.

(Enter LEONORA)

LEONORA   Mama, what's going on? I thought I heard shouting.

FRIEDA *(Unfreezes, looks disorientated, begins to mumble)* This is my house. This is my house...

LEONORA *(Holding her)* Mama...

FRIEDA *(Becoming aware of LEONORA. She grabs her hands and pulls her.)* Come Leonora. We mustn't let her win.

(Lights change. Lights up. MELISA'S room. She sits packing)

MELISA   Dear mama... Dear papa. Grandma and Grandpa. My great ancestors. The sun, the moon, the stars, the rain that makes the rice grow. I know I will bring shame on you my parents, my country, my ancestors – with my selfishness. I will wear my cheongsam, celebrate Chinese New Year. I will endeavour to speak Cantonese, even wear peach blossom in my hair on special occasions – but slave and chattel I shall be not. To endure marriage is to endure hell. Mama you should know that. I am too infatuated with freedom to sacrifice that. Mother. Father. I know you will

mourn me with chrysanthemums around the door as tradition requires.
But sometimes I think tradition is a dead man's revenge on the future.
Mama, I'm sorry you will never carry my trousseau as you have longed for
– but my chastity cannot be bartered for over a glass of chianti. Goodbye
mama. Goodbye papa.
*(MELISA rises with suitcase in hands. She leaves pausing momentarily
in the hallway to look around.)*

Lights change.

ACT TWO, SCENE 5
LEONORA'S room. FRIEDA acts urgently.

FRIEDA   Sit down. *(She pushes LEONORA into a chair. Then she
rushes to her bag and brings out a white dress.)* We must act quickly.
(She tries to put the dress on LEONORA. She resists at first) Trust me. I'm
your mother. *(She puts dress on LEONORA)* She's more powerful than I
thought. *(She brings out a bright sash from her bag and ties it around
LEONORA'S waist.)* I can sense her. She's darkening your aura – sapping
your energy. *(Ties scarf on LEONORA'S head)* She tink she can scare me,
well we'll see... *(She picks up cloak carefully and brings it towards
LEONORA reverently)*
LEONORA *(Stares at cloak. Stares at FRIEDA. She panics and jumps up)*
It's no use mother. It won't work. I'm not who you think I am any more.
(She pushes the cloak away.) This doesn't belong to me... *(FRIEDA stares
at her unable to take the cloak. LEONORA begins to take off scarf and
sash and hands them to FRIEDA.)* I don't deserve it. I'll get out of here
one day. I can make it on my own.
FRIEDA   You can't make it on your own. Look at you...
LEONORA   What's wrong with me? I'm still a good-looking woman. I
used to have plenty of beaus when I was young.
FRIEDA   Remember you're not young any more and your health is not
what it used to be.
LEONORA   I suffer from acute anxiety that's all.
FRIEDA   Rubbish, your behaviour is more than that.
LEONORA   My therapist Mrs. Brown, she says it's all the fault of the
modern world – makes you want to run away and hide. She gives me a lot
of support. She says that I'm making progress. So don't worry about me
mama. I'll work with children again, like I used to. You don't think I can
do it, do you mama? You've never believed in me. I was going to soar like a
bird.

FRIEDA   Face realities girl. Some of us are turkeys not meant for the sky. Come back home with me. You see what happens when you stay away too long – you forget where you belong. Divided loyalties.

LEONORA   But, can't you see mama, this is where I belong. This is my father's land. Where else should I belong? It's my birthright.

FRIEDA   But it's you mother's line that is important, after all who knows who your father is?

LEONORA   You see, it's all your fault. You've curse my life from the day I was born.

FRIEDA   Is the bad blood in you talking.

LEONORA   No matter how hard I tried. I could never amount to anything in your eyes. I could have been a great dancer...

FRIEDA   So what stopped you? Why didn't you make it? *(LEONORA shuffles away afraid of the question)* You know why... because you came here thinking they were going to welcome you with open arms. Instead all you got was a slap in the face and that set you back... forever. All these years Leonora you've been dancing, but you've been dancing in silence. Now it's time you faced the music.

LEONORA   Why do you hate me? Why? Because, I remind you of him. Daddy.

FRIEDA   Leonora chile I don't hate you. *(Approaches her warmly.)*I am not here out of malice. I know you think I'm an interfering old woman from backyard. But, I got eyes. I can see what they done to you – my sweet daughter. They twist you inside out. Yes, it's true what they say. The world is your oyster, but very few can reach the pearl. I believe you have tried and I respect you for that – but it's time to come home now. There's nothing left for you here now – nothing except empty shells.

LEONORA *(Laughing)* Imagine me a pearl diver and I can't even swim.

FRIEDA   That's because you were swimming against the tide. No-one swims against the tide for long.

LEONORA   Was I a fool to dream, mama?

FRIEDA   Come back home with me. They'll roll out the red carpet, sing the national anthem. You'll never see a finer set of people – the country is beautiful now. You know I build a big house on the plot of land your father left me in his will, we got goats, cows, pigs – plenty of plants, you won't miss a thing here. I am an old woman now Leonora. What's the use of all this knowledge if there's no-one to give it to. Back home you is their heroine.

LEONORA   But, you said it yourself, my life has been a complete failure. How could I go back and live another lie?

FRIEDA   Don't worry you'll be mother Frieda's daughter.

LEONORA *(Cynical)* Inherit mother Frieda's respect.

FRIEDA   Yes...

LEONORA   Mother Frieda's knowledge... Mother Frieda's wealth.

FRIEDA   Of course. You know I could have been a decent mother to you if it weren't for your father...

LEONORA   Don't bring daddy into this.

FRIEDA   I used to listen to the B.B.C. World Service my girl and think of you.

LEONORA   Well I'm not your girl any more. I'm a grown woman, can't you see? When I get out of here I'm going to sell the house and use the money to invest in a dance school. I'll invite the best foreign girls and the daughters of celebrities, the rich and famous. I've still got plenty of contacts. So you see you can take your mothering and your obeah back to the Caribbean with you. In fact on the way over, drop it in the ocean where it belongs.

FRIEDA   You can say that to me, after I spent fifteen years in penitentiary for you. *(LEONORA looks away scared.)* You thought I was dead didn't you? *(Walks up behind LEONORA who keeps her back to her)* You wanted me to die. You just like your father – deny me... deny me... and deny me again. You remember the lastday he came to our house?

LEONORA *(Turning round suddenly)* You promised.

FRIEDA   You remember what he looked like that day? I believed he was angry, very angry.

LEONORA   No.

FRIEDA   You saw his black wellington boots out on the verandah.

LEONORA   No.

FRIEDA   He always left his boots outside – caked with mud, and then you children knew he was there and not to disturb me.

LEONORA   I don't remember.

FRIEDA   He was angry that day because I'd told him I wanted more money for your school fees and your extra dancing lessons. He said he was proud you wanted to be a dancer but he couldn't give me any more money. I tried to blackmail him and he said he would stop supporting me altogether. I knew he was bluffing, after all he didn't want everyone to know you was his black daughter. Next thing I knew he was down on his knees begging me to keep his secret. I laughed – thinking all these years he been lying with his head on laced pillow – mine on straw. I manicured his finger nails. He wore three gold rings and drank wine from silver goblets. How they lived like kings and we like flies. All I was asking for was what was mine and yours. That was when he started – I should be lucky one of my children had good blood and how I lived better than any other negro on his land. I was mad. I curse him. I curse his wife. I curse his children. He boasted that he didn't believe in Mother Frieda's magic. That was when I felt the force driving my hands forward with the knife. *(FRIEDA carries out action)* He knocked me back and the knife went flying. I felt his hands on my neck. He was squeezing the life from me with the very hands that had stroked my back... *(Gasping)*... but you came didn't you Leonora?

LEONORA I must help mama... *(Crawling on the floor)*

FRIEDA The last breath was trickling from my body.

LEONORA I must help mama.

FRIEDA I don't know where you found that knife girl but you saved my life. *(LEONORA begins to stab at ground – crying.)* The police came with the catholic priest – Marshall Croft was lying dead in my arms. The priest gave him the last rites.

LEONORA *(Holding out her hands and looking at them with disgust)* I did it. I did it mama. *(Appearance of MEDUSA.)*

FRIEDA No, you didn't do it darling.

LEONORA I did mama. I remember it now – as if it was yesterday.

FRIEDA Your arms wasn't strong enough. He was a big man.

LEONORA That's why I'm being punished. Punished for my sins.

FRIEDA I did it. You hear me. I pushed the knife in.

LEONORA *(Looking with disbelief)* You. You did it. You killed my father.

FRIEDA It was him or me chile – you've got to understand...

LEONORA After all these years mama – now you tell me. You hated him. You hated him so much. You hate me...

FRIEDA Leonora, you must let me finish the ceremony –before it's too late. *(She goes towards LEONORA – who backs away.)*

LEONORA *(Frenzied screaming)* Get away from me. Don't you touch me. Don't you ever touch me again. It's all your fault. I hate you.

MEDUSA *(Beckons LEONORA toward the door.)* Like Cleopatra awakening from her mummified dream, wrapped in satin, porcelain smile... she took one step... *(LEONORA steps forward towards MEDUSA.)*

FRIEDA Leonora, don't give in to her now. Don't let her come between us. *(Notices LEONORA heading for the door in a trance)* Leonora... Leonora where are you going? Come back, you not ready yet.

MEDUSA ... at first her step is a little shaky, after all she's been asleep for hundreds of years – and she is not sure what awaits her outside her tomb... step... by step... getting stronger as she goes... Suddenly the doors of the pyramids are thrown open – she can smell the air... see the light... Come Leonora... come.

FRIEDA Come back, you must let me call them first – Koto the griot, Sylvia the marabout, Miriam who talks in spirit tongue. They will drive her out, she doesn't belong here... *(Intervenes, takes off symbolic necklace and places it around LEONORA'S neck.)*

MEDUSA *(Grabbing LEONORA by the hands)* Come Leonora. Don't listen to her. Where was she when you needed her? I was here, wasn't I? I looked after you, didn't I? She's never loved you. You know that now. After all, she killed your father. She killed your future. Come. You don't need her. *(Pulling LEONORA vigorously)*

MEDUSA   Step by step her strides are bolder, like a giant centurion on the run... nothing can hold her back now... Come Leonora. Come. *(Finally LEONORA reaches the door and steps out. MEDUSA follows after her. There is a flash of light. Door closes.)*

FRIEDA   Come great goddess of water, light walk with her, guide her, protect her. I can feel your strength, your presence is here. Intervene – intervene, do something now. Drive her – wretched demon from this place.

(Lights come up again, MELISA races onto the stage crying)

MELISA   I saw her. I saw her pulling Leonora into the road. I saw her. Her eyes were evil. Her face was twisted and full of anger and... and... hate. I saw the truck going towards them. I turned around and shouted for her to stop. I ran. I ran as fast as I could, my heart was beating ever so fast. I saw the truck and I managed to grab Leonora and pull her back... *(Crying)*... but it was too late... it was too late... *(DAPHINE consoles her)* You were right Daphine. She's not who I thought she was. She's not who I thought she was. I should have listened to you. All this time I've been running, hiding, pretending, looking for answers in storybooks. I've been such a damn fool.

FRIEDA looks crestfallen – lights change.

ACT TWO, SCENE 6
Lights up. DAPHINE sits with her head on FRIEDA'S lap.

DAPHINE   What's going to happen to her?

FRIEDA   They say she wasn't badly hurt. The truck just missed her. It was more the shock than anything. Thank god that girl was there in time. She saved Leonora's life.

DAPHINE   Are you going to take her back with you?

FRIEDA   I'll try. She's got a mind of her own that one. She always had ever since she was a girl.

DAPHINE   A change of environment is perhaps all she needs to get better. They'd only lock her away if you left her here. Although I'd do whatever I can to help her if she stayed.

FRIEDA   There is one thing you can do for me.

DAPHINE   What? *(FRIEDA gets up and gets a paper and her large bag. She hands it to DAPHINE.)*

FRIEDA   It's the deed to the house.

DAPHINE *(Disappointed)* Oh, I see you want me to put it on the market for you.

FRIEDA   No. It's yours. *(DAPHINE looks at her flabbergasted.)* Well, it's no use to me and Leonora won't be needing it for a while, if at all. And your friend, she can stay here as long as she likes. She's not a bad sort after all.

DAPHINE   Mine?

FRIEDA   ... and this too. *(She hands her the bag)*

DAPHINE   But...

FRIEDA   No buts... It seems my journey to England was twofold. I thought I was coming to initiate my daughter. But, what I found was not as simple as I thought. England needs Mother Frieda – You've been chosen – accept it with grace. *(DAPHINE takes the bag.)* When my mother was nine she had learnt all the names of over sixty-five herbs and plants. She could look into a person's eyes and tell what ails them – and she could certainly tell a good-natured person from a bad one. She passed the gift onto me. The light has settled in your eyes, my dear. That's how I know it is yours.

DAPHINE   Mine. *(Lights change. She places the robe on DAPHINE. FRIEDA begins to teach DAPHINE the names of herbs.)*

FRIEDA   Passion flower...

DAPHINE   Passion flower.

FRIEDA   Cures the ailment of...

DAPHINE   ... cures the ailment of...

FRIEDA   Kidney trouble.

DAPHINE   Kidney trouble.

FRIEDA   Kwaku bush, cerusi, oil of lavender...

DAPHINE   ... Kwaku bush... cerusi... oil of lavender...

FRIEDA   Dizziness.

DAPHINE   Dizziness.

(Music. DAPHINE walks forward in ceremonial cloak. The rest of the cast join in and follow behind her.)

FRIEDA   Mix five pints of water. Boil sour sop leave... tek one glass three times a day.

DAPHINE   Mix five pints of water. Boil sour sop leave – tek one glass three times a day.

FRIEDA   White sage, hug-me-close, bury you heart under coconut tree.

DAPHINE   White sage, hug-me-close, bury you heart under coconut tree.
FRIEDA   Search-me-heart, lily-of-the-valley and leaf-of-life.
DAPHINE   Search-me-heart, lily-of-the-valley and leaf-of-life.

They begin to dance. Lights down.

The End.

MY SISTER-WIFE

A Screenplay based upon an original idea by
Azmaa Pirzada

Meera Syal

OPENING TITLES:

SCENE 1
Int. MARYAM'S bedroom. ASIF'S house. Night.

(An Asian man, fortyish, handsome, is entwined with an Asian woman on the bed. He kisses her long hair which envelops her face. The bed is creaking under them.)

SCENE 2
Int. Landing/corridor. ASIF'S house. Night.

(A brown female hand carries a full decanter of water from her P.O.V. We move towards the door from behind which the sound of the lovers' moans and the creaking bed come. Her hand turns the handle and flings it open. The water decanter drops from her hand and smashes to the ground.)

END OPENING TITLES

SCENE 3
Int. FARAH'S bedroom (Parents' house) night.

(Close up of a love scene in an Indian film: two lovers reunited against a backdrop of screaming violins, passion, colour, over-the-top emotion alien to a western taste but somehow profoundly moving. A muffled sob.)

POPPY *(V.O.)* Oh God, I told you not to watch this.
(The television is switched off and the picture disappears. Pull back to reveal a suburban bedroom, feminine, relics of a teenage existence still apparent in the decor. FARAH is sitting up in bed tearful. She looks like a broken woman, in an old dressing-gown, dark rings under her eyes, her mouth full of chocolate which is open in a silent O of agony. POPPY sits

on the bed next to her, pushing a pile of used wet tissues and a nearly empty chocolate box to the side, to pat her on the back, making FARAH choke and breathe again. POPPY is one of life's doers, late twenties, cynical eyes in a wide open face, and FARAH'S closest friend.)

POPPY   You've just won a design award for your work, you're intelligent, beautiful...
(FARAH snorts, her nose is dripping. POPPY wipes it with a tissue.)
if a little messy, got a filofax of men of all shades and shapes panting to go out with you – you don't need him...
FARAH   I want to die.
POPPY   After weeks of holding up a female jelly, I'm feeling a bit suicidal myself...
(A telephone rings in the distance. FARAH'S ears cock, but POPPY takes her face in her hands, forcing her to listen.)
They all have something unique about them, a crinkly smile, the way they change gears, but not one of them is perfect or irreplaceable. That's what you used to tell me.
FARAH   He *is* unique. He's familiar. He understands all of me... both sides.
POPPY   Oh love... someone else will.
FARAH   I don't want to be out there, looking anymore. He was my future.
POPPY   He's married... isn't he? *(POPPY takes this in for a moment.)* All the best ones are. Bastards!

(There is a knock at the door which swings open. The first thing we see is the doorway carpeted in flowers, expensive bouquets still in their cellophane thrown and left where they landed. FARAH'S mother, MUMTAZ, an elegant, attractive woman in silk dressing-gown, stands holding out a telephone receiver, quizzical amongst the dying blooms. FARAH'S father, TARIQ, is just visible, a plump kindly man, his hair standing on end from disturbed sleep, his face etched with concern.)

MUMTAZ Darling... it's for you again.
(FARAH shakes her head and buries it in POPPY'S lap. MUMTAZ and TARIQ exchange an exasperated look.)

SCENE 4
Int. Kitchen. MUMTAZ'S house. Evening.

(MUMTAZ, resplendent in silk Pakistani suit, cool and impressive giving a cookery demonstration to a small group of retired English colonels. She mixes ingredients as they watch intently, making notes, savouring the smells and MUMTAZ'S expertise in silent reverence. From the adjoining room, the television with volume turned high, can be heard. MUMTAZ notes this with annoyance, trying to concentrate.)

MUMTAZ Now this is the most delicate part of the marinade preparation, too much heat and it curdles, too little and it sets...
COL. STEVENS This isn't how we did it in Derradoon.
(The television noise becomes deafening. We hear the channels flicked about. MUMTAZ carefully wipes her hands.)
MUMTAZ Col. Stevens, would you take over?
(She hands him an apron. He blinks nervously, regarding the bubbling mixture on the stove. He grabs a pot of curry powder violently, and bears it aloft over the mixture.)

SCENE 5
Int. Television room. MUMTAZ'S house. Evening.

(FARAH, in work clothes with her briefcase and portfolio at her feet, slumped in front of the television, flicking channels mindlessly. A full ashtray at her feet. MUMTAZ opens the door through which we glimpse the men crowding around the counter, watching COL. STEVENS getting down to work. MUMTAZ goes over to the television and switches it off. The door to the kitchen remains open.)

MUMTAZ Daddy was expecting you to take the new season's designs in today. *(Pause)* The boss's daughter still has responsibilities, Farah. You've sat here all day in your suit...
FARAH Changed my mind. Don't want to go anywhere.
MUMTAZ *(Sits next to her)* Oh, my daughter. You open like a flower and give everything. But your revenge is terrible, not only to yourself. This can't go on....
FARAH *(Whispering)* This will never heal.
MUMTAZ *(Takes a deep breath)* A very charming man, your Mr. Asif Shah. And very persistent. I can see what you see in him.
FARAH *(Shocked, looking at MUMTAZ for the first time)* You... saw him?... What did he say?
MUMTAZ A lot of things. He said he had to see me and explain...

FARAH   Explain what? About the wife and two kids that happen to slip his mind? You should have slammed the door in his face!

MUMTAZ   Farah, I'm so worried about you! The reason for your suffering was standing on my doorstep. How could I not let him in?

FARAH   He's a liar, mummy! He lied to me! No-one lies to me!

(Through the open door, we hear a gasp as a sudden burst of flame leaps from COL. STEVENS' frying pan. Neither mother nor daughter take any notice.)

MUMTAZ   Nothing is that simple. He said he was trying to protect you...

FARAH *(Spitting fire)* The old Asif Shah charm strikes again. God, whose side are you on? Well done, mum. Couldn't get me to marry the village idiots in flares your friends kept suggesting, Asif's rich and brown so he'll do... I'll look fab in a harem, and if my Maharajah gets bored, he can always swap me for a bloody camel!

(MUMTAZ moves to the door to the kitchen through which the men are peering in for a better look. She smiles with mock cheeriness and brings the door to.)

MUMTAZ *(Quietly)* We brought you up here. But have we left nothing of home in you?

FARAH *(Wearily)* What are you on about now?

MUMTAZ   Honour. Obligation. Duty to the family. Things we thought we had taught you. Perhaps he doesn't love his wife now...

FARAH   There is such a thing as an amicable divorce, you know.

MUMTAZ   An arranged match to a village girl, he told me. No real family besides his. He'd be no man in my eyes if he could forget his responsibilities towards her and...

FARAH   So where does that leave me?

MUMTAZ *(Sighing)* Well, he told me he wanted to marry you...

FARAH   What?... How...

MUMTAZ   Apparently his first marriage has never been registered here. She was brought over as his cousin... and as, he says, they've been emotionally apart for years, and she has given her permission...

FARAH *(Eyes shining)* Marry me!

MUMTAZ   I told him the word brings you out in a rash *(Hugs FARAH close)* If being apart is making you both so unhappy... I suppose we have to consider all the other options.

FARAH   It's as simple as that?

MUMTAZ *(Shakes her head)* Love used to be simple. I met your papa on our wedding day. I was lucky. We wanted you to make your own choices, hoping they would be sensible... God knows this isn't ideal. His family will always have a hold over him. I was brought up to accept such things. Could you? *(FARAH does not answer)* In the end, it's up to you. *(There's a cough coming from the doorway. COL STEVENS stands proudly in the doorway, holding aloft a perfect and steaming dish of tandoori chicken.)*

SCENE 6

Ext. Registry office. Day.

(A drizzly overcast day, made more depressing by the concrete bunker of the registry office, a building wholly unsuited to its task. A small group of wedding guests, including POPPY, MUMTAZ and TARIQ, exit the building, wincing at the rain and wind, the vivid colours of the women's traditional clothes a stark contrast to their surroundings. A gum-chewing photographer is waiting at the foot of the steps, camera at the ready.)

PHOTOGRAPHER   Right! Bride and groom first, then immediate family. Everybody else, move out of the way.

(Most of the guests begin filtering to the side. We see TARIQ and MUMTAZ looking behind them into the building, expectant. POPPY finds herself next to MARYAM, a plumpish, plain-looking Pakistani woman, late twenties, in a loud suit and obvious make-up. She is watching two young girls in matching suits running up and down the steps, playing tag. She seems to be unhappy. POPPY checks her gaze. The photographer's barks fill the air.)

POPPY *(Apologetic)* Chris is from my paper. One of the hard lads, he'd rather be doing a motorway pile up. More fun. *(MARYAM looks impassively at her)* If I know Farah. She's having a crafty fag in the bog. Who'd have thought it? The suicide rate of young males in South London will jump tonight!
(MARYAM does not find this amusing. POPPY shifts nervously. The guests are now murmuring, worried as MUMTAZ and TARIQ hover on the steps, looking inside anxiously.)
PHOTOGRAPHER *(Shouting)* The bride and groom... could someone go and find them? I haven't got all day...

SCENE 7
Ext. Registry office. (Back entrance) Day.

(A fire exit door leading into a back alley, tall steel bins, litter whisked about in the wind. The door bursts open, ASIF, in morning suit, drags FARAH into the alley. She looks exquisite in a Western ivory designer suit, clutching her bridal bouquet.)

FARAH *(Giggling)* Asif, what are you doing... they're all waiting.
ASIF I've been waiting all my life for this.
(He begins kissing her neck, trying to push her up against the bins)
FARAH *(Weakly)* My suit... they're calling us...
ASIF Are you really all mine now?
FARAH *(Melting)* Asif...
ASIF I love you so much.

(ASIF is showering FARAH in kisses, almost violent in their intensity. FARAH is trying to hold him off, protect her dress and make-up, but makes the mistake of looking into his eyes. She flings the bridal bouquet to the floor and pulls him to her, falling back against the bin, welding her body to his, drinking him in. We hear TARIQ and MUMTAZ'S voices from far away, caught in snatches by the breeze.)

SCENE 8
Ext. Registry office. Day.

(Still from POPPY and MARYAM'S P.O.V. A cheer goes up as ASIF and FARAH exit the building. The photographer hurriedly organises a family shot. The two girls run up to ASIF, clinging to him, wanting all his attention as he pulls them into place for the shot.)

POPPY Don't know how she'll handle this set up, being a stepmum and everything... Still, they're gorgeous girls. And once Farah's set her mind on something... or someone.
(The two little girls squeal loudly as the flash goes off)
Never seen her look so happy. You must be coming to the proper Pakistani do on the twentieth. Whose side are you on? Guest wise I mean?
(Suddenly the two girls rush over to MARYAM and fling themselves at her, over-excited)
GIRLS Mummy! Mummy! We had our photo taken with daddy! Did you see?

(POPPY stares at MARYAM, speechless with embarrassment. Cut to ASIF and FARAH in the middle of the guests, being congratulated. ASIF has

lipstick on his face. FARAH turns to him to quickly wipe it off, revealing a huge dirty black mark down the middle of her back. The guests exchange glances. MUMTAZ looks worriedly at TARIQ and wipes away a tear. TARIQ puts on a brave smile and begins throwing confetti, encouraging everyone else to follow suit. The confetti is whisked away by the wintry breeze.)

SCENE 9
Int. Lounge. MUMTAZ'S house. Night.

(A group of Pakistani women sit around the lounge sewing elaborate suits, writing out invites, matching up shoes with already finished suits. FARAH stands grumpily in the centre of the circle being measured by MUMTAZ, who has a long list of "tasks to do" pinned like a label onto her front. One of the older women comes up to read the list on MUMTAZ'S chest, which makes her laugh. The room is silent, industrious, peaceful.)

FARAH *(Shattering it)* We've still got a few weeks.
  (MUMTAZ squinting, then pausing to rub her eyes and press on her temples, feeling a headache coming on.)
MUMTAZ Which is nothing. Now stop fidgeting.
OLDER WOMAN *(Urdu, subtitles)* She's trembling at the thought of her wedding night!

(The women laugh. FARAH looks confusedly at MUMTAZ. FARAH'S dupatta has come away from her shoulders. MUMTAZ purposefully arranges it so it covers her breast. FARAH looks puzzled. Another woman begins humming a tune in the background.)

MUMTAZ Modesty.
OLDER WOMAN *(Urdu, subtitles)* Tell her Mumtaz, what she's got to look forward to! I can't, my memory doesn't go back that far!

(The women scream at this. The humming becomes a song, which all the women begin singing. It is a traditionally lewd folk number. The older woman pushes FARAH and MUMTAZ together, encouraging them to clap and dance.)

FARAH What are they singing? I wish I could understand...
  (MUMTAZ pulling her into the dance)

MUMTAZ There are many things I wish you could understand. Are you happy?
(FARAH swinging MUMTAZ round and whooping)
FARAH   Yes! Yes! Yes!

SCENE 10

Int. FARAH'S bedroom. MUMTAZ'S house. Night.

(Yellow neon light streams through the open curtains. FARAH sits at her dressing-table. She holds up the gold tikka (Headpiece) to her forehead, attempts a shy bride pose and bursts into giggles.)

FARAH *(To herself)* Finding respectability at twenty-nine and two thirds...
(FARAH stops, hearing stones patter at her window. She runs to it and throws it open.)

SCENE 11

Ext. FARAH'S bedroom window. Night.

(ASIF stands below, bathed in the headlights of his sports car.)

FARAH   Ey you, you're not supposed to see me till the wedding night!
ASIF   We're man and wife according to Her Majesty's government, and what's good enough for Queenie...
FARAH   Going to climb up the drain-pipe and ruin your creases?
ASIF *(Shy suddenly)* No. Some things we should stick to. Sounds daft...
FARAH *(Gently)* No. I feel the same.
(FARAH blows him a kiss. He mimes receiving it, and topples over a dustbin)
ASIF   I'm too old for this. *(FARAH shakes her head, grinning)* I never thought I'd get a second chance.
(They stare at each other. In the distance, the mournful wail of a siren.)

SCENE 12

Int. MUMTAZ'S house. Kitchen. Day.

(FARAH has the radio on full blast as she checks through MUMTAZ'S list at the kitchen counter. She pricks her ears, expecting to hear something. She goes over to the radio and turns it off. Sure enough, the doorbell is being pressed insistently.)

SCENE 13
Int. MUMTAZ'S house. Hallway/front door. Day.

(FARAH opens the door to ASIF. FARAH laughing, trying to close the door in his face.)

FARAH   Not before the suhaag raat! I told you...
(ASIF pushes the door open. FARAH giggles and runs back into the hallway. ASIF doesn't pursue her. She turns to laugh at him. She is stopped by the grave expression on his face. He holds her shoulders, soothing her like a child)
ASIF   Get your coat. It's your mama.

SCENE 14
Int. Hospital corridor. Day.

(A deserted hospital corridor; clinical white, plastic chairs, a lone muffled announcement over the tannoy. FARAH sits facing a closed ward door, ASIF next to her. She doesn't see him, all her energies are focused on that closed door. Suddenly from inside, there is a loud sobbing, FARAH'S father. FARAH looks at ASIF, his tears beginning to fall. She is dry-eyed, but takes his hand grips it so tightly his flesh turns from brown to white. We focus in on their clasped hands.)

SCENE 15
Int. FARAH'S bedroom. ASIF'S house. Night

(Close on ASIF gripping FARAH'S hand, which is decorated with bridal henna and weighed down with gold jewellery. FARAH'S new wedding ring winks in the half light. FARAH, in full bridal dress, her face completely covered by an embroidered veil, is being gently led through the door by a smiling ASIF in crumpled morning dress. MARYAM and SABIA are standing next to the bed, obviously surprised by this interruption. They quickly put their arms behind their backs, hiding something. We see FARAH'S hand clutch ASIF'S arm tightly. MARYAM notes this and smiles cruelly, then suddenly lifts her arms and throws a shower of rose petals up into the air, laughing loudly. SABIA, a woman of about sixty-five, in perpetual white widow's weeds, eyes closed behind her thick-lensed spectacles, deliberately sprinkles her petals over the bed, muttering to herself, not looking up. There is a commotion behind them, and we glimpse the two little Pakistani girls in bright salwar kameez, standing in the doorway. MARYAM'S face falls. She rushes over to them

*and gathers them into her arms, before bundling them out of the room.
SABIA glides after them, pausing only to press her hand in blessing on
ASIF'S forehead, ignoring FARAH completely. The door closes and the
sounds of the girls' chatter fades away. ASIF leads FARAH to the bed,
slowly lifts her veil. We see her face for the first time and she is crying.)*

ASIF *(Tenderly)* I'm here, Farah.
FARAH   I'm so glad you are.

SCENE 16
Int. Living-room. ASIF'S house. Night.

*(Some months later. A party, the house is buzzing with young rich
couples, half Pakistani, half white. FARAH and ASIF stand holding court,
both immaculately dressed and glowing with happiness. POPPY, on the
settee, holding hands with a burly, unshaven man, chatting to two
overdressed Pakistani women. POPPY breaks off her conversation to
search for an ashtray, one appears under her hand, held out by
MARYAM, who also goes on to refill everyone's glasses. POPPY and the
two women watch this in embarrassment. FARAH is gliding around the
room, greeting guests. She is gracious, but there still lurks a hint of
sadness about her. She looks over at ASIF, who watches her with obvious
pride. He gives a reassuring smile. Meanwhile, MARYAM threads her
way through the crowd handing out refills, clearing plates and never
acknowledged. She is invisible. Cut to ASIF standing in a group of his
male associates, both Pakistani and English, who are obviously amused
by something. One of the Pakistani men nudges his white neighbour and
leans forward to ASIF.)*

FIRST MAN   One woman for the kitchen and kids, another for the
bedroom.
(First man raises his glass to ASIF)
Mubarak!
(ASIF stiffens, his smile becomes fixed)
WHITE MAN Four wives is it, you chaps can have? So what about the four
mother-in-laws?
(The men guffaw at this. ASIF remains calm)
ASIF   Maryam lives with us because I think that's the civilised way to
treat the mother of my children...
WHITE MAN And what about the cat-fights?
ASIF   Maryam and Farah are not animals.

WHITE MAN *(Flustered)* 'course not, I just meant...

FIRST MAN He means you're a brave fellow. I couldn't live like that.

(The other men grunt in agreement)

ASIF I dare say you couldn't. *(ASIF turns to first man)* What, take Glenda, the Discipline Queen, home to meet Sufia? *(ASIF turns to white man)* Or maybe drag your secretary back for a game of strip scrabble with Susan? I am honest with my wife. Suppose that's my burden, coming from a primitive culture.

(Close up on the men's dumbfounded faces.)

SCENE 17

Int. Kitchen. ASIF'S house. Night.

(Cut to POPPY, lighting up by the open back door of the kitchen, FARAH standing next to her, anxiously looking over her shoulder. She grabs the lit cigarette off POPPY and takes a deep drag, exhaling gratefully.)

POPPY How are you coping?

FARAH Still not in the party mood.

POPPY *(Hesitantly)* Actually, I meant, with *her*. His other half. What do you say to her?

FARAH Nothing much. Three months of married bliss and I hardly see her. She's got her own routine, shopping, the kids...

POPPY *(Takes the cigarette off her for a drag)* She emptied my ashtray.

FARAH I know... I don't expect her to act as home-help, but Asif tells me not to interfere.

POPPY He's obviously tasted your cooking. *(They laugh)* The old hag in the bi-focals gives me the creeps.

FARAH Asif's mum. She only speaks Urdu and I don't. We get on just fine.

POPPY So long as they keep out of your way, you're happy?

FARAH *(Sighing)* She wants the girls educated here. They've lived separate lives in this house for years. It's big enough.

POPPY But, they aren't divorced, sweetie.

(She hands the cigarette back to FARAH)

FARAH Mentally they are. We can't just throw her out.

POPPY Why not? I bloody would.

FARAH Family, duty, responsibility... I've thrown so much of my past away without trying to understand. We do things differently, Poppy.

POPPY *(With raised eyebrows)* My paper would have a field day with this. Christ!

FARAH   Anyway, if this doesn't work, me and Asif just move out.
(POPPY looks at FARAH, but says nothing. She changes the mood)

POPPY *(Wickedly)* So can you give me an exclusive on your three-in-a-bed sessions?

FARAH   God, he hasn't slept with Maryam for years! *(For the first time, she breaks into a smile)* Do you blame him?

(FARAH and POPPY look up, hearing a noise. MARYAM stands at a counter calmly polishing glasses. How long has she been there? POPPY grabs the cigarette off FARAH and attempts a weak smile.)

POPPY *(Hurrying out)* Er, don't worry about that clean glass, Farah. This one's fine...
(FARAH and MARYAM face each other. MARYAM pushes past FARAH and opens a unit, she takes out a clean glass and begins wiping it.)

MARYAM You don't know where anything is in this kitchen yet.

FARAH   Haven't spent much time in here, I suppose.

MARYAM He's always preferred eating out to home cooking. Until he gets sick of too much rich food. Then he comes running back to me. *(She goes over to the sink with the glass)*

FARAH *(Rushing forward)* I'll do it.
(MARYAM turns on the tap, which suddenly explodes, belching out water and soaking FARAH'S embroidered suit. We are not sure if this is an accident.)

FARAH *(Jumping back too late)* Oh, no! It's ruined!
(MARYAM fetches a clean tea-towel and begins wiping down FARAH'S front. It is the closest the two women have ever been.)

MARYAM That tap has a temper sometimes. Excuse me.
(She lifts FARAH'S top and slides her hand underneath soaking up the water from inside with the tea-towel. MARYAM begins singing to herself, a strange discordant tune. FARAH feels very uncomfortable. MARYAM looks up into her face.)

Some of the others have been more beautiful, but you have something. You have fire.
(The door swings open. SABIA stands in the doorway.)

SABIA *(Urdu)* Don't touch her! You should be outside helping. Leave her alone.

(MARYAM extricates herself from FARAH and follows SABIA out of the room, FARAH watching them go.)

SCENE 18
Int. FARAH'S bedroom. ASIF'S house. Night.

(FARAH lying on her bed in her dressing-gown. She is sleeping fitfully and suddenly jerks awake. Disorientated for a moment, she consults the alarm clock. It is two – thirty a.m. and she is worried. She picks up the near empty water decanter from the bedside table and goes to the door.)

SCENE 19
Int. Corridor. ASIF'S house. Night.

(FARAH walks along the long corridor and is puzzled to see a light coming under a door at the end of the passageway. She creeps into the bathroom next to it. We hear FARAH fill the decanter at the tap without switching on the light. FARAH then emerges standing at the lit bedroom door and knocks gently. No reply. FARAH knocks again.)

FARAH *(Quietly)* Maryam?

(She pushes the door tentatively.)

SCENE 20
Int. MARYAM'S bedroom. ASIF'S house. Night.

(A woman's room, feminine and neat. Traditional Pakistani clothes and jewellery are strewn on the bed which is undisturbed and empty. FARAH blinks hard, looks again not sure she is still awake. She backs out of the room, some kind of realisation is dawning which she cannot yet face.)

SCENE 21
Int. Girls' bedroom. ASIF'S house. Night.

(At the next door the two girls sleep peacefully, arms wrapped round cuddly toys. She closes the door quietly.)

SCENE 22
Int. SABIA'S bedroom. ASIF'S house. Night.

(*At the next room she stands before the door, trying to steady her breathing before flinging it open. It is a strange room, the walls covered by religious prints, shelves of glass bottles, pills, potions, charts, more like a grotto. SABIA lies ramrod straight in bed, asleep, her thick spectacles next to her false teeth in a glass on the bedside table. There is no-one else in the room. FARAH'S breathing is now rapid. She closes the door behind her.*)

SCENE 23
Int. Corridor. ASIF'S house. Night.

(*FARAH approaches the bedroom next to hers almost reluctantly. She stands outside it, listening hard. Her hand moves towards the handle and is jerked back as she hears the noise. It is a woman's laughter, followed by bass male tones and an ominous silence. FARAH, alerted, drops the decanter in her hand which slowly pours water in a steady stream onto her bare feet.*)

SCENE 24
Int. Bathroom. ASIF'S house. Night.

(*Later: ASIF. sweaty and bare-chested in his pyjama bottoms, stands at the bathroom sink. ASIF half fills the decanter in his hand and gulps down the contents, almost choking as he looks up and sees FARAH'S reflection in the mirror, standing behind him.*)

FARAH   Thirsty work, Asif.

ASIF (*Spinning round to face her*) Farah...

FARAH   So now we take it in turns.

ASIF   What?

FARAH   So that's why we have separate bedrooms. When are the other two moving in?

ASIF   What's all this?

FARAH   Four wives, isn't it, according to the Koran. I'm sure you'll come up with some ancient family law to justify yourself.

ASIF (*Realisation dawning*) Oh!... Farah, we were talking.

FARAH   Talking?... Don't lie to me, Asif. Not again.

ASIF   ... Talking with the mother of my children. Your sister. Is that a crime? (*ASIF holds out his hand to her*) Come on. This is silly.

(FARAH looks at his hand, not taking it, wondering whether he's telling the truth.)

SCENE 25
Int. Living room. ASIF'S house. Day.

(The "Neighbours" theme tune, very loud. SABIA in front of the television screen watching intently. MAUREEN, a good-natured Irish woman in her fifties, is dusting and polishing the various expensive ornaments in the room.)

MAUREEN   Learn English from this stuff, Sabia, and when you open your gob they'll think you're Kylie Minogue.

SABIA *(Urdu)* Shut your mouth, I'm watching this.

MAUREEN   Are Sapana and Soraya back from their kiddies' party yet? Oh they're lovely little girls, so happy...

SABIA *(Urdu)* This man is cheating on his wife. I hope his manhood shrivels up and falls off.

MAUREEN   I reckon it's because you all live together, one big happy family, bit like us really...
(She has a good look at the statue in her hand, a graphic sexual coupling)
... though I'm not sure we'd have this in a good Catholic household. That's one thing you lot got right, you're not hung up about sex.

SABIA *(Urdu)* It's overrated. Give a man a son and he's yours for life. That's where Maryam went wrong.

MAUREEN   Maryam, did you say? She back yet?

SABIA *(Urdu)* Farah thinks sex will keep him happy, huh. Maryam knows what love is. She washes all his shirts by hand.

MAUREEN   Honestly, Sabia, I'd need subtitles to have a conversation with you.

SABIA *(Urdu)* She might win over Maryam, she has a good heart. But mine is made of stone.

MAUREEN *(Exasperated)* Eh?

SABIA *(Slowly)* Throw another prawn on the barbie.

MAUREEN *(Astonished)* Sabia, that was absolutely brilliant! *(She claps her hands, laughing.)* Say it again, go on!
(FARAH enters the room in her work clothes carrying a portfolio. The laughter stops abruptly. SABIA gets up and leaves the room.)

MAUREEN   Don't mind her. Maryam's not back from the shops yet.

FARAH   Oh. Yes.

MAUREEN   Must say, you don't look like sisters. Pardon me saying,   but you got the looks. Mind you she's a canny woman, Maryam. Clever.
Must have given you the runaround when you were kids.
(FARAH looks at MAUREEN, dumbfounded)
Well, better get on.
(MAUREEN moves into the hallway. We hear a hoover starting up.)

SCENE 26
Int. Kitchen. ASIF'S house. Day.

(FARAH goes into the kitchen and starts hunting round in cupboards. She gives up finding the bread and instead, takes a fag packet from her dressing-gown pocket, lights one and sits at the kitchen table, inhaling thoughtfully. She jumps, hearing the door swing to. MARYAM entering laden with shopping)

MARYAM   You won't keep your looks eating snacks like that. *(Pointedly opens a window to dispel the smoke, and then busies herself finding various utensils an ingredients)* A nice paratha dripping with ghee.
FARAH   No really, I'm not...
MARYAM   You are refusing a gift from a sister?
FARAH   No 'course not. I'm just not hungry.
(FARAH watches MARYAM expertly kneading dough, rolling it out into perfect rounds and throwing the paratha onto a sizzling hot griddle.)
MARYAM   Good day at the shop?
FARAH   Asif met me for lunch.
MARYAM   You look tired. Didn't sleep too well last night?
FARAH   You told the cleaning lady we were sisters.
MARYAM *(Unconcerned)* Maureen? *(She shrugs)* Told her what she wanted to hear. Besides, we are, aren't we?
(MARYAM puts a saucer in front of FARAH who is at first confused by this, then cottons on and meekly stubs out her cigarette in it. MARYAM empties the saucer in the pedal bin, washes the saucer, dries it, puts it away, then returns to the griddle. MARYAM then places a hot, sizzling paratha before FARAH, challenging her to refuse it. FARAH breaks off a small piece and chews it, swallowing it down with difficulty.)
Oh. Nearly forgot.
(She goes to a cupboard and brings out a small phial containing a greenish looking powder. She sprinkles some of it into a glass of water and drinks it down, wincing slightly.)
FARAH   What's that?

MARYAM *(Carefully replaces the stopper and hides the phial away in a cupboard)* One of Sabia's tonics. To give me back my sparkle. You should try it.

FARAH   Oh. Does it work?

MARYAM Took it for the first time last night. *(MARYAM licks her lips)* Tastes fine to me.

(Close up on FARAH'S horrified face.)

SCENE 27
Int. Back office. FARAH carpet factory. Day.

(Close up of a carpet design on a drawing-board. It depicts two voluptuous Indian women cavorting around a bored looking Maharajah, bordered with interlocking birds and beasts. The Artist's hand carefully inks around one of the women's profiles. The pen slips and a jagged scar appears on the beautiful face.)

FARAH *(V.O.)* Shit.

(Pan out to reveal FARAH in a back office surrounded by her pens and portfolios. She is simultaneously trying to draw and hold a telephone conversation.)

Get to the airport and pick up the order. Yes, in the van. You can't get sixty rugs in the boot of your bloody Mini-Metro.

(FARAH slams the telephone down. A knock on the door. MRS. SIDDIQUI popping her head round.)

MRS. SIDDIQUI   See you tomorrow, Farah dear. *(FARAH opens her mouth)* No. No phone calls. Sorry.

(She leaves. FARAH consults her watch, worried.)

SCENE 28
Ext. Street outside FARAH Carpets. Day.

(FARAH standing outside anxiously checking all the cars passing by. She turns hearing a car horn and runs towards it.)

SCENE 29
Ext/Int. ASIF'S car. Day.

(FARAH gets into the car, still worried.)

ASIF   Sorry, meeting ran on.
FARAH   You could have phoned.
ASIF *(Surprised)* Not like you to worry.
FARAH   I thought you weren't coming.
ASIF   Why? *(FARAH cannot answer. He breaks into a laugh)*
    Silly girl! How are the new season's designs coming on?
FARAH *(Relaxing)* The carpet world's equivalent of flock wallpaper.
    (ASIF laughs) I look forward to our evening jaunts. What's it to be
    tonight? Thai? French, maybe?
ASIF   I'm getting tired of rich restaurant food. Let's go home.
    (FARAH'S face falls a hundred feet. Slowly.)

SCENE 30
Int. Living room. ASIF'S house. Evening

*(FARAH sitting on the settee looking bored. The television is on loud,
some noisy comedy show with canned laughter. ASIF sits on the floor
with SAPNA and SORAYA cuddling under each arm. They are enjoying
the programme and squeal at all the jokes, looking up at ASIF, for
approval, vying for his attention. Through the kitchen door we see SABIA
and MARYAM finishing off the washing-up, laughing and chatting
together contentedly, occasionally calling out to the girls who run in and
out of the kitchen for forbidden tit-bits of food. FARAH is completely
ignored. At one point, she reaches over to the girls. Trying to make
conversation, offer them a hug. They both shy away from her, taking
refuge in ASIF'S arms. FARAH bad-temperedly takes out a cigarette and
goes to light it before catching ASIF'S stern look of disapproval. She puts
the cigarette away. FARAH picks up her empty cup, getting up to take it
to the kitchen. MARYAM takes it from her before she leaves the settee.
FARAH watches MARYAM move around the room, clearing cups,
plumping cushions, throwing smiles at the girls. She walks seductively,
slowly, tossing back her hair, which has just been washed and hangs in a
black curtain down her back. It is as if she knows she is being watched
and is putting on a performance. She is flirting. FARAH turns to ASIF to
see him following MARYAM'S every move with an obvious smile of
pleasure on his face. He then catches FARAH watching him and turns his
attention swiftly and guiltily to his daughters. MARYAM finishes tidying
up then turns her attention to the girls.)*

MARYAM *(Urdu)* Bedtime! Say goodnight to Papa.
GIRLS *(Urdu)* No! We want to stay up. Can we have a story?
    (SABIA coming from the kitchen carrying a medicine bottle and spoon)

SABIA *(Urdu)* No fuss please. Take your tonic before sleeping. *(The girls line up dutifully and each receive a spoonful of a reddish looking liquid from SABIA.) (English)* Good girls. Dadima's medicine. Makes you strong, yet?

(FARAH watches this with interest. MARYAM and SABIA push the girls towards ASIF. They cover him with kisses and hugs. He then turns them to face FARAH.)

ASIF   Say goodnight to Farah Auntie.

FARAH *(Amused whispering)* Auntie!

(The girls face FARAH uncertainly. FARAH smiles and holds out her arms. The girls dutifully come forward and allow themselves to be kissed. FARAH enjoys this, and hugs them a little too long, enjoying the feel and smell of them, smoothing their hair, eventually coaxing a smile out of SAPNA. FARAH looks up to see MARYAM looking at her with such hatred that she immediately pulls away. MARYAM calls sharply to the girls who run to her, and are bundled upstairs by the two women. ASIF watches the girls go.)

ASIF   Torn between two lovers.

FARAH   What?

ASIF   My girls. They have to get exactly the same number of kisses and cuddles or they start getting violent.

FARAH *(Trying to lighten the mood)* Well pass me my zimmer frame so old Auntie Farah can get to bed.

ASIF *(Laughing and hugging her)* I could hardly let them call you mummy, could I? *(FARAH does not think this is funny. She pushes him aside and goes upstairs.)*

SCENE 31
Int. ASIF'S room. ASIF'S house. Night.

(FARAH standing in the doorway of ASIF'S room. A neat, male room, open wardrobes reveal rows of hand-stitched suits, silk ties, designer shirts. But other wise it seems stark, no personal touches like photographs as if the occupant were not staying long. An angle-poise lamp lights up a desk upon which is a computer, scattered files and papers. The bed is undisturbed and empty. FARAH smiles in relief. She pulls the door to and walks towards the bathroom where there is light coming under the closed door. As FARAH passes SABIA'S room she stops, straining her ears. There is a faint sound of what? Chanting? Prayers? FARAH tries the bathroom door and is surprised to find it locked.)

SCENE 32
Int. Bathroom. ASIF'S house. Night.

(FARAH knocks gently and ASIF opens the door. ASIF returns immediately to washing at the sink.)

FARAH   You don't usually lock the door.
ASIF   Checking up on me, were you?
FARAH *(Flustered)* No. Of course not. *(She begins caressing his shoulders. He doesn't even turn round so she stops, helpless)* Come to bed.
ASIF *(Drying off and preparing to leave)* Being spied on doesn't put me in the mood.
FARAH   I wasn't.
ASIF   You're either pulling me in or locking me out...
FARAH   I want to be with you tonight. Can't I ask for it?
ASIF *(Half-smiling, attempting humour)* Seduction, is what our women are supposed to be good at.
FARAH *(Shouting)* I will not be compared to *her*!
ASIF *(Grabbing her)* You'll wake the children.
(FARAH picks up a container of powder from the overloaded cosmetics shelf and throws it against the wall. It smashes to pieces, loudly, filling the room with whirling scented clouds. ASIF is stunned.)
FARAH   Whoops.
ASIF   What the hell... *(He stops as FARAH calmly picks up a tub of cold cream and holds it in the air)*
FARAH   Who are the others?
(ASIF looks blank. FARAH throws the tub, it narrowly misses his head and breaks against the wall behind him, splattering him with white, sticky globs.)
FARAH   Maryam told me.
ASIF   I have never kept my affairs secret... our marriage was over by then, I wanted Maryam to know I was... she accepted it!
FARAH *(Momentarily shocked. She tries to recover)* Maryam is a good little Pakistani wife. I am nothing like her.
ASIF *(Moves towards her tentatively)* I took other lovers in front of her. Doesn't that prove anything to you?
FARAH   I think she still wants you.
ASIF   She wasn't interested before you arrived.
FARAH   Is that why I'm here?

(ASIF cannot answer. FARAH gently wipes away the mess from ASIF'S face and chest with her finger tips. ASIF sighs in relief They both try and relax, still shaky from the argument.)

SCENE 33
Int. Corridor. ASIF'S house. Night.

(FARAH takes ASIF'S hand, switches off the light, and leads him wordlessly down the corridor to her room. As they pass MARYAM'S door, we see it open a fraction. A glimpse of MARYAM watching them, and then the door closing shut.)

SCENE 34
Int. Large house. Pakistan. Day.

(This whole section has a dream-like surreal quality. The lighting is of paramount importance, it should be the warm golden relentless heat of Pakistan, putting everything in definite light and shade, creating an air of expectant stillness. We follow FARAH through a maze of marble corridors, exquisitely carved pillars, silk wall hangings, mughal miniatures. Somewhere there is sitar music playing.)

MUMTAZ *(V.O.)* Your father took me to see some cousins outside Lahore. We were just married. What I saw there, Farah. So perfect. Every last detail so clear.

(FARAH suddenly realises she is lost. She begins to panic, doubling back on herself only to find another marble corridor. She ends up facing a heavy carved wooden door, from behind which there is a murmur of women's voices and the occasional squeal of a young child. She pushes open the door. A group of four women, ranging in age from fifty to sixteen, all recline on silk cushions, drinking tea and feeding each other with sweet-meats whilst young children play around their feet. The music is now loud. Sunlight streams through the carved wooden shutters at the windows throwing moving spirals of pattern over their faces. Utter peace. The women smile at each other, beautiful in their contentment. They do not notice FARAH who retreats backwards from the room, closing the door reverently. She jumps as she is tapped on the shoulder, and turns to face a toothless crone of a servant.)

SERVANT *(Urdu)* You shouldn't be here.
FARAH Who are they?

SERVANT *(Urdu)* The ladies of the house.
FARAH *(Loudly)* I don't understand...
SERVANT *(Urdu)* My master's four wives, each one a jewel.
(The servant leads FARAH gently away. She keeps looking back at the room longingly, for one last glimpse of paradise.)

SCENE 35

Ext. Garden Centre. Day.
(Close up of a puppet display: an Arabian nights display is draped around a large Christmas tree; doe-eyed swaying maidens hover in the background with fixed painted smiles. It is near closing time. Not many people are about. FARAH, muffled up in winter clothes, is mesmerised by the display. She looks strained, dark circles under her eyes, pinched face. POPPY, in fake fur hat and coat, is dragging a large fir tree towards FARAH, who has a pile of shopping bags at her feet, crammed with parcels.)

POPPY   For someone who's not supposed to celebrate Christmas, this is a serious spending spree.
FARAH *(Listless)* I don't know if I need to get Asif's mother anything.
POPPY   How about rat poison?
FARAH   Probably got a supply in one of those glass bottles under her bed. Why bother?
POPPY   She's put a hex on you! That's why you're looking so rough!
FARAH *(Turning round, serious)* Do you think that too?
POPPY   It was a joke! Season of goodwill and all that...
FARAH *(Returns POPPY'S look steadily)* She's trying to get him back.
POPPY   Who?
FARAH   It's not love. She's just using him as a sperm bank.
POPPY   Asif and Maryam? They're not?
FARAH   I can't prove anything. But I hear noises. And if she gets pregnant, he could never leave her.
(FARAH walks towards the display, POPPY following her, alarmed)
POPPY   If this is going on how can you put up...
FARAH *(Slowing gazing at the display)* In my mother's story, all the women together, so happy. They seemed like the lovers and the husband the odd one out.
POPPY   What's this got to do with them sleeping together? Farah!...
FARAH   Sisterhood. The man, husband, he strutted around thinking, they all love me so much they are willing to share me, a quarter each. The joke is, none of them really loved him, they couldn't have done. Or they'd

have killed each other to have him all to themselves. *(POPPY looks puzzled)* I've stopped taking the pill.

SCENE 36
Int. Dining-room. ASIF'S house. Christmas day. Day.

(FARAH, ASIF, MARYAM, SABIA and the girls sit around a festive table surrounded by the remains of a traditional meal. MARYAM hands FARAH a present which she takes with a surprised smile and carefully unwraps. It is a cheap set of make-up, eye shadows, lipsticks, nail varnishes, in garish colours. FARAH looks up into MARYAM'S smiling face. MARYAM wears a loud salwar kameez and obviously badly applied make-up. All eyes are on FARAH except her father's, TARIQ. He is still trying to finish his meal, pathetically, chasing peas round his plate. He wears a crooked paper hat and has gravy on his tie.)

FARAH   Lovely. Thank you, Maryam.
MARYAM I thought your face could do with a bit of colour.

(ASIF rummages around the litter round his plate. He silently hands MARYAM and FARAH identically wrapped small boxes. FARAH unwraps hers and gasps at the exquisite solitaire diamond ring glittering inside. She looks over at MARYAM who is smiling, holding up exactly the same ring. ASIF takes the rings from both women and shows how they clip together; forming one perfect glittering circle.)

ASIF   Two halves. One ring. An original. Had my jeweller make them up 'specially. Happy Christmas.

SCENE 37
Int. Living-room. ASIF'S house. Day.

(They drink and laugh whilst the girls run around their feet, squealing.FARAH is tipsy, she watches as MARYAM clears up around her; pouring another glass of wine for herself. Suddenly ASIF is at her side and snatches the bottle from her hand.)

ASIF *(Whispering fiercely)* Don't you think you've had enough?
FARAH *(Stopping ASIF as he goes to leave)* And aren't you going to help clear up?
(ASIF throws her off and marches away. MARYAM continues tidying)

MARYAM *(Softly to FARAH)* That is not the way to keep him happy.

FARAH *(Snapping)* You've been his slave and chief bottom-wiper, no wonder he acts like God.

MARYAM Asif is cleverer than me. He knows more about the world...

FARAH You've lived here for twelve years, you can't drive a car, fill in a tax form. You don't even have your own bloody cheque book! Asif knows more about the world because he's kept you out of it!

MARYAM I know my place. Where do you fit in?

FARAH It's women like you who turn men like Asif into monsters. *(She grabs MARYAM'S hand. We see they are both wearing their matching diamond rings. They catch the light and sparkle, making little lights dance across their faces. MARYAM removing FARAH'S hand firmly from hers.)*

MARYAM A man should treat all his wives equally. It is written in the Koran.

FARAH *(Slowly)* You still consider yourself... his wife?

SCENE 38

Int. Conservatory. ASIF'S house. Evening.

(FARAH sits on the floor next to the French windows looking out at the garden. She watches the fir tree with its Christmas lights which blink off and on, taking a swig from the wine bottle in her hand. FARAH'S father, TARIQ stands in the doorway watching her, still in his crooked paper hat. He looks old and bewildered.)

TARIQ You never used to drink, Farah.

FARAH Things change.

TARIQ *(Looking out at the barren garden)* No flowers.

FARAH It's winter, daddyji.

TARIQ In Pakistan, flowers all year round. Your mother liked flowers very much.

FARAH *(Swigging from the bottle)* I remember.

TARIQ I'm selling the house. Too big. I want to go back and live where my bones keep warm.

FARAH *(Frightened)* What about me?

TARIQ Asif will look after you now.

FARAH Don't leave me here on my own.

TARIQ You're not on your own. You're married. You don't know what loneliness is.

(FARAH looks at him, then looks out at the garden.)

SCENE 39
Int. FARAH'S bedroom. ASIF'S house. Night.

(FARAH lying in bed, smoking and watching the smoke curl about her head. She wears an old T-shirt and bed socks. The room is littered with her unwrapped presents. There is a knock at the door. FARAH jumps up and begins flinging the litter into a cupboard.)

FARAH   Just a minute!
(She runs to the mirror, drags a brush through her hair, pulls her bed socks off and lies on the bed in what she hopes is a seductive position.)
Enter!
(Nothing happens. FARAH goes to the door, opens it. Nobody there. Then she sees a small parcel on the floor outside the door. She takes the parcel in. Reads the gift tab: 'From SABIA'.)
Well well.

(FARAH unwraps the parcel to reveal a small phial of black liquid, the label on it reads: 'for good health, one spoon each morning'. FARAH laughs out loud. She opens the phial and tips the liquid into the plant pot of a bizzy lizzy next to her bed.)

SCENE 40
Int. ASIF'S bedroom. ASIF'S house. Night.
(ASIF sitting at his word processor typing away. He looks up annoyed at the knock at the door.)

ASIF   I'm busy.
(The door opens and FARAH enters, now with a grubby sweat-shirt over the T-shirt, bed socks, fag in one hand and bottle of wine in the other.)
FARAH   Thought you'd like a festive tipple.
ASIF   I don't want smoke in here.
FARAH   Whoops. *(She spits on the fag to extinguish it and drops it in a bin)*
ASIF *(Finally looking up)* And I've got a large account to finish.
FARAH *(Holding out the bottle)* It's Christmas night!
(ASIF continues typing. FARAH goes up to him and begins nuzzling his ear)

I know we didn't have the best start to our marriage.

(ASIF stops typing but doesn't look round)

But, we can get back to how we were before... with a few changes.

(ASIF pushes FARAH away gently never taking his eyes from the screen)

Why Asif?

(She takes off her ring and puts it on the computer keyboard. ASIF stops typing)

ASIF   You know I have to get this ready for the Pakistan trip next week.

FARAH   Do you have to stay a whole month?

ASIF   Two, if that's how long it takes.

FARAH   I'll come with you.

ASIF   Farah, please!

FARAH   You don't want me.

ASIF *(Turning to her)* I love you, Farah, but you're stifling me. I feel like I'm constantly on trial...

FARAH   So do I! It's this house... It's Maryam.

ASIF   Please!

FARAH   And Sabia!

ASIF   My mother lived with my father's other wives for twenty years.

FARAH *(Shocked)* I never knew...

ASIF   You never asked. Me or her.

FARAH   Maybe I'm not selfless enough to share... my space.

(ASIF doesn't respond) Don't they have jealousy in Pakistan?

ASIF   It's a different way of seeing. Maybe we'll never get that back.

FARAH   We have tried, Asif. I didn't know what I was letting myself in for. Neither did you.

ASIF *(Wearily)* That's true.

FARAH   You see? We do agree! Let her have this place, we could find somewhere nearby. You would see the girls every day, I promise...

ASIF *(Coldly)* I don't need your permission to see my own children.

FARAH   No, of course.

(She thinks desperately trying to get him back)

Asif, we could have a child...

(He looks at her closely, wondering if this is a ploy) Our own baby, in our own house.

ASIF   And Farah Carpets?

FARAH *(She begins kissing his neck)* We could make a start tonight, if you like.

ASIF *(Manages a smile, gently pushing FARAH away)* I promise to think it over while I'm away. The practicalities. *(He turns back to the computer)* I must get on.

FARAH *(Watches for a while, gathering up courage)* Have you been sleeping with her? *(ASIF stiffens but does not respond)* I have to know.

ASIF *(Not turning round)* Farah, at the moment, I can't even sleep with myself... *(FARAH leaves. He hears the door close and sighs in relief Goes over to the water decanter and gulps the whole thing down from the bottle. There is a knock at the door. He rubs his forehead despairingly.)* Come in.

(MARYAM enters, still in her embroidered suit, her jewellery jingling and eyes downcast. She places a hot cup of tea on ASIF'S desk and refills his water decanter from a jug. ASIF watches MARYAM, notes her bare feet, and her silver anklets which jangle enticingly as she walks. MARYAM exits almost backwards, still not looking up. ASIF stops her in the doorway.)

Maryam.

(She looks up for the first time and looks down, lowering her eyes slowly, deliberately, a flicker of a smile on her lips.)

SCENE 41
Int. FARAH'S bedroom. ASIF'S house. Day.

(FARAH rushes into the bedroom and pulls open the drawers of her bedside cabinet, frantically searching. She wears an old salwar kameez with a jumper over it, and sneakers with thick socks. She finds what she was searching for, a wedding photograph of her and ASIF. She is about to leave when she notices the bizzy lizzy on the cabinet. It is completely shrivelled, brown and dead. She takes this in with horror, then rushes out.)

SCENE 42
Ext. ASIF'S house, driveway. Day.

(ASIF sits in the back of a chauffeur driven car in the driveway, its engine running. In the doorway, MARYAM, SABIA and the girls waving goodbye. FARAH comes running past them, opens the car door and flings herself inside.)

FARAH   I'm coming with you.
ASIF   Farah darling. I haven't got time...

FARAH   They're trying to kill me! You can't leave me here on my own!

ASIF *(Incredulous, shoots a look at the happy family standing in the doorway. FARAH slams the car door, shutting them out.)* What on earth...

FARAH *(Shivering)* I poured Sabia's tonic into my pot plant, you know, the one Maureen gave me, a cutting from her sister's bizzy lizzy...I wasn't going to drink it... does she think I'm stupid? Anyway, now the plant's dead like someone sucked the life from it. Sabia's poison was meant for me! How do you explain the plant dying just like that?

ASIF *(A long pause whilst ASIF assesses FARAH'S desperate face)* You probably forgot to water it. Farah.

(FARAH deflates, slumping onto ASIF'S shoulder. He uncurls her tightly balled hand. She is gripping their wedding photograph and a slip of paper with an address written on it.)

FARAH *(Faintly)* My father's address.

ASIF *(Taking photograph and slip)* Of course I'll look him up. Send your love.

FARAH *(Gripping him hard enough to make him wince)* Are we going to move out of here? Promise me!

ASIF *(Uncomfortable)* I'll think about it. I promise.

FARAH *(Getting out of the car)* That's all I wanted to hear.

ASIF *(Calling after her)* Farah?

(FARAH taps the car roof which pulls out of the drive, ASIF straining his head to see FARAH waving to him.)

FARAH *(Whispering)* I'll be waiting.

(She turns round to see SABIA and MARYAM still standing in the doorway, staring at her, immobile like statues.)

SCENE 43
Ext. ASIF'S house, driveway. Night.

(FARAH standing in the pouring rain at the end of the driveway. She seems oblivious to the rain, the ink from her designs running down her hand. She watches until all the lights in the house are gradually switched off one by one. Then she slowly walks up the drive towards the house.)

SCENE 44
Int. Hallway. ASIF'S house. Night.

(FARAH entering the hallway. The house is dark. She removes her soaking coat, shoes, and pads quietly in. She switches on the light and jumps in fright. MARYAM is sitting on the stairs, motionless.)

FARAH   Maryam?

(FARAH approaches MARYAM and sees that she is crying, soundlessly, without emotion)

MARYAM   Asif went to England one week after we got married. For five years I lived in Pakistan waiting for him. Me and Sabia, sometimes we forgot Asif existed. Then we came here. I knew nobody. Asif would pretend I was a servant when his business people came for dinner. Then the girls were born. I did not give him a son. He was so disappointed. When I found out about the girlfriends I said I didn't mind. They were only white women, so I knew they didn't matter. When I found out about you... I was so happy. Someone to talk with, go shopping with, cook with. The sister I never had, with one thing in common we both love... and now you will leave and take him with you.

FARAH *(Gently)* I am glad Asif told you of our plans...

(MARYAM registers surprise, but only we see it before she arranges her features back into a mask of pain)

(Quietly)... I'm suffering too, Maryam.

MARYAM *(Wiping her face resolutely)* We only have a short time together. We should be good to each other.

(FARAH tentatively hugs MARYAM, the first time they have done so. At the top of the stairway, we see SABIA'S shadowy figure, watching.)

SCENE 45
Int. ASIF'S house. Kitchen. Day.

(The following scenes to the accompaniment of a traditional Punjabi folk song, woman's guttural voice in a minor key. FARAH watching MARYAM plop perfect pakora into boiling fat. They come out crisp and perfect. FARAH, covered in flour, attempts to fry her pakora.)

SCENE 46
Int. FARAH'S bedroom. Day.

(FARAH standing behind MARYAM, showing her how to apply eyeliner and blusher in subtle definite strokes. MARYAM watching carefully, copying her. The result is quite impressive. MARYAM glows with pride, her face suddenly looking younger and prettier. FARAH opens a drawer beneath the dressing table, bringing out a scarf which trails items of

*skimpy underwear with it. FARAH is embarrassed, tries to hide the items
out of sight. MARYAM grabs them off her. She holds up negligees and
suspender belts to the light, shooting FARAH a look of amusement and
longing.)*

SCENE 47
Int. Living-room. ASIF'S house. Night.

*(FARAH and MARYAM in front of a soppy film on the video, both in
green face masks and their hair in towels. Piles of empty take-away
cartons around the room. MARYAM takes off FARAH'S towel and begins
massaging oil into FARAH'S hair. FARAH lies back, uncertain, trying to
enjoy it.)*

SCENE 48
Int. Lounge. Empty house. Day.

*(FARAH leading a sun-tanned POPPY around a huge empty house.
FARAH is dressed in a silk salwar kameez.)*

POPPY   So it's all settled then?
FARAH   More or less. He's told Maryam we're moving out...
POPPY   How do you know?
FARAH   She told me. I thought I'd save time by lining up a few
suggestions.
(POPPY looks doubtful)

SCENE 49
Int. Living-room. Suburban house. London. Day.

*(A large comfortable house. Pakistani women of different ages sit quietly
with their tea and snacks listening to FAUZIA, a fifty-year-old, talking.
Children run about the room and are grabbed and hushed. Next to
FAUZIA, a young woman, ABIDA, occasionally chips in. They work as a
double act. SABIA sits alone in a corner glowering, but FARAH is
mesmerised. MARYAM, next to her, leans in to whisper.)*

MARYAM You see why I wanted to bring you here?
*(FARAH nods, and motions MARYAM to keep quiet as FAUZIA
continues)*

FAUZIA *(Halting English)* We look after each other, her children are mine. No difference. If she is hurt, I bleed. One person.

(The women all exchange looks, some nodding approvingly, others suspicious. One young woman, in Western dress, clears her throat.)

YOUNG WOMAN But your husband I mean, do you share *everything*?

(The women giggle. FAUZIA and ABIDA smile)

FAUZIA Only the English think love is made in the bedroom. In the Koran, it says a man who will care for another wife will sit at the left hand side of Mohammed and the right hand of God. We are both equal. Both loved. Why should we feel afraid?

(FARAH shoots a look at MARYAM who suppresses a wicked smile.)

SCENE 50

Int. Hallway. Suburban house. London. Day.

(Later: FARAH is clearing up cups and plates from the hallway. She stops, hearing MARYAM'S laughter coming from the kitchen. FARAH hears MARYAM in the centre of a circle of friends, shrieking with joy at her jokes.)

MARYAM *(V.O.)* Western women, what do they know?

(The others laugh in agreement.) They think knowing lots of positions and silly underwear keeps a man happy but what about modesty? Silence?

(FARAH has stopped, cups in hand. She is listening hard.)

SCENE 51

Int. ASIF'S room. ASIF'S house. Night.

(A day-dream life sequence begins to form. We are in ASIF'S room at night. Discordant music, the same tune MARYAM hummed when wiping water from FARAH'S suit. We hear MARYAM'S voice, but this is FARAH'S vision. MARYAM and ASIF circle each other, she is shy, looking away, he grabs her face and lifts it to his lips. He runs his hands over the softness of her throat. She looks up at him appealingly. He is bare-chested. He throws her onto the bed and she feigns resistance, struggling until he pins her arms down and looks into her eyes. Only then does she smile, radiating submissive adoration.)

MARYAM *(V.O.)* And it is not how often you do it, but for how long, never demanding your own satisfaction but making sure he feels strong, in control and he will come back for more…

SCENE 52
Int. Hallway. Suburban house. London. Day.

(We are back in the suburban house. Close up on FARAH'S face, sick with realisation as the women applaud MARYAM, and she exits from the kitchen, bumping into FARAH. The two women face each other a moment. FARAH is trembling with anger. She hisses into MARYAM'S face.)

FARAH   How long has this been going on?
(MARYAM stares back at FARAH innocently, giving nothing away.)

SCENE 53
Int. Living room. MATA-JI'S. Southall. Day.

(A suburban living room converted into a kind of waiting room, rows of chairs, Indian calendars on the wall. Indian film magazines on coffee tables. Various Pakistani and Indian women of all ages sit quietly waiting, some clutching small bottles of indeterminate powders, others containing urine samples. The atmosphere is tense, secretive. The room is badly-lit and the air hung low with incense smoke. FARAH enters, blinking in the gloom. She eventually sits down next to a young pretty woman who is obviously a new bride from her jewellery and dress.)

BRIDE   Got the time?
FARAH *(Consulting her wristwatch)* Seven-thirty.
BRIDE   Soddit. My old man's going to be yelling for his roti. Married five weeks and already going hungry. What you in for?
FARAH   Actually, I was out shopping and my-er-cousin came in here. I'm not sure...
BRIDE   Oh your cousin, eh? *(She laughs)* I know it's embarrassing. I mean I had to tell a complete stranger I don't like sex. But she's heard it all before.
FARAH   Who?
BRIDE   Mata-ji. Some say she's a hundred and three and a witch. I said I don't care if she's got hooves and a hairy chest, her stuff works. It works like magic.
(She indicates a middle-aged woman opposite)
Her husband started seeing this white bit, she comes here, two weeks later, whitey's got shingles and he's ironing his wife's sari blouses...
(She indicates a heavily pregnant woman near the door)

That one, seven years married, no kids, still she started seeing Mata-ji last spring. So what's your problem?

FARAH *(Taking this in, her face hardening)* My problem? I think someone is telling me lies.

SCENE 54
Int. MATA-JI'S boudoir. Day.

(SABIA and MARYAM sit at a table in a low-ceilinged room hung with bottles, dried herbs, pickled oddities in jars. No sound but that of laboured breathing from an unseen person at the opposite end of the table.)

SABIA   A son. She wants a son.
(A wrinkled old woman's hand pushes a packet of powder across the table. SABIA picks it up and presses it to her hand in reverence.)

SCENE 55
Int. FARAH Carpets. Day.

(FARAH, in smart traditional dress, is on the telephone whilst keeping an eye on the browsing customers. Her hair is growing. She looks tired and has put on weight. She is alternatively smoking and munching on a chocolate bar. She is obviously stressed.)

FARAH   No, I'm fine Poppy, just keeping well out of her way until Asif gets back. Week after next, as far as I'm concerned, we move out... you have?... Pharmacist?*(She chokes with laughter)* Henry the Pharmacist!

MRS. SIDDIQUI *(Coming up)* Sorry to disturb you, Farah...

FARAH   Got to go, call me back in five. Okay? *(She replaces the receiver)* Something wrong, Mrs. Siddiqui?

MRS. SIDDIQUI   Not really. There's a woman who's been looking round the offices, asking all kinds of questions. She says she knows you, so we let her in...
(FARAH pushes past MRS. SIDDIQUI, heading for the offices at the back of the counter. Calling after her) She only asked about vacancies.

SCENE 56
Int. Back office. FARAH Carpets. Day.

(FARAH running through the back office to the outside door. In the darkness is a figure, a dark woman in a semi-smart fitted suit with short hair, cut in a fashionable style, reaches the exit door and disappears.)

SCENE 57

Ext. Back alley. FARAH Carpets. Day.

(FARAH pushes open the exit door and finds herself in the back alley, dustbins, cardboard boxes, the faint sound of traffic. She looks up and down the alley. It is deserted.)

SCENE 58

Int. Stairway landing. ASIF'S house. Day.

(FARAH walking up the stairs, balancing a plate of chocolate-ice cream in one hand and details of properties for sale in the other. As she reaches the top, she hears running footsteps and a door slamming. She pauses, listening. The sound of someone laboriously tapping on a typewriter begins. She turns into the passageway to see her bedroom door slowly swinging shut. She hurries to the door opening it carefully.)

SCENE 59

Int. FARAH'S room. ASIF'S house. Day.

(The room is empty, but the make-up on her dressing-table is in disarray. FARAH quickly picks up a perfume bottle which has started to leak onto the wood, replaces stoppers on cosmetic tubes, runs her fingers through a powdery pool of blusher.)

SCENE 60

Ext. Driveway. ASIF'S house. Day.

(ASIF'S limousine pulling into the drive. The chauffeur getting out and holding open the back passenger door. The trees in the front garden are beginning to bud, the crocuses are already out.)

SCENE 61

Int. Hallway. ASIF'S house. Day.

(ASIF entering the house loaded with Duty-Free bags, a suitcase, coat. He throws his coat onto the floor and stops, listening. The house is strangely quiet.)

SCENE 62
Int. Living room. ASIF'S house. Day.

(ASIF moves slowly into the living area and stops, mouth open. SAPNA and SORAYA sit on the settee in matching dresses, SABIA in the middle of them. On her left stands MARYAM, short hair, impeccably made-up, in an elegant lounge suit. On the right stands FARAH in a bright salwar kameez, hair now long and tied back, her curves now straining at the seams of the suit. FARAH and MARYAM come forward at the same time to greet ASIF.)

MARYAM/FARAH   Welcome home, darling.
(ASIF looks from one to the other)

SCENE 63
Int. ASIF'S bedroom. ASIF'S house. Night.

(Close up of ASIF emptying the whole of his water decanter down his throat. He is still recovering, panting breath, sweaty brow. The door opens and a smiling FARAH enters and throws a mass of papers onto the bed. ASIF smiles at her and begins to go through them, his smile gradually fading. ASIF, holding up a paper.)

ASIF   What's this?
FARAH   Oh I'm so glad! That's my favourite too. *(She comes to sit by ASIF, pointing out a paragraph)* Just look at this dining-room, wooden panels, and this area, we could turn into a playroom for the girls when they visit. *(FARAH trails off, seeing ASIF'S cold expression)* I explained everything in my letters...
ASIF *(Slowly)* I visited Maryam's family when I was in Pakistan. They're very unhappy at the idea of me leaving her alone.
FARAH   You promised.
ASIF *(Gently)* Farah darling, I only said I'd think about it. My chacha and her mama are business partners – think of the repercussions back home...
FARAH   What about here? Our home? She's taking over!

SCENE 64
Int. MARYAM'S bedroom. ASIF'S house. Night.

(The sounds of FARAH and ASIF arguing next door. MARYAM opens a drawer in her bedside cabinet, brings out a letter addressed to 'MRS. SIDDIQUI', FARAH Carpets. MARYAM also takes out a packet of powder given to her by MATA-JI. She pours herself a glass of water from her decanter, empties the powder into it and drinks it down.)

ASIF *(V.O.)* Over what? Who? I can't talk to you sensibly when you're like this.

FARAH *(V.O.)* I can't live like this. I have tried. You don't know what she's really like. I've been alone with her. I know!

SCENE 65
Int. Chemist's shop. Day.

(FARAH sitting slumped on a chair amongst the baby foods and nappies. We see POPPY behind the counter in the dispensary talking to HENRY, white coat, sensible face. They occasionally glance over at FARAH who is looking rundown, overweight, and miserable. POPPY kisses HENRY, takes a white paper bag from him and goes over to FARAH, handing her the bag with a concerned smile.)

FARAH *(Calling over)* Thank you Henry. *(HENRY raises his hand shyly. FARAH fumbles for her purse)* How much?

POPPY *(Stopping FARAH)* Silly. One of the advantages of sleeping with the management. *(POPPY takes in FARAH'S face)* Better take some of these vitamins now. You look bloody awful.
(FARAH gets up, hurt, attempting to leave. POPPY catching hold of her) What's going on? You can't carry on suffering like this...

FARAH   It's because I kept pestering him to move out, that's why he started sleeping with her again!

POPPY   What are you saying? That this is all your fault?

FARAH   How can we resolve anything when there's always another person to run to when things go wrong? She's got some potion from that Mata-ji witch in Southall. She's put a spell on him...

POPPY   Listen to yourself. You're an intelligent women, you've got a career... you have to get out of there!

FARAH   My Mum warned me. Some kinds of love I'll never understand.

POPPY *(Taking FARAH'S face in her hands)* Are you moving out?

FARAH   Yes... I think so...
POPPY   Hallelujah!
FARAH   Because if I can get him into my own space, I can fight her! If I could have a baby, I know I could get him back!
POPPY *(Kneeling beside her)* I think you're blaming the wrong person for all this. *(FARAH looks at her)* He's the one with the best of both worlds.
FARAH   You don't understand.
POPPY   I'm a woman. No woman I know could live like this.

SCENE 66
Int. Suburban house. London. Day.

(FARAH perched uncomfortably on the edge of a settee balancing a cup and saucer on her knees. FAUZIA sits opposite. In between is a table laden with the obligatory snacks. It is just getting dark.)

FAUZIA   You are a mirror. Everything you do reflects back on the people around you. You have responsibilities, a family name. Now you want to break up this family. What will people say?
FARAH *(Attempting smiling politeness)* I know all this, bibiji. I have tried to do my... duty, accepting Maryam...
FAUZIA   It is she who has accepted you. She is a good lady.
FARAH *(Struggling for control)* Of course *(She loses it)* Why aren't I good enough for him? Why does he need somebody else?
FAUZIA *(Smiling)* You think to share is a weak thing? *(FARAH says nothing)* I understand. You have grown up in a selfish country. Me. Mine. This is all girls like you know.
FARAH   Like me? What's wrong with me?
FAUZIA *(Laughing, kindly for the first time)* Nothing, beti. Look at you. Big job. Car. And too much fire inside.
FARAH   I wouldn't have survived here without it.
FAUZIA   You will never understand...
FARAH   I have to! Why can't I accept...?
FAUZIA   You are too foreign. You wear our clothes, eat our food, but your heart has changed too much living here.
FARAH   You're saying I'm not Pakistani enough? *(FAUZIA shakes her head almost sadly. FARAH is gripped with fury. She turns on FAUZIA.)* That makes me like a bastard to my own people. What have *you* achieved here? What makes *you* better? *(FARAH stands up. Her dupatta falls to the floor. She turns to FAUZIA. FAUZIA picks up the dupatta and arranges it deliberately over FARAH'S breasts.)*

FAUZIA   *You* knocked on my door.
   (FARAH is stopped in her tracks, conceding defeat.)
FARAH *(Quieter now)* I suppose I should leave him *(She looks up at FAUZIA, almost pleading)...* shouldn't I? *(The clock strikes eight. FAUZIA refills FARAH'S cup which trembles in her hand.)*

SCENE 67
Int. Lounge. ASIF'S house. Morning

   (ASIF sitting bolt upright on the sofa. Unshaven. Frightened. The front door slams. He jumps up and sees FARAH standing in the hallway, the sun rising behind her.)

ASIF   Farah...
   (FARAH is quite calm. She pushes past him and goes upstairs. He follows.)

SCENE 68
Int. FARAH'S room. ASIF'S house. Morning.

ASIF *(Watches as FARAH throws a few belongings into a suitcase)* Farah, listen to me... *(FARAH closing the case and picking it up)*
FARAH   I'm leaving. Out of my way. *(ASIF doesn't move, she screams)* Get out of my way!
   (As she goes into the hallway, MARYAM and SABIA rush from their respective rooms in their nightwear)
SABIA *(Shouting in Urdu)* Leave her! Let her go! We don't want her here! I'll pay for her taxi myself!

   (FARAH suddenly stops in the hallway. She sways, gulping for air. Then rushes out. We hear FARAH being violently sick.)

SCENE 69
Int. Bathroom. ASIF'S house. Morning.

   (FARAH is slumped over the toilet bowl, ASIF next to her holding her hand, his eyes worried. MARYAM and SABIA standing in the doorway, their faces set and angry.)

ASIF *(Concerned)* Janoo, what's wrong? What is it?
SABIA *(Urdu)* Can't you tell by now? Are you sure it's yours, Asif?

(FARAH heaves again, leaning over the toilet. ASIF looks at SABIA, stunned, and then back at FARAH. ASIF, overwhelmed, joyful as realisation dawns.)

ASIF   We'll call him Tariq, after your father. You'd like that wouldn't you? Stop this nonsense. You're not going anywhere. We're all here, Farah...

(Close up on MARYAM and SABIA'S faces.)

SCENE 70
Ext. Doctor's surgery. London. Day.

(ASIF'S car is parked outside a Central London surgery. MARYAM stands at the top of the steps with FARAH until the buzzer sounds and FARAH is admitted. ASIF watches MARYAM descend the steps, smart in a simple business suit. She sits in the passenger seat and begins sorting through her bag.)

ASIF   So you're going through with this interview?

MARYAM I know the people there. It would be like working for family.

ASIF   But you haven't told Farah...

MARYAM *(Soothing)* Asif, I might not even get the job, what's the point?

ASIF   And I don't like you working. I provide you with everything you need.

MARYAM *(Laughing loudly, seeing ASIF'S angry face and stopping)* Farah's in the house now, if the girls need company after school.
(MARYAM gets out of the car) Besides, if you leave me, I'll need to be able to support myself, won't I Asif?
(MARYAM slams the door and clicks off down the road, ASIF watching her go with something almost like admiration.)

SCENE 71
Int. Doctor's surgery. London. Day.

(FARAH facing the doctor over her desk. She is completing a medical history form.)

FARAH   I just want to know why I feel so ill all the time.

DOCTOR   The first three months can be the most difficult, your hormones are running riot, your body is going through the most massive changes and you will feel tired. Exhausted. Having said that, I am worried about your blood pressure, and you do seem to be retaining an unusual amount of fluid for this early stage in your pregnancy. And you're slightly anaemic. *(FARAH looks worried)* But these are all things we can monitor, so please don't worry. First of all, I'm going to put you on iron tablets.

FARAH *(Quickly)* I'm not taking any tablets. Or potions or pills. This child is very important to me. I'm not taking any chances.

SCENE 72
Int. Dining room. ASIF'S house. Morning.

(Close up of ASIF'S hand fiddling with the top button of MARYAM'S stiff new blouse. He manages, finally to fasten it. ASIF and MARYAM stand before the dining table. The girls are eating cereal. ASIF holds open a mock-leather executive briefcase into which MARYAM puts new biros, a notepad, a new calculator and some make-up. She is dressed in a smart suit, also new, and glows with satisfaction. ASIF watches her, amused. In the background, FARAH shuffles slowly around the breakfast table, piling away dishes. She is dressed in an old shalwar kameez. Her hair, now longer, is lank and tied back. She moves with difficulty, horribly swollen, not with the natural swell of pregnancy – but something bloated and unnatural.)

SAPNA   You don't go to work, Mummy.
MARYAM I do now.
ASIF   It's your mum's first day. We mustn't let her be late. Come on.
(ASIF organises the girls, wiping milky mouths and teasing on coats)
SAPNA   Who's going to pick us up at school?
ASIF   Farah auntie, will. *(Pushing SAPNA'S arm into a sleeve)* Put this on.
SAPNA   Why? Why can't Mummy...?
ASIF   The doctor says Farah auntie must take a rest.
SAPNA   Is she sick?

SCENE 73
Int. Kitchen. ASIF'S house. Morning.

(FARAH is piling the dirty breakfast dishes in the sink. MARYAM enters and begins searching through cupboards.)

ASIF *(V.O.)* You'll be late!

MARYAM *(Shouting back)* Can't find my vitamins!

FARAH *(Without looking up)* Second cupboard on the left. Top shelf.

MARYAM *(Finds them, looks over at FARAH)* Leave those for Maureen. That's why we pay her. *(FARAH ignores her. MARYAM moves closer)* You don't mind, do you? About me working...

FARAH *(Turning to look, patting her stomach)* I've got more important things to worry about now.

MARYAM *(Takes this in, impassive. She goes back to the cupboard and brings out a bottle of green tonic.)* Oh Farah. You haven't been taking Sabia's tonic? She made it up specially for you.

FARAH *(Eyes the bottle suspiciously, backing off)* No.

MARYAM *(Picking up a spoon)* Come on. You do have more important things to worry about...

(MARYAM pours out a spoonful. FARAH'S eyes widen in terror. MARYAM begins moving forward with the spoon.)

FARAH   No. Don't you come near me...

MARYAM Don't be silly... just a mouthful...

FARAH *(Backing off)* Get back... get away from me.

MARYAM *(Coming closer)* No! No! No!

(FARAH knocks the spoon out of MARYAM'S hand, sending her sprawling. MARYAM stumbles backwards into ASIF who comes rushing in)

ASIF *(Holding up MARYAM)* What the hell... *(ASIF looks over at FARAH who is shaking with fear and anger. The girls stand in the doorway, wide-eyed, anxiously watching this)* What did you do?

MARYAM *(Shaken)* It's okay... the tonic... I just asked...

ASIF *(Turning on FARAH)* What's happening to you? *(He indicates the girls)* They're scared of you, do you know that?... sulking around in your room, not eating with us... now this...

MARYAM Asif...

ASIF *(Ignoring her, to FARAH)* I have to drag you to your check-ups! Don't you care? You're carrying my son! Pregnancy should be the happiest time in a woman's life.

MARYAM *(Coolly)* Oh shut up Asif! You don't know what you're talking about.

ASIF *(Turns to MARYAM, incredulous)* What did you say?

(They turn, hearing SABIA shouting in the doorway)

SABIA *(In Urdu, to MARYAM)* How dare you talk to my son like this!

MARYAM Every step he takes you put your neck under his foot! What have you ever taught him!

SABIA *(English, pointing at FARAH)* You learn this from her! Her fault!
(FARAH stifles a sob and runs upstairs. A long silence. ASIF pushes SABIA and the girls out of the kitchen.)

ASIF *(To SABIA)* Take them to the car. *(They leave. He turns to MARYAM)* This time last year you couldn't even look me in the eye.

MARYAM *(Responds with a mocking gaze. ASIF goes to the door, looking up the stairs after FARAH)* Go on then. Go after her.

ASIF *(Defeated)* I... I don't know what to say to her. I think she hates me.

SCENE 74
Int. FARAH'S bedroom. ASIF'S house. Night.

(FARAH at her wallchart with a red biro. We see it is entitled 'MARYAM and ASIF'. It is divided up into columns, dates, some red stars next to them. FARAH puts a red star next to the most recent date.)

FARAH *(Muttering to herself)* Lovemaking began at eleven forty-five, ended eleven fifty-five. Huh, big stud Asif, that the best you can do?
(Next door the bedsprings suddenly start up again. FARAH bites her pen absent-mindedly, smearing her mouth and lips with red.)

SCENE 75
Int. FARAH Carpets. Day.

(POPPY enters the shop. She is smartly dressed. She pauses a second in front of a mirror near the doorway and checks her hair, messing it up a little. She then catches sight of the large diamond ring on her wedding finger, holds it up to the mirror to watch it sparkle. She smiles a huge smile to herself and marches up to the counter.)

POPPY I'd like to talk to Mrs. Shah please.

MRS. SIDDIQUI *(Looking up)* One minute, madam.
(She disappears into the back office. POPPY looks round the shop, holding her hand ostentatiously on her face in case anyone's looking. A door opens behind her and she swings round expectantly.)

POPPY You'll never guess what Henry bought me...
(She stops, coming face to face with MARYAM. POPPY'S face falls. MARYAM'S betrays nothing)

MARYAM Yes madam, can I help you?

SCENE 76
Int. Lounge. ASIF'S house. Day.

(Saturday lunchtime. Children's television programmes in the background. ASIF, SABIA, MARYAM and the girls sitting on the floor in front of the television eating snacks. The door slams. FARAH enters in an old salwar kameez with woolly cardigan over it, socks with Indian sandals. She clutches a McDonald's takeaway carton. She ignores the family and walks through the room and out of the door.)

ASIF   She's like the madwoman in the attic. Talk to her.
MARYAM You talk to her. She's your wife. Tell her to stay in her room when your clients come round. That's what you used to do with me.

SCENE 77
Int. FARAH'S room. ASIF'S house. Day.

(FARAH finishing off her McDonald's. She stops, fingers to her mouth, hearing some noise. She listens harder. Bedsprings coming from next door. FARAH throws down her carton, furious.)

FARAH   In the daytime! Can't do that, haven't got a space in my chart for the daytime you can't.
(She rushes out.)

SCENE 78
Int. Hallway. ASIF'S house. Day.
(FARAH rushing down the hallway. Flings the door open screaming.)

SCENE 79
Int. MARYAM'S room. ASIF'S house. Day.

(SAPNA and SORAYA are bouncing on the bed, giggling. They stop dead as FARAH enters. SORAYA begins to whimper in fear. FARAH begins to giggle, then chuckle, then laughs hysterically, pointing at the girls who stand still and mute with fright.)

SCENE 80
Int. FARAH'S room. ASIF'S house. Day.

(FARAH standing at her bedroom door, listening. Sounds of the children's voices disappearing down the stairs, the front door slamming shut, a car starting up and driving away. FARAH smiles. Runs to her bedside cabinet and pulls out an oil can.)

SCENE 81

Int. MARYAM'S room. ASIF'S house. Day.

(FARAH begins stripping the bed wildly, throwing sheets, pillows and blankets off until the bed frame is exposed. She sits on the bed and bounces around, testing it, listening for where the squeaks come from. She locates the main area and tries to oil the springs. They are underneath and just out of reach. She then heaves the frame on its side. This is a long and difficult task, with many stops to catch her breath. At last the frame is balancing precariously on one side. FARAH leans the frame against the wall, but we see it is not secure. She takes the oil can and crawls underneath, trying to reach the rusty springs. Close up of the frame which sways just a second before it comes crashing down.)

SCENE 82

Int. Private room. Hospital. Day.

(Close up of FARAH'S hand clamped tightly over another woman's hand. Pull back to reveal MARYAM sitting next to FARAH'S bed, FARAH sleeping but still holding onto MARYAM'S hand like a vice. Away from the bed, ASIF stands talking with an English woman doctor. He is red-eyed and unshaven.)

DOCTOR   I am sorry, Mr. Shah. Let her sleep as long as she wants now, she should be out of here in a week. And then it's up to you.

ASIF   But you say there's no lasting damage. We can have more children?

DOCTOR *(Her face hardening)* Give your wife a chance to get over this, don't you think? A miscarriage is like a death for many women, they need to mourn. They need support, Mr. Shah.

(Cut to MARYAM at FARAH'S bedside. She is very calm. She talks to FARAH who is still out cold)

MARYAM *(Quietly)* Now, my sister, we are equal.

SCENE 83

Int. Chemist shop. London. Day.

(Close up of the bottle containing SABIA'S green 'Health Tonic'. It is now half full. Pull back to reveal POPPY and FARAH standing at the Chemist's counter. FARAH is wrapped up in a heavy, winter coat, and men's socks.POPPY and HENRY are in short sleeves. It is a warm May day)

FARAH   Can Henry analyse this?

POPPY   What is it?

FARAH   It was a full bottle. I know what they're up to.

POPPY   Who?

FARAH *(Taking the bottle over to HENRY and placing it in his hands)* I want to know every ingredient in this.

POPPY   I've been calling you for days...

FARAH   I don't answer the phone any more.

POPPY *(Looking over FARAH with real concern, taking in her sunken eyes, the woolly coat)* Why don't you come and stay with us?

FARAH   Oh, she's being so nice to me now. Isn't that the behaviour of a guilty woman?

POPPY   I thought you had a fall...

FARAH   So you believe them too? I thought you were my friend.

POPPY   I am...!

FARAH   This baby would have changed everything. You know the first thing Asif asked when I came round? 'Was it a boy?'

HENRY *(Calling over)* I'll have to send this off to the lab. Take a couple of weeks.

FARAH   I should never have let her get close. That was my big mistake. No one's going to do that to me again.

POPPY   Farah...

FARAH   I can't see you any more, Poppy. I'm sorry.
(FARAH leaves the shop.)

SCENE 84
Int. Stairway. ASIF'S house. Evening.

(A dinner party is just coming to a close. FARAH sits in the dark at the top of the stairs smoking, flicking ash onto the carpet. She is listening in to the farewell conversations at the door. She is unseen.)

SCENE 85
Int. Hallway. ASIF'S house. Evening.

(ASIF is helping one of his Pakistani business friends on with his coat. MARYAM stands next to him, dressed up to the nines.)

MAN   I'm sorry that Farah couldn't join us tonight. *(Looking at MARYAM)* But I can see you're more than taken care of.

ASIF   We're hoping Farah will be better soon. Thanks for coming.
(The man leaves.)

SCENE 86
Int. Stairway. ASIF'S house. Evening.

(FARAH hears the front door. As soon as the front door closes, there is a brief scuffle in the hallway.)

MARYAM *(V.O.)* Stop it, Asif.

ASIF *(V.O.)* Don't turn me away. *(Urdu)* I'm not sure of anything any more. I need to hold somebody.
(Focus in on FARAH, wishing she could understand)
(Urdu V.O.) I can't cope with her. *(English)* You're a woman. You should understand...

MARYAM *(English V.O.)* About the baby. *(FARAH listening intently. Urdu V.O.)* I should. You put me through the same thing... *(English)* But it wasn't an accident.

FARAH *(Alert, breathing hard)* I knew it.

MARYAM *(Urdu V.O.)* You have to cope. With both of us, Asif. You brought us both into this house.

SCENE 87
Int. Hallway. ASIF'S house. Evening.

(ASIF grabs MARYAM and kisses her. FARAH is watching through the railings. She ducks out of sight as MARYAM breaks away.)

MARYAM *(Taking ASIF'S hand)* Come then. Come to bed.
(FARAH ducks away, out of sight, and disappears.)

SCENE 88
Int. ASIF'S room. ASIF'S house. Day.

(FARAH, still in her nightwear enters with a jug of water. She fills ASIF'S jug and looks round the bedroom. Opens the wardrobes, faces the rows of hand-stitched suits and runs her hands along the material. She sniffs the sleeves, trying to recall his scent. She searches through the pockets, finding nothing but pressed silk hankies.)

SCENE 89
Int. MARYAM'S room. Day.

(Next FARAH goes to MARYAM'S room, no more Indian suits lying around, but opens a wardrobe to reveal rows of smart, tailored suits. There is now a filing cabinet next to the bed. After filling MARYAM'S water decanter, FARAH begins searching through her drawers and cupboards. She discovers a brown paper bag, opens it to reveal a pregnancy testing kit, unused.)

FARAH   Kill one baby. Start another. So you want to fight dirty, my sister-wife. I haven't even begun.

SCENE 90
Int. FARAH'S room. ASIF'S house. Night.

(FARAH looking at a water decanter, completely full. She tears open a sachet and sprinkles a little of the powdery contents into the water. She watches, fascinated, as it clouds and then clears.)

FARAH *(V.O.)* I know Mata-ji I cannot be the first to make you this request. I swear on my husband's life I will tell no-one of this.
(Cut to close up of an old woman's hand sliding the sachet across the table. A young woman's hand closes over it)
I think you must be the only friend I have in the world.

SCENE 91
Ext. Park. London. Day.

(FARAH sitting on the swing, warm day, though she is wrapped up as if it was winter. She is swinging and watching the girls playing on the slide, aided by MARYAM and SABIA. MARYAM is taking the girls up the stairs and SABIA catching them at the bottom of the slide. Suddenly MARYAM seems to go dizzy a moment. She sits down on the stairs and

breathes hard, trying to fight off fainting. SABIA runs to MARYAM'S aid. SABIA turns to look at FARAH who is still swinging, expressionless.)

SCENE 92
Int. Bathroom. ASIF'S house. Day.

(MARYAM is sitting on the toilet seat, flushed and weak. FARAH enters, checks her temperature, wets a face flannel and places it on MARYAM'S forehead who sighs in relief.)

MARYAM I've been feeling a bit strange this last week. Must be the bug going round the office.

FARAH   Good. I thought for a moment it might be my cooking.

MARYAM No no, you're very good now. Better than me, I think. When you first came here, you could not boil an egg.

FARAH   I've learned fast.

MARYAM Don't you want to come back to Farah Carpets? Everyone asks about you...?

FARAH *(Quickly)* I like it at home.

(MARYAM'S teeth begin chattering uncontrollably)

MARYAM I think I should lie down.

(FARAH helps her up. MARYAM leans on her, their faces very close.)
Farah, when you lost the baby... wasn't your fault...

FARAH *(Looking at her now)* I know.

SCENE 93
Int. MARYAM'S bedroom. ASIF'S house. Day.

(MARYAM is now lying in bed, still shivering but calmer and drowsy now. FARAH is drawing the curtains.)

MARYAM I'm not used to this. Someone looking after me...
(MARYAM smiles uncertainly at FARAH who forces a smile back)
Will you come up and see me later?
(FARAH nods, picks up the empty water decanter from the bedside table and exits quickly.)

SCENE 94
Int. Kitchen/garden. ASIF'S house. Day.

(FARAH stands at the sink, rinsing out the decanter. She suddenly wants to cry, she leans forward onto the sink, fighting back tears, frightened by something unknown which threatens to overpower her. FARAH looks up through the window and sees the FOUR WOMEN from the house in Pakistan sitting in the back garden. They are reclining in the sunlight, beautiful profiles to the sky, smiling and waving towards FARAH who does not seem surprised to see them. THE WOMEN are lit in such a way we cannot be sure whether they are real or in FARAH'S mind.)

SCENE 95
Ext. Garden. ASIF'S house. Day.

(FARAH opens the kitchen door, still holding the water decanter, and walks towards THE WOMEN. She breaks into a smile, her walk turns into a run. As soon as she reaches them, they begin pointing to the house, and put their fingers on their lips, motioning her to not give them away.)

ASIF   Farah? *(FARAH swings round to face ASIF. She is   bewildered, out of breath)* What are you doing out here?
(FARAH looks nervously from THE WOMEN to ASIF. He obviously cannot see them. THE WOMEN laugh slyly. Enjoying the joke. ASIF checking the decanter in FARAH'S hands.)
Watering the plants, were you?
(One of the younger women, vivacious, in bright colours, leans forward to whisper.)
FIRST WOMAN   Don't give anything away, sister.
FARAH *(Looking back at ASIF)* Er, yes. No. *(THE WOMEN giggle again, FARAH tries not to grin, motioning them to be quiet.)* A walk. In the fresh air.
ASIF *(Looking straight at THE WOMEN who loll on the grass and hang from the trees)* What are you... *(FARAH looks at ASIF innocently)* Never mind. How's Maryam?
(THE WOMEN all look at each other, and then accusingly at FARAH.)
FARAH   Sleeping.
(SECOND WOMAN, an older one, chewing betel nut, and spitting out a stream of red juice which just misses ASIF'S foot.)
SECOND WOMAN   Not permanently, I hope.
FARAH *(Defensively, to the women)* I have been looking after her!
ASIF *(Confused, still trying to work out where she's looking)* Yes, yes, you have been. And I'm very pleased to see it.
(ASIF is awkward, searching for words.)

Actually, I have been meaning to talk to you for some time.
(THE WOMEN all make groaning noises.)

FIRST WOMAN   You'd better sit down. This could take a long time.
(FARAH sits down on the grass. ASIF is surprised at this, but smiles and complies, sitting down next to her.)

ASIF   I... er, I wanted to apologise... since the baby... the miscarriage, I know I have been avoiding you. It hurt me to see you... I...
(This is obviously difficult for ASIF. He is confused, little boy lost. FARAH visibly softens, but stops herself from giving in. THIRD WOMAN, the eldest one of the group, dignified and beautiful.)

THIRD WOMAN He has swallowed his pride. Can you force down your pain?

FARAH *(Quietly)* No.

ASIF   Pardon?

FARAH   No apology needed, Asif.

ASIF *(Relieved)* Good. *(Reaches out tentatively to touch her hair, now long and in a plait.)* You've grown it like a village girl.

FARAH   You like it like this?
(FOURTH WOMAN, the youngest, pretty and adorned with jewels.)

FOURTH WOMAN   Don't beg for compliments! He should worship the earth you tread!

ASIF   Since our marriage, you're not the same... I mean, I appreciate the way you have adapted.

FARAH   What do you mean?

ASIF   To our... situation. Trying to work together, all of us. As one family. It was hard at first, but I think we'll be O.K.

FARAH   I thought...
(THE WOMEN crane forward to listen closely.)

FARAH   We talked about us moving out.

ASIF   But you and Maryam are getting on so well now. You've changed.

FARAH *(Desperate)* To please you!

ASIF *(Taking FARAH'S hand)* Thank you. And I am.
(THE WOMEN break into spontaneous applause which FARAH shouts over.)

FARAH   I married for love, Asif.

ASIF *(Puzzled)* And so did I.

FIRST WOMAN *(Shouting)* She means sex!

FARAH   No!

ASIF   Do you think I don't love you any more?

FARAH   I... *(Looks at THE WOMEN for help)*

SECOND WOMAN   You have lived in the West too long. Can't you see anything beyond your own desire?

THIRD WOMAN You will be provided for all your life. Poverty is the greatest murderer of love.

FOURTH WOMAN   Your sister-wife knows you better than your husband. Together you can play him like a sitar.

FIRST WOMAN   Sex is best when it is fought for, sister.

(THE WOMEN'S voices rise, a shrieking cacophony of sound. FARAH covers her ears, closes her eyes.)

ASIF   Farah? *(He takes her hands away, forces her to look into his eyes.)* I want you to get... better. Work, stay at home, whatever makes you happy. Stop torturing yourself. You don't have to fight for me. I will always be here. Till death us do part... *(He smiles)*... isn't that what these degenerate white people say?

SCENE 96

Int. MARYAM'S bedroom. ASIF'S house. Day.

(SABIA is making MARYAM comfortable, plumping pillows, etc. MARYAM is still groggy but looking better. SABIA goes to draw the curtains and sees FARAH in the garden. She is standing at the base of the largest tree, looking up and seemingly talking to someone.)

SABIA *(Laughing to herself)* Barking mad.

SCENE 97

Int. MARYAM'S bedroom. ASIF'S house. Night.

(The room is dark. FARAH, clutching her packet of 'Medicine' from MATA-JI quietly enters with the water decanter. She creeps over to place it on the bedside table, opens the packet preparing to sprinkle some of the powder into it, and jumps hearing MARYAM'S voice.)

MARYAM Farah?

FARAH *(Stuffs the packet down her cleavage and turns round to face the bed.)* Sorry. Didn't mean to wake you.

MARYAM *(Still groggy, between sleep and waking)* Can't sleep.

FARAH   Shall I put on the light?

MARYAM No. *(Mumbling)* Curtains... open. *(FARAH opens the curtains. Moonlight floods the room, giving the two women's faces an eerie glow.)* My legs... the cramps.

(FARAH moves to the bed and begins massaging MARYAM'S legs gently)
I'm scared.

FARAH   Why?

MARYAM The pain.

FARAH *(Nervous)* You're not thinking of calling in the doctor?

MARYAM The same when I lost my baby.

FARAH *(Puzzled)* What baby?

MARYAM Nasreen. *(MARYAM is drifting in and out of sleep now, slightly delirious.)* Asif wanted a boy. Scan. The scan said a girl...

FARAH *(Holding her breath)* Go on.

MARYAM Dangerous, doctor said. No more children.

FARAH *(Stopping the massage)* What do you mean?

MARYAM *(Almost asleep)* Clinic nice. Only the best, Asif said. No pain. No more girls you see.

FARAH *(Incredulous)* He made you have an abortion?

MARYAM I'm safe with you. Two wives, more chance of a boy. I'm free Farah. I'm not scared of him any more.

(MARYAM is asleep. FARAH takes out the packet of medicine from her front. She opens it, goes to pour it in and looks across at MARYAM'S sleeping face. She hesitates, not knowing what to do. The sound of women's voices come through the open window. She moves slowly towards it and looks out.)

SCENE 98
Ext. Garden. ASIF'S house. Night.

(The FOUR WIVES are sitting in the branches of the tree, waving and calling to FARAH. They are beautiful, bathed in soft moonlight. FARAH watches as the eldest wife stretches out her arms which hold a small baby, wriggling and gurgling, playing with her jewellery.)

FIRST WIFE Don't do it, Farah. She's a woman, too – your sister. Think of your ma.

SCENE 99
Int. MARYAM'S bedroom. ASIF'S house. Night.

(FARAH looks down at the sachet in her palm. She closes her fingers around it, squeezing until it's completely crumpled. She flings it out of the window.)

SCENE 100
Int. Lounge. ASIF'S house. Evening.

(The sound of laughter and talk coming from the dining room, a party obviously in full swing, full of media types, amongst them ASIF and MARYAM, looking stunning. ASIF seems to be holding court. JANE, a producer, walks towards the kitchen. JANE stops at the door, hearing raised laughing female voices coming from inside.)

SCENE 101
Int. Kitchen. ASIF'S house. Night.

(She pushes open the door and stops, confused. The room is empty except for FARAH who seems to have been in conversation with – who? FARAH looks up, unembarrassed, seeing JANE in the doorway.)

FARAH   Yes?

JANE   Sorry, I thought there was a group of revellers in here.

FARAH   No. Just us.

JANE *(Confused)* Oh, of course... what a super spread! *(She lingers over the food)* I love curry, try to make it at home but it's just never the same as the genuine article, is it? Still, no expense spared with Asif. I'm really excited he's agreed to come and do our programme – 'Business in the Nineties'. We feel it's so important to represent the Asian community and their successes. Do you watch it?

FARAH   No.

JANE   I expect you're too busy running this place, eh? *(She waits for a reaction. There is none.)* Anyway, must go and mingle. *(JANE exits as MARYAM enters, looking stunning in a silk suit.)*

MARYAM I thought Asif's business friends drank a lot, but everyone in television must be an alcoholic. *(MARYAM begins hunting around in cupboards, oblivious to FARAH.)* Where's the damn corkscrew? *(FARAH glides over to a drawer pulls it out and hands it to MARYAM. MARYAM is momentarily wrong-footed, maybe struck with deja-vu.)* Thank you. *(MARYAM indicates the lavish spread)* The food...

FARAH *(Interrupting)* You are better now, aren't you...? You do feel...

MARYAM *(Smiling)* I'm very well, Farah. Thank you. *(MARYAM awkward, indicating the party)* You're not joining us?

FARAH   Why?

MARYAM   Because... *(Angry now, not at FARAH)* Because it's our
party? *(MARYAM and FARAH stand face to face. It is MARYAM who
turns and leaves. FARAH addresses the tree in the garden.)*
FARAH   You heard Maryam. Our party. Shall we go?

SCENE 102
Int. Lounge. ASIF'S house. Evening.

*(A gathering of various media types in animated conversation over wine
and Indian snacks. SABIA moves through the crowd with a tray,
obviously put out at having to play the servant. She stands before TIM, a
young fashionably scruffy television director, who does not look at her as
he puts down his empty glass on the tray and picks up a refill.)*

SABIA *(Urdu)* This is not my job. We have an Irish servant. Now you are
waiting on us. Have you got a house this big?
TIM   Eh?
SABIA *(English)* Please have some more.
TIM   Great... yeah.
SABIA *(Urdu)* And I hope you choke on it.
　　*(TIM nods and joins a group standing around ASIF and MARYAM,
　　including JANE and her P.A., LOTTIE. They are hanging on ASIF'S every
　　word, marvelling at his story-telling. It is only MARYAM, who is slightly
　　aloof, watching ASIF closely. She turns to LOTTIE at her side who is
　　gazing adoringly at ASIF.)*
MARYAM   Of course he's irresistible. But I never know when he's
telling the truth.

SCENE 103
Int. FARAH'S bedroom. ASIF'S house. Evening.

*(Close up on FARAH and ASIF'S wedding photograph, dusty and askew
in its frame. We pan to the bed where FARAH'S wedding suit is laid out,
her jewellery carefully placed on top of it. We hear women's laughter and
see four pairs of brown, bejewelled hands carefully lifting the jewellery
from the bed. FARAH is being dressed by the FOUR WOMEN. They tie
her 'langa' (long silk skirt) and smoothe her tunic over her hips. They
fasten the gold 'tikka' into her centre parting in her newly oiled hair.
They fasten her wedding necklace and nose-ring with reverence as if
preparing her for battle. All the while, they murmur softly in Urdu,
sweet nothings.)*

THIRD WIFE *(Urdu)* My, how beautiful she is!
SECOND WIFE *(Urdu)* A real Pakistani bride.

FIRST WIFE *(Holds FARAH'S chin in her palm. English)* Your ma would be
so proud. He is yours Farah. Take him.
*(FARAH is almost ready except for one detail. She picks up the wedding
dupatta and arranges it meticulously round her head and over her
breasts.)*

SCENE 104
Int. Lounge. ASIF'S house. Evening.

(ASIF still holding court)

JANE   If we could fix a day to film in your office. The end of
next week would be good for us. Is that O.K.?
ASIF *(Checking MARYAM)* You do understand, I don't want to talk about my
family life.
JANE   Oh of course. No, it's the businessman in you we're   interested
in. *(JANE looks at MARYAM, joking)* No skeletons in your husband's
closets?

*(She trails off realising ASIF and MARYAM are no longer listening, and
the room has gone very quiet. All eyes are on the doorway where FARAH
has entered and is standing as if waiting to be announced. She is dressed
in her wedding suit and full jewellery, carefully applied bright make-up
and a radiant smile. FARAH moves around the room shaking everyone's
hands, dispensing greetings like a Royal on walkabout. People begin
whispering to each other as she passes, bemused but too polite to laugh.
ASIF stands stiff and taut as FARAH approaches. FARAH smiles sweetly
at the group and turns to JANE, shaking her by the hand.)*

FARAH   How do you do. I am Mrs. Shah.
*(The group look confusedly at each other, and then from FARAH to
MARYAM to ASIF who is about to explode)*
JANE   I'm sorry... *(Looks at MARYAM)...* I thought...
FARAH   Oh yes! *(She laughs gaily)* I mean, the second Mrs. Shah.
Maryam's sister-wife.
*(JANE nudges LOTTIE furiously who takes out a notebook and pen. The
rest of the group stand waiting, ears pricked. Taking FARAH by the arm)*
ASIF   Farah, I think maybe you should rest like the doctor said...

FARAH (*Resisting him*) No! Listen to me! Asif, I don't want to be
   selfish any more, I can't exist wanting all of you, it's too painful. What's
   best for the family is best for me.
   (*MARYAM begins pulling FARAH away, who tries to resist. She then
   catches sight of ASIF'S face, pale and trembling with anger, and gives in,
   allowing herself to be pulled away.*)

SCENE 105
Int. Hallway. ASIF'S house. Evening.

MARYAM (*Pulling FARAH through the hallway and up the stairs*) That
   was a spiteful thing to do, Farah.
FARAH (*Genuinely bewildered*) Why?
MARYAM Don't be so stupid.
FARAH   Why should we be ashamed? I don't understand...
   (*They are by now at the top of the stairs. They see ASIF appear below in
   the hallway and begin purposefully following them.*)
MARYAM God.
   (*ASIF ascends the stairs. He grabs FARAH by the arm, making her wince
   with pain. MARYAM placing her hand on ASIF'S chest.*)
   Asif.
ASIF (*Shaking off MARYAM, face to face with FARAH*) Just what the hell
   are you trying to do?
FARAH (*Confused*) I thought you'd be pleased...
ASIF (*Incredulous*) What! (*He swings round to MARYAM*) Did you two
   plan this together?
MARYAM No! You think I'm mad too?
   (*ASIF looking at MARYAM with new eyes*)
FARAH   Mad?
ASIF   There's a room full of TV people downstairs... can you see
   tomorrow's headlines? Barbaric Pakistani in Love Triangle? Asif Shah and
   his bloody harem.
MARYAM (*To FARAH*) Some things we keep within the family. The outside
   world would not understand.
FARAH   Maryam needs me, don't you Maryam.
   (*MARYAM lowers her eyes, avoiding FARAH'S appeal. Close up to
   FARAH'S face.*)
ASIF   Maryam was with me long before you!
   (*He stops, realising that was an awful thing to say. He is completely
   drained. ASIF goes downstairs, leaving the two women facing each
   other.*)

MARYAM   He didn't mean what he said. You know what he's like when he's angry.

FARAH   You win. *(Smiles sadly)* This is what you've been waiting for, isn't it?

SCENE 106
Int. Kitchen. ASIF'S house. Night.

(FARAH washing up at the kitchen sink surrounded by the debris of the party. The FOUR WOMEN from Pakistan loll around the room, pinching leftovers, swigging from discarded wine bottles, bored and lazy. FARAH moves around them, shoving them out of her way as she tries to clear up.)

SCENE 107
Int. ASIF'S bedroom. ASIF'S house. Night.

(ASIF is sitting on his bed with his head in his hands, distraught. MARYAM stands watching him.)

ASIF   What's happened to her? I can't bear to see her like this... *(He begins crying, helpless. MARYAM hesitates, then goes to him, cradling him like a child.)*

SCENE 108
Int. Kitchen. ASIF'S house. Night.

(The FOUR WOMEN are all chatting loudly whilst FARAH watches them. FARAH stands in the centre of the room and addresses them.)

FARAH   You don't belong here. You can't exist here. You are redundant. *(FARAH claps her hands. The FOUR WOMEN look alarmed as they slowly fade away before FARAH'S eyes. FARAH makes sure they have gone, then slowly moves to the kitchen, lounge, television room, switching all the lights off behind her.)*

SCENE 109
Int. Hallway. ASIF'S house. Night.

(FARAH carrying a water jug walks down the hallway. She pauses outside ASIF'S room and moves on to MARYAM'S bedroom.)

SCENE 110

Int. MARYAM'S bedroom. ASIF'S house. Night.

(FARAH pouring water into MARYAM'S empty decanter. She is zombie-like, removed, completely empty. Her hands slip and water spills out onto the cabinet and carpet. This wakes her a little, she panics, throws open the cabinet looking for a cloth. FARAH finds something at the back, a cardboard box, carefully placed upright. She opens it. It is the pregnancy test, which has been opened and used. In the box are various papers, she searches through and finds an official looking letter, opens it. We see it is a letter of confirmation from a doctor that MARYAM is four weeks pregnant. FARAH reads this through twice, mouthing the words to herself. She slumps onto the bed. We have never seen FARAH cry before, not fully, without restraint. A silent scream of grief begins, which she stifles with a pillow over her mouth. She begins rocking it like a baby. She looks up when she hears the bedsprings creak. A peal of female laughter rings out.)

FARAH *(Sobbing)* Where are you now? Where...?
(FARAH is inconsolable, raw, mad. She looks about her and up at the ceiling, as if looking for the FOUR WOMEN. They are nowhere to be found.)

SCENE 111

Int. FARAH'S bedroom. ASIF'S house. Night.

(FARAH is dry-eyed now, is searching through her drawers, methodical, unhurried. She finds what she is looking for, the packet of powder from MATA-JI)

SCENE 112

Int. MARYAM'S bedroom. ASIF'S house. Night.

(FARAH empties the whole packet of powder into MARYAM'S water decanter. She is shaking, holding back tears. The water fizzes and clouds up, gradually going crystal clear and still. The surface is momentarily broken by one of FARAH'S tears which drop into the decanter and is lost.)

SCENE 113
Int. ASIF'S bedroom. ASIF'S house. Night.

(MARYAM still comforting ASIF. She kisses him. He kisses her back, they cling together, it is sexual but mostly healing. ASIF begins to pull off MARYAM'S clothes.)

MARYAM No don't!
ASIF Why?
MARYAM Tonight I feel... ashamed.
(ASIF reaches over to the bedside table. Pours himself a glass of water from the decanter, gulps it down, flicks the light switch, and the room goes dark.)
MARYAM *(V.O.)* No Asif... *(They begin struggling)*

SCENE 114
Int. FARAH'S bedroom. ASIF'S house. Night.

(FARAH lying fully dressed, ramrod straight on her bed, clutching her wedding photograph to her chest. The curtains are open, the light off. There is a roaring   sound in the room, or maybe inside FARAH'S head.)

SCENE 115
Int. Hallway. ASIF'S house. Night.

(The roaring sound continues. MARYAM comes flying out of ASIF'S bedroom distressed, half-dressed, and runs into her bedroom, slamming the door behind her. ASIF follows, clutching a sheet to his naked body. He knocks softly on the door. She opens it, confused, torn between disgust and desire. ASIF, standing facing MARYAM. He turns to go and she stops him, opening the door to let him in, hating herself for it.)

SCENE 116
Int. FARAH'S bedroom. ASIF'S house. Dawn.

(FARAH lying on her bed in darkness. The roaring sound gets louder, to unbearable pitch, and suddenly stops. Suddenly she realises it is early morning, dead silent, not even birds singing. FARAH is motionless as if dead. The peace is shattered by an unearthly scream which reverberates through the house. FARAH jumps up and rushes out.)

SCENE 117
Int. Hallway. ASIF'S house. Morning.

(*FARAH runs into MARYAM'S room and the screaming. She flings open the door. ASIF is lying open-eyed and motionless on MARYAM'S lap. She is still screaming, but now almost silently, just gasping for air. Close up of water decanter on ASIF'S side of the bed, lying on it's side, empty. SABIA rushes in and immediately begins wailing. Unearthly, ritualistic, kissing her dead son over and over. The girls stand at the bedroom door in their night-clothes, mute with shock. FARAH gathers the girls to her side and stands still, dry-eyed, calm.*)

SCENE 118
Int. Kitchen. ASIF'S house. Day.

(*FARAH stands at the kitchen window looking out at the garden which is rain-swept and grey. She is dressed in a white salwar kameez. No make-up or jewellery. Her face looks younger and unlined. Through the open door we see a small group of people, the English ones in black, the Pakistani in white. MARYAM, similarly dressed to FARAH, moves among them accepting condolences. SABIA sits in a huddle of older Pakistani women. She is inconsolable.*)

SABIA (*Urdu*) My son... my life. (*English*) I am alone. Heart attack! I know the truth. Ask her!
(*SABIA points a finger at FARAH, but no-one is taking her seriously, they smile apologetically at FARAH, soothing SABIA. Many of the guests say their farewells and begin leaving. The sound of cars revving up and pulling off. POPPY enters the kitchen, HENRY hovers at the door. She hugs FARAH, smoothing her hair.*)
POPPY   We'll come back later this evening if you like.
FARAH (*Shaking her head*) Maryam's here. I'll be fine.
POPPY   Maybe this isn't the time. (*She fishes around in her bag, brings out the bottle containing SABIA's green 'tonic' and a letter*) Sorry, it took so long.
FARAH (*Taking the bottle, confused*) What's this?
POPPY   That medicine you wanted analysed. It's all here.
(*FARAH opens up the letter and runs her finger down the list.*)
Ginseng, Vitamin C, amino acids, fructose a nice healthy pick-me-up. I should take a swig now, might help you through today.

FARAH *(Looks over to SABIA who is now being comforted by MARYAM, faintly)* Pick-me-up?

POPPY *(Putting the bottle on the table)* Sorry. Not important now...

FARAH *(Begins shaking)* Oh God, oh my God...

POPPY *(Mistaking this for grief, holding her tight)* It's alright, love. Let it out now. It's alright.

FARAH *(In shock)* I don't think I even loved him any more, at the end... I don't think I did.

SCENE 119

Int. MARYAM'S bedroom. ASIF'S house. Day.

(FARAH and MARYAM sit together on the bed. FARAH is in MARYAM'S arms, drained. A shaft of sunlight breaks through the grey and momentarily lights up their faces, now so similar, so beautiful. MARYAM is talking to FARAH soothingly, as if comforting a child. FARAH closes her eyes. MARYAM rocks her gently and the bed springs creak in their familiar, regular rhythm. FARAH opens her eyes wide.)

FADE OUT.

The End.

Song for a Sanctuary

Song for a Sanctuary was written partly in response to the murder of an Asian woman at a refuge. It is not however, a documentary or a biographical play. It is a fiction, concerned as much with conflicts which arise between women who are under siege and are at a crisis point in their lives, as it is with domestic violence.

It took a long while to evolve into its present form. Earlier drafts, presented as readings at the Soho Poly Theatre, at Common Stock, and at the Riverside Studios had a much larger cast and more of a 'slice of life' feel to them. Rita Wolf and I managed to set up the Kali Theatre Company, largely through her dedicated efforts and commitment to the play, which raised the finance for the workshops and reading at Riverside Studios and eventually, the funds to produce and tour the play nationally, with the support of the Arts Council in Spring and Autumn 1991.

We played to mixed audiences, occasionally small but always enthusiastic. The response of women who had been, or were at the time, living in refuges themselves was deeply moving for both of us, and for the cast. It made all the effort seem worthwhile.

I would like to thank the women and workers in refuges who made time to see me when I was researching the play, all those actors who committed time and effort generously to the readings and the theatre venues which welcomed it. I would also like to thank Sue Parrish of the Women's Theatre Group for her careful criticism and clear-sighted analysis which helped me enormously with the final draft. But above all, I feel indebted to Rita Wolf for her consistent support and her faith in the play.

A radio version of *Song for a Sanctuary* was broadcast on B.B.C. Radio 4 on the 18th February 1993.

Rukhsana Ahmad

SONG FOR A SANCTUARY

Rukhsana Ahmad

First performed by Kali Theatre Company at the Worcester Arts Workshop in Worcester on 8th May 1990. Directed by Rita Wolf.

CHARACTERS:

RAJINDER, a resident	**Kusum Haider**
SAVITA, her daughter	**Sanny Bharti**
PRADEEP, her husband	**Simon Nagra**
AMRIT, her older sister	**Simon Nagra**
SONIA, another resident	**Jackie Cowper**
CLIENT	**Simon Nagra**
KAMLA &	**Sayan Akkadas**
EILEEN refuge workers	**Joanna Bacon**

ACT ONE, SCENE 1

Thursday morning. RAJINDER is unpacking in the refuge kitchen. She is lining shelves with sheets of old newspaper and wiping and scrubbing with dedication grumbling under her breath.

RAJINDER   Hai, hai, ainna gund! You'd never guess how filthy it is inside, disgraceful... Where is it now? I thought I had some *Dettox* here...

SONIA *(Enters)* Hello, there!

RAJINDER   Good morning.

SONIA   Welcome aboard! You've got into it nice an' early.

RAJINDER   Mmm... I came a couple of hours ago.

SONIA   Jesus! You've got loads of stuff there! I came with just one Tesco carrier bag.

RAJINDER   I don't like to run out of things at odd times... it's taken an hour to get the locker and shelves into order. Looks as though they've never been cleaned since they were put up.

SONIA   Possible. Good housekeepin' ain't a huge priority round these parts specially as you don't 'ave to bother with coffee mornings and ladies' lunches in 'ere.

RAJINDER   I don't do it for show. It's hygiene I'm worried about. Can you imagine all the millions of germs in here?

SONIA   Creepin' an' crawlin'! Ugh. Do I have to?

RAJINDER   There's bits of cheese and breadcrumbs and stale crisps everywhere. You can actually smell the fungus.

SONIA   Hmm. Not very nice at all, is it?

RAJINDER   Just look at that... that was a forgotten banana I think. It's got no business to be here in the first place.

SONIA   None at all! The locker on the right's mine if you've got some energy left when you've finished yours. It looks a treat already.
(RAJINDER only glares and turns back to her work.)

SONIA   Coffee?

RAJINDER   No thanks.

SONIA   I think it'll be good to introduce ourselves before we start rowin', shall we? I'm Sonia.

RAJINDER   My name's Rajinder, Rajinder Basi.

SONIA   Hi, Rajinder, nice to meet you. You're goin' into the room next to me, aren't you?

RAJINDER   The room at the back, on the ground floor.

SONIA   Yeah, that's the one. You got any kids?

RAJINDA *(Nods)* Three. Two girls and a boy.

SONIA   Oh! Are they young?

RAJINDER   Fourteen, eleven and eight. Sanjay, my son's the youngest and I have two daughters.

SONIA   Oh, well, that's handy. They must be a help.

RAJINDER   They are, sometimes.

SONIA   At least they don't want feedin' in the middle of the night, like Barbara's little one. You can set your watch to his howlin', two a.m. every mornin' he starts.

RAJINDER   No, I've been through all of that. And how about yours?

SONIA   I 'aven't bothered with any of that yet.

RAJINDER   Oh, really?

SONIA   It's hit me now you must be the lady who came on the inspection last week? So, you forgot to look inside the cupboards then?

RAJINDER   Is that what she called it, 'an inspection visit'?

SONIA   Well, you made history apparently; no one's ever done that before.

RAJINDER   I've always lived in a nice house. I thought it best to see the place beforehand, for the children's sake. I don't know why she got so resentful about that.

SONIA   Who did?

RAJINDER   Kamla, I think she said her name was. Indian name but   she didn't look very Indian.

SONIA   Her soul's Indian I think.

RAJINDER   Do we have souls that are brown too, then?

SONIA   You are spoilin' for a row, aren't ya? Perhaps I sh'd take my coffee an' go to my own room?

RAJINDER   Sorry! I don't think I know what an Indian soul's really like?

SONIA   Unworldly? Committed, in some way... quite determined, maybe, like old Gandhi... bit like them Indian monks, you know, the ones who decide to give up the material world?

RAJINDER   I see.

SONIA   Oh, well. It was only an idea. *(Pause)* Maybe we haven't got any souls anyway.

RAJINDER   I don't know that life's worth living if we don't.

SONIA   Yeah, you wonder sometimes if it is? Too heavy, all that for me this time of the mornin'. Got to get a move on. I do a Yoga class lunchtime on Thursdays. I think I need another coffee to get the ol' system goin'. *(SONIA winks at RAJINDER who looks unamused and concentrates on cleaning again. SONIA pulls up a chair, lights a cigarette and settles down to a comfortable silence with a newspaper and coffee.)*

RAJINDER   Have you been here long?

SONIA   Five weeks this time.

RAJINDER   So it isn't your first time?

SONIA   Oh, no! An' yours?

RAJINDER   I've been in a refuge before... couple of years ago, I went in an emergency situation, and it was a mistake. That's why I planned it all carefully this time. I think you need to.

SONIA   Maybe you'll stick with it better. I've been in an' out of here a lot. Get's up Kamla's nose. She doesn't like Returners, *(Pause)* that's women who go back to their blokes.

RAJINDER   Doesn't she?

SONIA   I don't think she knows how hard it is to pull yourself out of it, for good. It's really tough.

RAJINDER   It's not easy when you go back either because husbands hate you so much for trying to get away, don't they?

SONIA   It's different I think with Gary. I'm not married, see, an' Gary, my partner, is actually quite nice for a bit when I go back to him.

RAJINDER   Not married!

SONIA   I think all men are different. An' he really tries to be nice when I go back, at least in the beginnin'; he'll get me presents, take me out for a drink, be quite lovin'. Then he falls into his ole habits. First it's a slap, and then maybe a fist or two, then a couple of kicks, until one day he has to let it all out on me. Last time he messed me up really bad... The worse it is the longer it takes me to get back to him, but I always do in the end. See my back?

RAJINDER   It looks dreadful. Five weeks, did you say?

SONIA   It doesn't hurt any more.

RAJINDER *(Shakes her head in dismay)* You shouldn't go back this time. You're not even married to him. And it is so much... harder to leave, you know, once you have children, and then before you know it your whole life's gone. That is awful.

SONIA   He doesn't mean to be nasty or anythin' but you know what men are like. They only understand violence and they want to feel in charge, but me with my big mouth, I always slip out the wrong thing.

RAJlNDER *(Tries to distance herself a little)* They can't all be like that; my brothers are so good to their wives... Oh well...

SONIA   Lucky devils!

RAJINDER   God only knows what people do to deserve their luck.

KAMLA *(Enters)* Hi. So you've met Sonia? I thought I'd come and say hello and get the papers out of the way.

RAJINDER   Sure.

KAMLA   Some details got left last week since you were in such a hurry.

RAJINDER   I only just made it in time. Pradeep got in a few minutes after I did.

KAMLA   That's okay. All I need is the names of the children here and your signatures.

RAJINDER   Savita, Bela and Sanjay.

KAMLA   Right, got that. Now, there's one other thing, would you mind running through... a few details with me... just a couple of questions about what happened? *(RAJINDER looks annoyed but says nothing.)* Have you taken out an injunction against him? Have you ever been to the police about your husband?

RAJINDER   Never. They open an inquiry and make your life hell with questions and questions and questions. The one who reports has to answer all their questions. They never catch the thugs; everyone knows that.

KAMLA   So was there an incident which made you leave?

RAJINDER   You're doing the same thing! I was told there would be no prying.

KAMLA   I'm sorry if it seems like that.

RAJINDER   This isn't easy for me, as it is.

KAMLA   Of course. Normally it isn't necessary.

RAJINDER   Then I would like to be treated 'normally', please.

KAMLA   Trouble is you haven't been referred by anyone, like a social worker or a doctor so, it is necessary. I'm sorry but resources are precious, we do need to prioritise in some way... to establish need.

RAJINDER   Do you imagine anyone would want to come to a refuge unless they needed to?

KAMLA   It's possible.

RAJINDER   Definitely not – if they've been in one before.

KAMLA   You may be right.

RAJINDER   I know I am right. It may look as though I have a choice, but I haven't really. I need to be two steps ahead of him.

KAMLA   Oh?

RAJINDER   I'm trying to escape from a man who's cunning, and strong, and tough as a bull; he can see through curtains, he can hear through walls. I am really frightened of him.

KAMLA   I'm sorry, I had to ask.

RAJINDER   It's all right. It's the haste of the young, isn't it, judging like that.

KAMLA   I'm not that young.

RAJINDER   You look very young to me. Where do you come from, Kamla?

KAMLA   South London.

RAJINDER   Oh, I see! *(Pause)* 'Tusi Punjabi boalday o?

KAMLA   I'm sorry, I don't.

RAJINDER   It's... just, that I wondered about what other languages   you spoke, if any?

KAMLA   Some French.

RAJINDER   Maybe I shouldn't have asked.

KAMLA   No, that was silly of me. I'm sure we can do better than this. Two grown women!

RAJINDER   Can we really?

KAMLA   Yes, I believe in friendship between women.

RAJINDER   I've heard about it too.

KAMLA   This language thing, it's just that, it looks like an inadequacy and it isn't. Names are all they had left to them, in the Caribbean; to keep the languages going seemed a bit pointless in the end.

RAJINDER   So you're not from India?

KAMLA   No, not quite. *(Pause)* They struggled to make us Indian, in some sense. But it was hard; there probably isn't a lot we have in common.

RAJINDER   You're right, I'm sure.

KAMLA   It needn't be a problem though.

RAJINDER   I certainly hope not. *(Enter EILEEN.)*

KAMLA   Hi, didn't know you were back! Rajinder this is Eileen, my colleague. She's been here since the refuge was set up.

EILEEN   Ages and ages ago! Hello.

RAJINDER   Pleased to meet you Eileen.

EILEEN   Me too.

RAJINDER   Could I talk to *you*, if that's all right, about 'my case'.

EILEEN   Sure, whenever you like.

RAJINDER   Tomorrow, maybe? It seems I need to justify my being here.

EILEEN   You're welcome to be here if you need to, no questions asked.

RAJINDER   Thank you. I'm glad to hear that. Now if you'll excuse me, I must go. They get quite upset in the school if mums are late. *(Exit RAJINDER.)*

EILEEN   Phew! Been stepping on toes, eh?

KAMLA   She would say nothing of her circumstances and she seems totally calm.

EILEEN   Could just be a layer, like her make-up.

KAMLA   Pretty thick layer, then!

EILEEN   Come on! There's nothing wrong with a bit of make-up, K!

KAMLA   Well... *(Pause)* The thing is she looks able... and quite well-off. I have to ask, do people like her deserve to use up room?

EILEEN   I don't think anyone comes here, if they have a choice, Kamla.

KAMLA   Hmm. She did claim that she has no family here.

EILEEN   Exactly, and maybe no friends.

KAMLA   I dunno about that. I'd be very surprised! You become that smug only when you've got everything; and then, of course, good luck follows you wherever you go. You're never short of friends.

EILEEN   She's not your type, that's all.

KAMLA   No, she isn't. I wonder if she's using us, in some way, for some strange game of her own. She's not the kind who needs help!

EILEEN   Oh, Kamla, what's that supposed to mean? Stop being suspicious. How many times've you said yourself that class divides women, amongst other things. Don't let it do that to you now.

KAMLA   Just found her a bit... annoying...

EILEEN   Try to find the common ground, there must be some, somewhere within her, there must be the woman who needs help... I think ou're being quite irrational about her.

(KAMLA only shrugs. Exit EILEEN a little annoyed. KAMLA picks up RAJINDER'S shawl and sits down on a chair. She opens the shawl and drapes it round her shoulders and walks slowly up and down the stage. She strokes the shawl and then lifts a finger to warn.)

KAMLA   You wrap it up carefully in old muslin if you can't find a polythene bag... you don't just leave good shawls lying around. Don't you know moths get at them if you're not careful? *(Carefully folds shawl and puts it back.)* Oh, sorry I nearly forgot. *(Pause. Hums to herself, then tries to sing a snatch of an Indian song.)* Aaj sajan mohay ang laga lo, janam safal ho jaai / 'Any languages?' Riday ki peera, birha ki agni, sub sheetal jo jaai... Language classes, music lessons, dance lessons, they tried it all... it was no use to me. Who cares for all that crap anyway? *(Then she gets up and tries a few steps of Kathak holding her hands together in front of her looking stiff and awkward.)* Tut, taa, thai, thai, tut, taa, thai, thai and now double *(Faster)* taa, thai, thai tut, taa, thai, thai. *(Enter RAJINDER.)*

RAJINDER   I forgot my... shawl... oh?

KAMLA   Here it is. *(Exit KAMLA, flustered)*

SCENE 2

Friday night. RAJINDER'S bedroom in the refuge. The stage is in complete darkness. SAVITA has woken up after a nightmare. PRADEEP walks onto the stage and stands silently behind them. His shadow falling across them. SAVITA shuffles softly to her mother and whispers.

SAVITA   Mummyji! Wake up, please Mummy!

RAJINDER   What is it, for God's sake, sshh quiet, Savita, you'll wake up the others. Hush, meray bachchay, you're shivering, what happened?
(RAJINDER moves and lights a lamp. A small spotlight comes on above them emphasising the darkness.)

SAVITA   There's someone in here.

RAJINDER   Where? Are you crazy, darling! There's no-one here. Try to sleep, you'll wake up the whole house.

SAVITA   I saw him getting into the room. He broke in through the window.

RAJINDER   Who?

SAVITA   Maybe it was Papaji. I couldn't tell, his face was hidden in his turban, and, and he had his kirpaan, he was holding it like that, like a flag, above his head.

RAJINDER   Stop being so silly, Savita, there's no one here.

SAVITA   You know how he looked that day when he went mad 'cause you got back late... He just stood there, he was polishing his... kirpaan... and his eyes looked strange... I really felt so terrified of him.

RAJINDER   Yes, I remember it.

SAVITA   And you know, that time... when he flung his plate at you, for talking back at him?

RAJINDER   Savita, stop it. I won't be able to sleep, don't stir it all up in my head at this time.

SAVITA   He wouldn't, he wouldn't force us to go back, would he, really, Ammah?

RAJINDER   I don't think so. Calm down, Savita. He can't find us here.

SAVITA   But if he does? Would he beat you in front of the other women here?

RAJINDER   He won't, he can never trace us to this place. Hush...

SAVITA   You can take self-defence classes at my school.

RAJINDER *(Kisses her.)* I'll think about it.

SAVITA   We could keep a hammer under the pillow. I kept Sanjay's bat under the bed, last night.

RAJINDER   Savita, what shall I do with you, my child, you're impossible...!

SAVITA   Ammah, I'm scared, don't laugh please.

RAJINDER   I'll cry if I don't.

SAVITA   Don't laugh, you sound strange. Why does everyone sound so different in the dark?

RAJINDER   Try to sleep, jaan. *(Pause)* Hold on, what's that smell? Oh, Savita!

SAVITA   Ammah, I'm really, really sorry.

RAJINDER   Not again, I could kill you. All that washing it makes!

SAVITA   I never mean to. I don't know how it happens.

RAJINDER   Go and wash and then change your clothes. You're fourteen! What if someone finds out? *(SAVITA gets off the floor.)*

RAJINDER   And just leave the wet things on the floor, I'll get up and rinse them out myself.

SAVITA   I *can* wash them out you know.

RAJINDER   I'll do it, then I know it's done properly and they won't smell. *(Exit SAVITA. Sound of a light switching on off-stage. Water running, then sound of a small baby crying.)* Curse the day that brought us together, Pradeep! God forgive me, but I'll never let you find me ever again... I swear never to let you touch me again, Pradeep *(Exit PRADEEP in silence.)* Wash the bedclothes, your hands, your face, your body, once, twice, three times and pray for it to be cleansed. Then wash him off your body, Rajinder... and never let him touch you again...

Light fades slowly on RAJINDER.

SCENE 3

A bench in a park is set out at the front. RAJINDER walks on dressed for a walk. She sits down 'feeding the birds'. EILEEN follows her and joins her on the bench.

EILEEN   Mind if I join you? I saw you from the window and I felt like a walk too. We all stay cooped up indoors too much.

RAJINDER   Not at all. *(Moves to make room for EILEEN.)* I love this half hour of peace and quiet, before the children return from school.

EILEEN   Look at that cheeky thing, they seem to know you already. D'you come out here every day?

RAJINDER   Just to get rid of the old bread and rice. I just collect it all from everyone. It's sinful to throw food in the bin.

EILEEN   Didn't I see you pourin' a pint of milk down the sink only yesterday?

RAJINDER   That was different... it... it got polluted.

EILEEN   Oh! *(Pause)*

RAJINDER   I didn't mean to make a scene, but it matters to me, a lot. They don't seem to understand how much. How someone can just leave meat to defrost in a bag on the shelf, I don't understand...? The blood from it just dripped on to the milk.

EILEEN   Was only on the carton though, wasn't it?

RAJINDER   But still. It was... it is disgusting. It only needs for them to keep out of my bit of fridge and there wouldn't be a problem. Tell me how long have you been here Eileen?

EILEEN   Almost eleven years now.

RAJINDER   We must all sound the same to you!

EILEEN   Not at all. The situation is the same but women are so different, I'm not bored. No. A bit thrown by the enormity of it sometimes, but not bored, never that.

RAJINDER   You really care, don't you?

EILEEN   I think all of us do, in our own ways. Kamla does too, and the others.

RAJINDER   Maybe it's because you're older I felt I'd find it easier talking to you. I thought you'd understand more... than Kamla?

EILEEN   Perhaps I do, just a tiny bit more, an' that because I've been there.

RAJINDER   Meaning?

EILEEN   I came to this place for refuge myself, it was different then, a couple of women had set it up as a safe house. Then they gave me the job.

RAJINDER   I didn't know that. Do you ever get over it? I dunno if I should ask?

EILEEN   I don't mind talking about it now. It hurts, but I'm not bitter any more. I feel angry, more with myself for having stood it so long.

RAJINDER   You must have hoped he would change.

EILEEN   Yes, don't we all do that? I gave him a good ten years, and you? More than that, I s'pose?

RAJINDER   Fifteen. Sometimes people repent, they say.

EILEEN   I just couldn't take it any more. Bullyin', beatin', abuse and insults – an' he'd torment me over the money an' the housework. I became so nervous I'd be shakin' at ten o'clock when it was time for him to come home. He'd walk in and start pickin' on me. The night I left, he actually came at me with a hammer. I was so shit-scared I ran all the way to the police station in my slippers.

RAJINDER   How terrible! God, I can just imagine what you went through.

EILEEN   You know what the coppers did? Dumped me right back with him again. 'Domestic', they said. I nearly died when he finished with me that night. That was it. I had to leave after that. I was too scared to go back.

RAJINDER   Hmm.

EILEEN   That was it.

RAJINDER   Yes. No-one can really understand what it's like inside your four walls. (*RAJINDER is silent. Enter PRADEEP. Watches from a distance.*) Do you have any children?

EILEEN   Two, they're grown now; wasn't much of a life for them I can tell you, all that bashin' an' terror day and night.

RAJINDER   It's the children you have to think of.

EILEEN   Are yours very disturbed by it all?

RAJINDER   Hmm.

EILEEN   For a long time I couldn't talk about it either. And for a long time, I never really felt safe. I'd be scared at night thinkin' he'd found me and was staring through the window panes.

RAJINDER   But he couldn't have, I suppose?

EILEEN   No. I'd put miles and miles between us.

RAJINDER   That means you can get away if you really want to. Can't you?

SCENE 4

KAMLA and EILEEN are working in the refuge office. Typing accompanied by some muttering from KAMLA.

KAMLA   When's the next management committee meeting, d'you know Eileen?

EILEEN   Twenty-seventh, I think.

KAMLA   Is there still time to put something on the agenda then?

EILEEN   Bit tight, I think, what did you?...

KAMLA   Just an idea, I had.

EILEEN   Hum?

KAMLA   Perhaps we should have a registration form for women to fill... to detail their case histories a bit more.

EILEEN   You must be joking.

KAMLA   We need to know everything... when they come.

EILEEN   There's plenty to do here without adding to the bureaucracy.

KAMLA   But... *(SONIA knocks and enters.)*

SONIA   Are you two busy or can I come in and have a word?

EILEEN   Come in Sonia.

KAMLA   Tisn't the best of times, though.

SONIA   Won't be long, I promise.

EILEEN   Right, what's the problem?

SONIA   I want to change my room.

KAMLA   What's wrong with yours?

SONIA   Rajinder and family next door. I can't believe it, the place is dead as a morgue in the morning and it sounds like Piccadilly Circus in the middle of the night, there's noises through the night. You know how the water works go pumping and whistling and rattling the whole place up every time someone opens a tap or somethin'.

EILEEN   It's these old houses.

KAMLA   So they have baths in the middle of the night to keep the smell of curry down?

SONIA   Look here, Kamla, don't jump down my throat. It's nothin' like that. I'm no racist. You're new here, but Eileen knows me over the years. I've been in an' out of this place you know.

KAMLA   That gets no medals in my book.

EILEEN   Let's not get into a state over this. Isn't it best for you to have a chat with her yourself, in the first place, Sonia?

SONIA   I've done that. This is a lady with a big problem.

EILEEN   Well, ain't we all?

SONIA   Naw, it's different.

KAMLA   What's that supposed to mean? I won't listen to this Eileen. There's rules about racism written out somewhere.

EILEEN   Would you let me deal with this please, Kamla. So what did she say when you asked her about the baths?

SONIA   She sez her youngest wets the bed sometimes. Well, would you call three nights out of seven sometimes?

EILEEN   No.

SONIA   And she says all the washing can't be left. Anyway she's got a thing about washin'. She's in the bathroom for hours an' hours.

EILEEN   She's right, the others won't want stinkin' bedsheets soakin' in the bath first thing in the morning; that would be a bigger nuisance, I reckon.

SONIA   I can't sleep with all the bloody racket so what am I to do?

EILEEN   He'll stop wettin' the bed as soon as he settles down.

SONIA   That might take weeks, besides she's not helpin' any. She gets quite wound up if they start gettin' matey with the other kids. Her li'l girl likes to 'ave a chat with me an' you can see her gettin' pretty uptight about that. Then there's Barbara on my other side, and her Ricky starts screeching two a.m. sharp.

EILEEN   Tough! Babies have to be fed and changed.

SONIA   For fuck's sake, that kid's not a baby. Maybe she should have him down to the doctor's.

KAMLA   Surely noise can be kept down a little in consideration of others.

SONIA   Exactly. An' that's not all. Last night at about five I got my head cleared of all the cobwebs an' I thought, here goes, I was droppin' off and then I heard someone singin'! I couldn't believe it.

KAMLA   Singing?

SONIA   Yeah, I asked her. Well, what d'you know, it's 'er prayin' first thing in the morning.

KAMLA   Praying! In this day and age?

EILEEN   People do, you know.

SONIA   I don't mind 'er prayin' even at that time of the mornin' but not that loud, please!

EILEEN   I do think Sonia that is the kind of thing best dealt with, directly by yourself. Just ask her, nicely, over a cup of tea.

SONIA   Well if that isn't a fuckin' cop out. You two really want to sort this out, don't ya? Is it 'cos they're hard-pressed mums or 'cos they're both black?

EILEEN   You've got more sense than that Sonia!

(SONIA stamps out angrily.)

KAMLA   I knew there'd be trouble with Rajinder.

EILEEN   Sonia'll soon come round to it.

KAMLA   I see the point of making concessions to the mums but I think you should've had a word with her yourself.

EILEEN   When you've been here as long as I have...

KAMLA   That's another thing! I'm sick to death of having the weight of your experience thrown at me all the time.

EILEEN   Sorry, not very tactful. It gets heavy if I interfere, spoils things. It's best if they talk to each other an' deal with it. They're adult women.

KAMLA   But praying in the middle of the night is a bit much! It's not adult behaviour. We really do need to do some consciousness-raising work here.

EILEEN   I don't see much wrong with that. Praying's only a step away from wishing. Anyway, for some women, it's the only thing that keeps them goin'. Who are we to destroy that?

KAMLA   She's just like my mother. You won't destroy her faith. It would take a bloody miracle to do that!

EILEEN   So what d'you want me to do?

KAMLA   She can't relate to me at all, won't even talk to me. At least she talks to you, so you've got to do some work with her, you know... just to make sure she doesn't go back. She's done that once before.

EILEEN   I'd rather she chooses herself Kamla. I'm not into mind-bending.

KAMLA   Look at the world we live in Eileen, it pushes women into marriage. There's always pressure to save the 'home', keep the family together. They need support to get out and to stay out of a bad marriage and we've got to give that support. Sometimes it does mean challenging their beliefs, yeah?

EILEEN   Well, if you must!

KAMLA   She stays aloof, won't talk to the others. She's putting their backs up. She doesn't mix, won't give support or take it. Then her whole attitude and manner... it is so critical of what we try to do and so... uncritical of the outside world. It's too insidious. We've got to take her on.

EILEEN   I tried to draw her out, but I couldn't.

KAMLA   Why won't she talk of what's brought her here? Has she said anything to you?

EILEEN   She's not ready to talk yet. Takes a lot of trust to share the shame and humiliation you've hidden from the world for so long. Why should it be a problem? It's not right to try and prise it out of her. I'll fight you on that one, if you do put it on the agenda.

KAMLA   Maybe she'll never be ready. She's not facing up to it, is she? I am suspicious of secrecy. Just typical of this kind of woman, isn't it?

EILEEN   Kind of woman! Crap! All that stuff you chum out about stereotypes... if only you could listen to yourself talking!

KAMLA   See! She's divided us already! Some women are collaborators by nature, they're the ones who'll always sell you out, beat you down... with their mad, suicidal fanaticism. We need to fight that kind, specially in here.

EILEEN   I don't like the tone of any of that, Kamla. Just lay off – leave her be, till she asks for help. All kinds of women have a right to their views.

KAMLA   And I have a right to persuade them to change those views.

EILEEN   Only persuade, not pressure. The women who come to us are... stuck, they're stranded, they're shipwrecked if you like... they don't know where to start. They need space okay?

KAMLA   Sure. I'll give her space, all the space she needs... but I won't let her undermine the work we have to do.

EILEEN   She's hardly in a position to do that! *(Exit EILEEN.)*

KAMLA   Maybe she'll change, but... maybe she can't. *(Pause)* I'm not going to be sentimental and gush over her just cause she's Indian. No guilt trips on that one!

SCENE 5

Short stylized sequence. SONIA, KAMLA, SAVITA and EILEEN are playing cards. We watch them playing and arguing for a few minutes. They bid, argue and shout excitedly as they play. KAMLA claims victory at the end and then KAMLA and EILEEN go off-stage leaving SONIA and SAVITA to review the game.

SONIA   That was a bloody lousy game. You just can't afford to lose count of how many aces are out, Savita.

SAVITA   I didn't do too badly, I got such rotten cards.

SONIA   We're three down: not good enough, darlin'. If this was money, an' not match sticks, we'd be broke. By the way did you ask yer mum 'bout going to the film, Friday. Kamla wanted to know. She's booked six tickets, I think.

SAVITA   No, I think the only way she'll let me go is if she doesn't know it's a Fifteen film.

SONIA   I'm not tellin' any lies. Never have done, even to save myself a hidin'. I think it's best to tell her. Sanjay'll tell her if you don't.

SAVITA   Oh, he's such a tell-tit. Rotten brat! Then she won't let me go. I want to go... so badly. Everyone in my class has seen it.

SONIA   I'll put in a word. I dunno if it'll help any, ah... *(Enter RAJINDER.)* Here Raji, could Savita come to see a film with all of us... it's me birthday.

RAJINDER   I don't think she's old enough for a night out yet. You always have homework and things to do at the weekend, Savita. You don't really want to go.

SAVITA   Please, Ammah. I do. Just for the film.

SONIA   That's all we're doin' really, probably get a takeaway after, everyone's skint.

SAVITA   Please. It's a film I really want to see. They've all seen it in my class. I'll do anything you say. Please.

RAJINDER   Never mind if they have. We're different from them, you know that.

SONIA   Only a bit of fun for her. She'll be okay.

RAJINDER   What film is it?

SONIA   Pretty...

SAVITA   Out of Africa *(Together)*

SONIA   A-aa! Savita?

RAJINDER   Hmm. All right then, but make sure you're not moaning on Sunday night about homework.

SAVITA   Thanks Ammah, you're so sweet, you're brilliant.

KAMLA *(Enters)* Hi, Rajinder, just the person I wanted to see.

RAJINDER   Hello.

SAVITA   Kamla I meant to ask you, could I type something on your typewriter? We're doing an anonymous letter to our Head Teacher.

KAMLA   That sounds a bit dicey, why should it be anonymous now?

RAJINDER   Don't you dare get involved in silly things like that. You need to do your homework now, you better be off.

SAVITA   I'm going, I'm going. *(Exit SAVITA.)*

KAMLA   Just wanted you to know I've made an appointment for you to see the housing bloke tomorrow morning. Is that still okay? And I'd quite like us to have a chat about things after that.

RAJINDER   I thought Eileen was to be my caseworker.

KAMLA   She's got all she can handle at the moment. I'm sorry, but here women don't get to choose their caseworkers.

SONIA   Don't you think that's quite unfair, Kamla?

KAMLA   No, I don't. How does someone choose a caseworker? Because of the colour of her eyes, skin, her smile, what? It's nonsense, really. Choice can be just a pointless complication sometimes. Anyway, people don't always know what's best for them.

SONIA   Sure. You love to cluck over us, your chickens, don't you
Kamla? Then you can peck at the ones who try to get away. So now you
know why they call her THE COLONEL...! Oh, well...

KAMLA   Meanwhile, I'll see you tomorrow afternoon, won't I?

RAJINDER   All right, if there isn't a choice.

KAMLA   By the way, Sonia. I got the tickets for 'Pretty Woman' for
your birthday. Would you tell the others please.

RAJINDER   I thought you said 'Out of Africa'!

SONIA   There was some confusion about this, I think.

KAMLA   But that's what you told me, six tickets for 'Pretty Woman',
I'm quite sure.

SONIA   Yes, yes, I know.

RAJINDER   So what's 'Pretty Woman' about? Why didn't you want me to
know it was that film?

KAMLA   It's nothing special, just an entertainer, I think. Are you going
too?

RAJINDER   I'm not actually.

SONIA   Savita was scared you wouldn't let her go 'cos it's a Fifteen.

RAJINDER   If it is she certainly can't go to see it. I don't think it's
suitable.

KAMLA   They see worse on T.V. sometimes, I have to say.

RAJINDER   The others do, mine don't. I'd like my children to grow up
with some sense of who they are. We're different.

KAMLA   Sometimes children are older than you think they are.

RAJINDER: I take it I can still make these choices at least for my own
children.

SONIA   Sure. You're the boss. She'll go by what you say, Raji.

KAMLA   But, of course.

RAJINDER   I'm quite shocked, I didn't expect to be lied to by you,
Sonia!

SONIA   I'm sorry. It was difficult. I, I didn't know quite... what... to
say then.

RAJINDER   Sure. Because you felt she was right and I was wrong.
Well, let me tell you, we've taken refuge here but that doesn't mean my
children have to be taken over and re-modelled into something that
belongs neither here nor there. (*Throws a contemptuous glance at
KAMLA and walks out. Ruffled, KAMLA avoids SONIA'S look, tries to
shrug it off and exits.*

Lights fade on the scene.

SCENE 6
AMRIT appears behind the gauze. Stands squarely facing the audience.
RAJINDER follows her and stands alongside.

RAJINDER   No-one cared when he tried to push me over the window sill.
I could have died then, his bride of six months carrying his child in my
     body – he meant it to happen. I felt it in his grip. None of you believed me.
AMRIT   But you're so wrong! We all love you. In any case you only
     ever complained about little things, Rajo. Trivial things.
RAJINDER   Not for me, they weren't. I'd have washed and cooked and
     cleaned for all of you. Maaji just had to say yes, once. There were only the
     two of us to feed then but you forgave him, all of you. I can't forgive you
     for that now.
AMRIT   You don't make sense to me. To put this on Maaji's shoulders,
     at her age. It'll kill both of them, the shame of it all, the disgrace! You
     could have tried harder.
RAJINDER   I did my best.
AMRIT   There's no sweat on your brow, no tears in your eyes. Your
     hands are neither sore nor bloody.
RAJINDER   Must you have blood always? Would you rather I died, so you
     wouldn't have to explain to your friends? Look into my eyes and say it,
     why don't you look into my eyes and then say I should go back to him?
AMRIT   What of the children? They will be asking, 'What'll become of
     them'?
RAJINDER   Don't you care for me at all? I've adored you Amrit, ever
     since I was tiny. Why do you hate me so?
AMRIT   You'll be sorry. I'm warning you. Your selfishness will ruin
     your daughters, I can tell you that. They'll learn all the self-indulgent, sick
     ways of the West... their crazy, blind cult of the body – face creams, diet
     pills, and keep fit, you'll see. You'll regret this.
RAJINDER   Would you rather I set myself alight in my back garden?
AMRIT   Honour is always preferable to disgrace, but the choice of
     course is yours.

Exit AMRIT. Light fades on RAJINDER.

SCENE 7
SONIA'S bedroom. Stage is dimly lit. Soft mournful music is playing on the
radio. SONIA is reading. SAVITA emerges from the wings and looks on
uncertainly. Then tiptoes forward gently. Before she can surprise her,
SONIA turns round and spots her. She shows no sign of welcome.

SAVITA   Hi, Sonia. Listening to the radio?

SONIA   Hmm.

SAVITA   Dull, isn't it? *(SONIA just shrugs indifferently.)* Shall I turn it off? Doesn't it make you a bit sad?

SONIA   I don't mind.

SAVITA   You can always find some good music on the radio, try Choice FM. I can find it for you if you want.

SONIA   I don't want to listen to Choice bloody FM.

SAVITA   Okay, so don't. You don't have to shout.

SONIA   Can't you see I want to be left a – *(Stops as she sees SAVITA'S face crumbling.)* to choose my own music at least when I am in my own room, if I can't choose the T.V. I want to watch. I'm sick to death of watching 'Neighbours' and 'Blind Date'.

SAVITA   Did you watch any T.V. today?

SONIA   No.

SAVITA   So you've been here all day?

SONIA   What is this? Some kind of a 'Question Time' or somethin'. I'm just fine. I'm my own boss. I get up when I please an' I stop in when I please.

SAVITA   Why do you look so miserable then? Are you missing Gary?

SONIA   I'm just a bit fed up with myself. *(Pause)* You don't look that chirpy yourself, come to think of it. D'you miss your dad at all?

SAVITA   Sometimes. I feel a bit sorry for him. *(Pause. She pulls out a small square envelope from her pocket.)* Look, I've got these.

SONIA   What are they?

SAVITA   Rude pictures.

SONIA   Gawd! *(SONIA jumps up in horror.)* Fuckin' hell. *(SAVITA watches her calmly.)* These are not rude. Savita... they're filthy. Black and white originals like that! Where the hell did you get this lot from? *(Puts them back into the envelope hurriedly.)*

SAVITA   Bit disgusting. Aren't they?

SONIA   Come on, tell me, was it someone in school? Who gave them to you. You'll have to tell me now. Savita.

SAVITA   I took them.

SONIA   Where from?

SAVITA   I saw her hiding them behind the wardrobe in the bedroom.

SONIA   Who?

SAVITA   My mum. She must have been hiding them from him. She doesn't like this sort of thing. I don't know where he gets them from.

SONIA   Blimey! Does your mum know you've got these?

SAVITA   Of course not.

SONIA   Christ! Why do you keep them?

SAVITA   Dunno. *(Pause)*

SONIA   Oh, Savita, love... what is it?

SAVITA   I never mean to do it. I've these horrible dreams. I wake up
and the bed is all squelchy and warm and wet and I feel so ashamed of
everything.

SONIA   You poor kid. I didn't guess... I'm sorry.

SAVITA   Promise me you won't tell anyone. It hurts Mummyji so
much and it makes her really cross with me. I'm so bad.

SONIA   You're not, you're all right. What's these bad dreams, eh?

SAVITA *(Pause)* I can't even remember that much when I wake up... but I'm
cold and I'm scared. *(Pause)*

SONIA   What do you see, then? Burglars, devils, witches, what?

SAVITA   Nothing like that...

SONIA   You can tell me, if you want to. Might help you get rid of
them.

SAVITA   I always see... Papaji... that's my dad.

SONIA   Is he that scary then? Was he violent a lot?

SAVITA   He's angry with me and he gets into my room and he sits on
my bed. His eyes look strange and his lips curl up, like that, and his teeth
are set.

SONIA   Angry with you. for what?

SAVITA   It's night time and I want him to go away. but he won't and
he sits and sits. His hands are so big, and rough and hairy... and in his
clothes he's hiding this... this dagger. to kill Mummyji... and, I think he
might stick this into me... he won't go away and he won't leave me alone.

SONIA *(Puts her arms round her and holds her close.)* Awright. C'mon. Just
leave it for now. Forget it. It's just a bad dream.

SAVITA   He said, it was my fault... that I made him come to me.

SONIA   ... come to you...?

SAVITA   ... to my room... because I was too lovely. But I never... And
he said he would tell Mummyji it was my fault if I didn't let him come any
more...

SONIA   Oh. Savita! *(Pause)* 'Course it's not your fault, love. *(SAVITA
looks confused and tearful. SONIA takes both her hands and sits beside
her on the floor.)* You must know that it weren't your fault.

SAVITA   But I should've... made him stop. I should have tried to.

SONIA   You've got to tell your mum.

SAVITA   NO. No, no, please, Sonia. I beg of you don't make me. I'd rather die than tell her. She'll never forgive me. Never... if she thinks it's my fault she'll never talk to me again. I'm too frightened.

SONIA   You've got to tell someone.

SAVITA   If you say a word of this to anyone, I'll run away. I can't bear it if she doesn't talk to me any more. You won't tell her. will you Sonia? Swear to me you won't, please!

SONIA   Oh, all right, I swear I won't.

SAVITA   D'you believe me Sonia?

SONIA   I believe you, pet.

SAVITA   You wouldn't stop talking to me, would you?

SONIA   NO, of course not, silly.

SAVITA   What if he finds us and takes us back?

SONIA   No, he won't, I'm sure.

SAVITA   And, Sonia?... Sometimes...

SONIA   Yes?

SAVITA   I do miss him, sometimes... *(SAVITA bursts into tears and SONIA holds her in both her arms and soothes her.)*

ACT TWO, SCENE 1

KAMLA is speaking on the telephone to KATIE in the refuge office.

KAMLA   Now listen, Katie, you'll get worse sleeping rough like that. We'll have you as soon as we have place... Why don't you put Bev on the phone, I'll speak to her she'll get you fixed up for a few days... See you soon. *(Enter RAJINDER)* Won't keep you a moment. *(RAJINDER sits)* Bev, I don't think we can offer her a room for a couple of weeks yet... Could you not have her for now?... Wonderful, I'll speak to you very soon... Okay. Bye now. *(Pause)* Sorry about that.

RAJINDER   That's all right.

KAMLA   Can I get you a tea or coffee?

RAJINDER   No, thanks.

KAMLA   Well, how are things?

RAJINDER   Not too bad.

KAMLA   Good, good. *(Pause)* What about school? Are they all settled?

RAJINDER   Yes. They seem happy enough.

KAMLA   Finances? Everything running smoothly.

RAJINDER   It's all right, at the moment.

KAMLA   So, no problems at all? *(Pause)* What am I saying? Of course there are problems. Dumb question. I mean any problems to do with the refuge, with other residents, or with facilities?

RAJINDER   Sharing a house isn't easy, even with your own family sometimes there are problems. There's been a few, but only little ones. I'm managing.

KAMLA   Good. Great to hear that. *(Pause)* Have you thought of some training for yourself?

RAJINDER   I got a B.A. in India. You can't do much with it here.

KAMLA   So what've you thought about doing?

RAJINDER   Horoscopes... I mean professionally. I could do that from home, charge people, it would fit in with the children's timings.

KAMLA   You can't make enough doing that.

RAJINDER   That depends on what you call enough, and on your luck.

KAMLA   You don't believe in all that seriously though, do you? I couldn't. It leaves no room for human effort. How can you ask people to work towards change if you believe that someone else is pulling the strings?

RAJINDER   It doesn't mean you can't make any choices... just that... the circumstances in which you have to make them are often beyond your control. Like birth, or death.

KAMLA   Hmm. I hadn't thought of it like that. *(Pause)* But there's a real world out there where you need a certain minimum to survive. Might be useful for you to think of some retraining, in more practical terms, hmm? Now, how did it go with the housing officer today?

RAJINDER   Not very well, I'm afraid.

KAMLA   Any special reason?

RAJINDER   It wasn't so much what he said... it's... what I couldn't say. I hadn't realized, until today that... you... have to go through all that in order to get a place. I've decided I can't take that.

KAMLA   What! You can't afford to decide those things any more.

RAJINDER   What do you mean? It's my life we're talking about. I'm not one of your illiterate working class women to be managed by you.

KAMLA   Well, that's how it's done whatever class you are. You've got to establish your need to separate from your husband, that's all.

RAJINDER   I've to explain to some stranger the history of fifteen years of marriage, expose every intimate detail of my life and you say, 'that's all', haan? But then you wouldn't know about it.

KAMLA   It's not pleasant, or easy, I know, but that is the procedure, for everyone, regardless of race and religion.

RAJINDER   I see.

KAMLA   In any case, you don't have to feel ashamed of anything. The shame's all his.

RAJINDER   Are you married, Kamla?

KAMLA   No. Fortunately. What's that got to do with anything?

RAJINDER   How can you understand what's involved then?

KAMLA   With respect, I can see marriage, as an institution, without the rose-coloured glasses.

RAJINDER   Aren't we allowed to have privacy any more just because we left our homes?

KAMLA   What's the big deal in privacy?

RAJINDER   It's important to me.

KAMLA   Don't you see, it's the 'privatisation' of women's lives which keeps us from seeing domestic violence in a socio-political context?

RAJINDER   I don't need your political analysis. I have to deal with my life as I think best.

KAMLA   Your story is common enough, believe me. It's part of a pattern of how men have used women over the years. That's why we started the support group sessions. You haven't been to any of those yet, have you?

RAJINDER   I don't believe in washing my dirty linen in public. Thank you.

KAMLA   There's something positive about sharing.

RAJINDER   Sharing your troubles seems more like a sign of weakness to me.

KAMLA   Perhaps if you try a session some time...

RAJINDER   I don't think you understand my language Kamla. I didn't marry in a registry office. I married before God. It wasn't just a social arrangement, it was a sacred bond, made with body and soul.

KAMLA   Something broke that bond for you and exposing that something now is part of the price you pay for your release.

RAJINDER   What do I want release for? I'm not going to marry anyone else. I just left, because...

KAMLA   Because...?

RAJINDER   ... there was no other way.

KAMLA   I'm sorry, I know it still hurts.

RAJINDER   I need time to think through things.

KAMLA   Time just goes by, women forget the hurt, their wounds begin to heal and then, they start imagining that things might get better, simply if they go back. That's what looks the easiest, if you don't have accommodation.

RAJINDER   I've done my bit of going back to him and I won't make the same mistake again, you'll see. I don't need to take a begging bowl to anyone. I can survive.

KAMLA   It's not begging. You have a right to housing. You need a place to live and a proper source of income. You're living in bloody cloud-cuckoo land.

RAJINDER   It's strange – this passion that you put into destroying other people's marriages. All that matters to you is that I should never go back to him!

KAMLA   You're still hankering for some woolly romantic dream of saving your marriage with your heroism. Can't you see there's nothing left for me to destroy? You ran away to hide from that awful shell of a relationship that you can't even speak about to others...

RAJINDER   I don't need to. *(Exit RAJINDER. KAMLA gets up and paces to calm herself down.)*

KAMLA   Stupid fool! *(KAMLA tries to return to her work.)*

ACT TWO, SCENE 2

SAVITA'S bedroom. F/X pop music playing. SAVITA is singing along tunelessly. She is dressing up before the mirror.

SAVITA   I look cool in that, don't I Ma?

RAJINDER   Sorry, Savita, you'll have to change.

SAVITA   Why? It looks fine to me.

RAJINDER   I don't want any discussion, or argument about this. You'll change, or else, you can't go to the party. It's as simple as that.

SAVITA   That's not fair. You have to say why.

RAJINDER   All right, then. The skirt's too short, the blouse is too grown up, together they look tartish.

SAVITA   Talk about stereotypes, Ammah! They're doing 'tart with a heart' films even in Bombay now. What have you got against them anyway?

RAJINDER   I hate to hear you talk like this.

SAVITA   Like what? What's wrong with it?

RAJINDER   As if... you're all smart and sophisticated and grown-up   and know everything.

SAVITA   Maybe I do know more than you think I know. How's that for a possibility?

RAJINDER   Not very likely.

SAVITA   Do you like Sonia, Ma?

RAJINDER   She's okay.

SAVITA   Well, she's been on the game, off and on, she told me.

RAJINDER   What do you mean?

SAVITA   Don't you know what that means?

RAJINDER   Well, would I ask if I did?

SAVITA   See, I do know more than you think. She's what they call a 'hooker', a prostitute!

RAJINDER   Don't you dare talk to me like that. I don't want to hear you talk, crudely, like this, even if it's true. I wouldn't believe that, even of her.

SAVITA   It's true, she's not ashamed of it. She says she's in charge of her own body, that's all it means. *(Pause)* Housewives sell their bodies too, you know. Only it's to one man, and that must be so boring, and they have no control over... their... bodies.

RAJINDER   Savita, shut up, that's enough out of you.
  (RAJINDER slaps SAVITA as she speaks. SAVITA is stunned for a second or two, then she tries to make light of it.)

SAVITA   Ammah! That hurt! It's not fair. I was only... joking. You're too strict you know.

RAJINDER   I've told you, we're different from all these people here. Don't you forget that.

SAVITA   Yeah, I know, we're Pakis.

RAJINDER   Behave yourself. I'm not going to let any of you out of this room any more, except for meals.

SAVITA   Brilliant. NO more school.

RAJINDER   I'm not joking, Savita. I'm dead serious.

SAVITA   So am I.

RAJINDER   Don't answer back.

SAVITA   You sound evil like him now. You're missing him aren't you?

RAJINDER   Shut up.

SAVITA   We'll be going back next, I suppose. We always do when you get like this.

RAJINDER   Like what?

SAVITA   Nasty, like him, and violent. Kamla said I could talk to her, anytime, if something bothered me. No violence, remember? It's a house rule. I could tell on you.

RAJINDER   Are you trying to threaten me now? She's put you up to it, hasn't she, the scheming little bitch! Tell her what?

SAVITA   Everything.

RAJINDER   About what?

SAVITA   All that you've been too coy to say...

RAJINDER   Don't try to play games with me Savita... what are you talking about now?

SAVITA   I know about the porno films, in the house... he forced you to drink, and... and... he made you do things you didn't want to do.

RAJINDER   That's not true... there was nothing like that. You're lying. You've no right to do this to me. Make things like this up, just to... humiliate me...

SAVITA   I heard you some nights.

RAJINDER   Shut up, Savita. For God's sake, be quiet. Someone'll hear you.

SAVITA   I don't care if they do. I hate you. I hate you even more than I hate him, you're such a bloody hypocrite.

RAJINDER *(Bursts into sobs)* Meri tauba, Guruji. Forgive my sins. What did I do to deserve this?

SAVITA *(Defiance slips away and she slips into childish protest.)* I don't want to go any more. I wish I was dead. You spoil everything. I'm telling you, I'll... I'll run away if you hit me again. I mean it. *(RAJINDER says nothing but tries to calm herself. SAVITA watches her for a few seconds then goes and puts her arms round her and kisses her.)* I'm sorry, Ammah. I was so horrible to you. I don't know what came over me.

RAJINDER *(Takes her arms away gently but firmly and turns her face away from her.)* You better go and get ready. They'll be here to pick you up soon.

SAVITA   Are you OK now? *(RAJINDER only nods.)* I'm only going because I hate this place. I wish I could get out of here for good.

Exit SAVITA. RAJINDER slowly gets up and begins to undress. Takes off her chunni and folds it. Takes off her jewellery slowly, lets her hair down. F/X music flowing into the next sequence.

ACT TWO, SCENE 3

Int. SONIA'S bedroom. Soft romantic music is playing gently in the background. SONIA is giggling and chatting in a husky whisper as she 'slips out' of a few things, slowly. The client she's entertaining sounds a bit drunk.

SONIA   So what kind of music d'ya like? I mean what turns you on?

CLIENT   Who said I need music? You turn me on, baby. You can turn the bloody thing off, does nothing for me.

SONIA   I like it. *(Pause)* Besides, it's good cover for any noise, 'en it?

CLIENT   Anythin's all right by me, darlin'. Keep it on if you want. To me it's all fuckin' noise that means nothin'. I was born tone deaf.

SONIA   Do you want a drink, to relax you, get you in the moodbe only another two quid on top?

CLIENT   Why not? We'll 'ave a drink together. Rip me off while I'm in the mood, I don' mind. I'll drink to your health. What've you got?

SONIA   A drop of whisky, if ya fancy that.

CLIENT   I fancy that. I fancy that very much, thank you.

SONIA   I'll 'ave to nip down to the kitchen to get some glasses, tho'. You don't move, or open the door to anyone, O.K?

CLIENT   Sure, I understand.

SONIA   Told you about the crabby old bat, my landlady. She doesn't allow no gentlemen visitors in the bedrooms.

CLIENT   Shh... I won't move.

SONIA   Shan't be a minute. Be a good boy now, won't you?

CLIENT (*Whispers*) I'll be quiet, as a grave... Promise. Cross my heart.

SONIA (*Giggles nervously*) Shhhhh... (*Opens the door quietly, it creaks, and she tiptoes out shuffling a little. Bumps into RAJINDER who is coming across tiptoeing quietly from the other end of the stage. Both of them startle and gasp together.*)

RAJINDER   God, you scared the life out of me.

SONIA   Rajinder! You made me jump!

RAJINDER   I'm sorry.

SONIA   What the bloody hell are you up to at this time of night?

RAJINDER   I'm just going to get a hot water bottle for Sanjay. He's wheezing. Are you all right?

SONIA   Er, I was just gonna get some glasses.

RAJINDER   Glasses? Yeah, sure, go on.

(*SONIA sighs and steps forward. CLIENTshouts off.*)

CLIENT   Hey, Sylvie, baby? Hurry up. Where are ya?

RAJINDER   Oh, my God! There's someone... in your... You've got a man in there?

SONIA   Naw, it's just the radio.

RAJINDER   Yes, the radio's on, it's playing music.

SONIA   The wretched fool!

RAJINDER   You, you... Oh God, how could you!

SONIA   He's just someone from down the local. He's drunk to the eyeballs. I don't think he knows where he is.

RAJINDER   It's disgraceful, this whole business!

SONIA   Listen, love, I'm too old for a lecture. Once in three friggin' months isn't a lot of business, what the hell difference does it make to anyone? Why don't you just shut your mouth and go back to bed?

RAJINDER There's a no-men rule in the house.
SONIA Bloody stupid rule. Doesn't mean anything.
RAJINDER I'll talk to Eileen tomorrow about this!
SONIA Do that. Eileen's a soft touch, she'll give me a warnin' an' I'll take it. O.K?
CLIENT How long 'ave I gotta wait in the fuckin' dark?

ACT TWO, SCENE 4

Refuge office. EILEEN and KAMLA are busy with paperwork. Enter RAJINDER dressed to go out. Agitated.

RAJINDER I came to return the key, and I thought there might be things to sign again.
KAMLA Where do you think you're going?
RAJINDER I'm going back.
KAMLA But where to?
EILEEN What happened?
RAJINDER I kept thinking about how to tell you all this. When I came here, this place seemed to be okay. Now I find something horrible's going on here. Late last night, Sonia had a man in her room, he was drunk and I know what they were up to. I was a bit silly, I really saw this place as special in some way. Now, I see how filthy it really is and dangerous for my children. To think I brought them into this hell. Savita's been going shopping and for walks with her, no wonder she's been behaving so... shockingly. I've no choice but to go back home.
KAMLA But you said you'd never do that!
RAJINDER Barbara said you can get a court order to keep your husband out, I'll try to do that.
KAMLA But that's a long process... Why don't you wait, let me ring round and try to get you into another refuge...
RAJINDER I won't live under the same roof as a common prostitute! I can't.
SONIA *(Walks in breezily)* Morning. I thought she'd be in here grassing me up, first thing!
RAJINDER I don't want to get into a discussion with her either, so if you'll excuse me...
SONIA Now, look 'ere... Rajinder... *(Exit RAJINDER.)*
EILEEN Shit! I could've done without this today.
KAMLA How the fuck did you have the gall to do that anyway?
EILEEN It's not the first time, either.

KAMLA   Maybe if she'd been dealt with severely the first time it
wouldn't have happened again. She's leaving because of what you did last
night.

SONIA   Isn't she a bloody loony!

EILEEN   That's beside the point. What's your excuse for fetchin' a man
into the house when you know it's against the bloody rules?

SONIA   What did she say? Don't fall into her trap. She's exaggerated,
you can be sure.

KAMLA   I'm absolutely furious. You seem to have no idea of how
dangerous it is.

SONIA   Gus is somebody I knew when I was a girl. Like we nearly got
married, at one time. I just asked him in for a laugh. He's such a scream,
kept shoutin' 'Sylvie, Sylvie baby', just 'cause I said he should keep his
voice down. Anyway, he was too drunk to know where he was or what was
goin' on.

EILEEN   Don't you understand Sonia, it's a rule you can't afford to
break. You risk the safety of others and that's not on!

KAMLA   We haven't had a chance to discuss this between us, but we'll
come back to you on this, you can be sure of that.

SONIA   What's a gel to do if her giro's late then? It's a bloody jackpot
for you, I reckon, show all of us how tough you are, eh?

EILEEN   I'm sorry not to see any sign of apology or regret from you,
Sonia, in spite of what's happened.

SONIA   Hold on! She's not some poor twit who got scared of a bloke
on the premises. She's into this fuckin' self-righteousness. Don't look at
me like that, Eileen. 'Course I'm sorry. How was I to know that stupid
Indian woman would make such a bloody drama out of it?

EILEEN   What's bein' Indian got to do with it?

SONIA   You know what she's like. Makes you feel like that.

KAMLA   I wish you'd learn the house rules, once and for all.

SONIA   I hope she won't get into trouble because of me. I've got
nothin' 'gainst her. And I'm quite fond of Savita. That poor kid didn't want
to go back at all. Her old man's been messin' her about. Did she tell you
that?

EILEEN   I don't know anything about this. Do you Kamla?

KAMLA   Are you saying Savita was being abused by her father? You
sure? How do you know this?

SONIA   She told me, that's how.

EILEEN   How dreadful... and we'd no idea.

SONIA   She's been wettin' the bed, it's her who does it.

EILEEN   Does Rajinder know?

SONIA	Dunno. Savita didn't think so. *(KAMLA goes for the telephone.)*
EILEEN	Hang on!
KAMLA	The child's at risk, don't you see?
EILEEN	That's not the way to handle this. You don't want to rush in with a sledge-hammer at this point. What if she doesn't know?
SONIA	Look, I am real sorry about this, Eileen.
KAMLA	I'm concerned about Rajinder too, but the child's interest takes priority. There's a legal requirement. We must inform the authorities within a week of discovering abuse.
EILEEN	I'll go and see her first. We're dealin' with people here, not just cases, Kamla. No good creatin' another trauma for the kid.
KAMLA	You've got a day to fetch her back, after that I'll take action on my own if necessary.

ACT TWO, SCENE 5

Int. RAJINDER'S bedroom at home. Bed is prominent, covered with a bright red bedspread. RAJINDER and SAVITA walk into the bedroom carrying bags in both hands.

RAJINDER	Everything looks the same, doesn't it, Savita? As if we'd never left this place.
SAVITA	Yes, it does. How long were we away?
RAJINDER	Three weeks and three days. Seems longer somehow. Wa-ay Guruji! Only you know the future. I vowed never to return to this house. I never thought such a time would come that will bring me back to these walls!
SAVITA	Feel as if he's here, somewhere.
RAJINDER	He won't be back till five. He hasn't made the bed, of course. *(Enter PRADEEP from the left. He comes and stands squarely behind the bed.)*
SAVITA	I knew we would come back.
RAJINDER	Why?
SAVITA	Papaji always has his way in the end.
RAJINDER	I thought you were unhappy there, you complained enough. Put that back.
	(SAVITA has picked up the 'Kirpaan' from the wall and is looking at it.)
SAVITA	I'm only looking. It wasn't exactly a holiday. If we had our own place it would have been different. We could've made it nice. Got little bits an' pieces, and made it our own.

RAJINDER   Time wasn't on our side. Maybe some good will come of this. Maybe we can stay here and keep him out of this place. At least it's comfortable. There's a lot to be said for mixer taps and central heating that works.

SAVITA   The blade's still sharp.

RAJINDER   I said put that back. Why've you become so disobedient, child?

SAVITA   Just looking. Why did we come back? Like this, all of a sudden? I didn't even get to say goodbye to Sonia and the rest, and people at school, 'cos you made me miss school.

RAJINDER   God must have meant us to come back.

SAVITA   So why did he send us away in the first place, Ammah?

RAJINDER   Only he knows why he made us do that. I don't know   all the answers. Go to your room and put your things away. *(Exit SAVITA.)* Well, Pradeep. I'm back. But I'm not the same woman who walked out of that door three weeks ago. Your hold over me is broken now, forever. I know now what I have to do. I must safeguard my honour. That is my duty to myself and to Guruji. He'll protect me now. *(PRADEEP stands still behind her. Pause. Enter SAVITA wearing a short frilly black 'naughty' nightie. Stands on the side watching RAJINDER. RAJINDER moves into the spotlight with SAVITA.)*

SAVITA   Here I am Mummy...

RAJINDER   Where did you get that?

SAVITA   It was a secret present from Papaji.

RAJINDER   What are you saying, Savita?

SAVITA   Here's the card, I've still got it. Read it, if you don't believe me. *(RAJINDER takes the card. PRADEEP reads out.)*

PRADEEP   To Savita, for being so lovely, Papa. *(Pause. SAVITA holds out two porn magazines to RAJINDER.)*

SAVITA   He gave me these too. *(RAJINDER says nothing.)* He said, you'd never believe me if I tried to tell you anything. He said he'd kill me if I tried to tell you. I never asked for any of this, I swear it by Guruji. He was lying, wasn't he? You believe me, don't you Ammah? Why don't you say something, then? Please, believe me, Ammah, please...

RAJINDER *(Walks slowly up to SAVITA. Puts her shawl round SAVITA'S shoulders and walks her away.)* We better get back before he returns.

ACT THREE, SCENE 1
Int. Refuge lounge. RAJINDER is ironing clothes. Daytime live is on a low volume. Enter KAMLA.

KAMLA   We've got to talk before I leave today, Rajinder. O.K?

RAJINDER   What about?

KAMLA   Savita.

RAJINDER   What have you got to do with Savita?

KAMLA   Both Eileen and I know about Savita. She told Sonia. You must see that the moment I discovered abuse, Savita became my client and I have to make sure that what's best for her should happen.

RAJINDER   I don't know what you're talking about. She told Sonia nothing. Sonia's lying.

KAMLA   If you continue to deny it I shall assume your collusion.

RAJINDER   What do you mean by that?

KAMLA   That means you knew what was happening and you didn't do anything to stop it.

RAJINDER   What are you saying, are you mad? She's my daughter, I'm more concerned about her welfare than you can ever be. You know what they say in India? 'Only crafty old witches pretend to love you more than your own mother'.

KAMLA   We all know about mothers, no-one's born without one. A lot of the bull-shit about love is to do with control.

RAJINDER   So what do you want from me now, Kamla?

KAMLA   I'd like to set up a case conference next week to deal with it.

RAJINDER   So what happens then?

KAMLA   Social Services get involved. She has to have a medical and then all the parties talk and decide what to do next.

RAJINDER   I can't agree to that. Why should I talk to strangers about my daughter? Where I come from we deal with things within the family.

KAMLA   That doesn't get you very far! There's two things you will get out of this if we go to court. You'll get housed and Savita'll get counselling and so would you. You've been through a lot.

RAJINDER   I'm not going to use her to get round your stupid, racist housing people.

KAMLA   I hope you'd have more sense than that. It is in your interest and hers.

RAJINDER   So, you want to deal with it your way. Do I have a choice?

KAMLA   Not really.

RAJINDER   All that talk about liberating women is just talk, isn't it?

KAMLA   There's a principle involved here and I do think men like him should be prosecuted.

RAJINDER   Ah! So that's it! I wondered about your motives. What if I told you she's lying, there was no abuse. She's always imagining things...

sometimes, she exaggerates... but he couldn't have... touched her, really. I was home most nights.

KAMLA   Obviously you need counselling, too. I can arrange that.

RAJINDER   There's no reason to justify your doing anything. She said nothing concrete to Sonia, and she never confided in you, anyway. What's more, I'll not let you talk to her and harass her over this. I want her to forget what... might have happened. And, probably didn't happen.

KAMLA   You've decided to cover this up. If she blocks it off, it'll cause problems later.

RAJINDER   You know what the trouble is with the West? There's fads here. People think they think for themselves, but they're never allowed to. One day someone decides to worry about salmonella in eggs and people give up eating eggs. Someone decides to worry about child abuse and the cases multiply. There's always been salmonella in eggs, don't you know?

KAMLA   So you're not going to co-operate?

RAJINDER   I came back didn't I?

KAMLA   You're still avoiding facing it.

RAJINDER   I'd like to avoid a scandal. She's got to marry one day. But then you don't know what it is to live within the community. I don't know where women like you come from. Call yourself an Asian, do you?

KAMLA   I am one.

RAJINDER   I wouldn't go that far! Black you may be, Asian you certainly are not.

KAMLA   You can't deny me my identity. I won't let you. You people with your saris and your bloody lingo and all your certainties about the universe, you don't have a monopoly on being Asian. You can't box it and contain it and exclude others. I'll define myself as I bloody well want to.

RAJINDER   You don't try to attack my beliefs, okay?

KAMLA   This is hypocrisy and I won't let you cover it up. I'm getting in touch with Social Services.

RAJINDER   Don't you dare do that.

KAMLA   You try and stop me.

RAJINDER   You bitch! I curse you to misery forever!

KAMLA   I'm not trying to hurt her. I only want to help...

EILEEN *(Enters. Stands and watches for a few seconds before KAMLA notices her.)* What a shouting match! I heard you in the office. I think I've got to take over this business from you, Kamla.

RAJINDER   Thank you. I'd appreciate that.

EILEEN   This isn't right. We all need to be calmer before we can deal with this, it's obvious. *(EILEEN puts her hand on KAMLA'S arm and wheels her away. RAJINDER begins pacing the room.)*

RAJINDER   There must be a way out, there must be one. If only he would die. I wish I had the courage to kill him, then maybe we could go back and live there, in the safety of our own home.

(RAJINDER collapses on a chair, covers her face with both her hands. Sobbing. Re-enter EILEEN. Pause)

EILEEN   Rajinder, please, don't. It doesn't have to be like this.

RAJINDER   I'm sorry, I can't help it.

EILEEN   We're on the same side, believe me.

RAJINDER   I don't know what to do any more. I feel, as if I'm running out of time and, and there's nowhere to go.

EILEEN   I'll see to it that you get the time to take it all in before you have to deal with anything, O.K.?

RAJINDER   And Kamla?

EILEEN   She's worried, partly because you went back once.

RAJINDER   But I didn't know...

EILEEN   I know. *(Pause)*

RAJINDER   I sold my bangles today. But I still won't have enough to rent a place unless I get a job first. It'll take time... and, and he might find us.

EILEEN   We'll deal with it together, one thing at a time. It'll work out, you'll see. So you're looking for a job. I'm glad you're doing that. Kamla couldn't believe your career plans when you told her all that.

RAJINDER   I'm sorry, I shouldn't really have shouted at her. But... she thinks she knows everything. If she'd grown up in India maybe she'd know there's more to life than you can ever hope to learn in one lifetime, and she thinks she knows it all at thirty.

EILEEN   Her heart's in the right place.

RAJINDER   If she's got one!

ACT THREE, SCENE 2

PRADEEP enters the stage facing the 'outside' of the door. Looks around. He is wearing a cap pulled over his eyes and dark glasses which mask his face. He is carrying a large bag. Puts it on the floor. Stands beside the door and stares at it for a few seconds, then presses the entry phone. EILEEN answers.

PRADEEP   Hello.

EILEEN   Hello, who is it please?

PRADEEP   Good afternoon, Madam. Collecting for a children's charity.

EILEEN   I'm sorry. Try next door. *(Replaces the 'phone. PRADEEP stands beside the door and smiles. He looks at his watch and leans*

against the wall in a leisurely manner. KAMLA enters refuge office looking rushed and hurried as she rifles through papers.)
You were going to tell me how much you can spare from the petty cash for the cake.

KAMLA   Sometimes you absolutely amaze me, Eileen. I am utterly thrown by the biggest problem that's hit us in months and you're worrying about how much you can have for the birthday cake. Does Sonia deserve a bloody surprise party after what she's been up to?

EILEEN   We need the bloody parties even more when there are problems. I wish I could wave a wand and get them both talking to each other; I want the tension and unpleasantness to go from the house.

KAMLA   Don't we all. *(Sits resignedly, opens the petty cash box.)* I expect you're bloody right as well, as always. Twelve pounds. Here it is. Parties are nice, they do help. You know, we never had parties when we were little.

EILEEN   Was that a cultural thing, then?

KAMLA   That too. But mostly it was to do with money. God, I hate the meanness of poverty, the penny-pinching, the skimping, the making-do.

EILEEN   Don't remind us.

KAMLA   But it never affected me the way it did my brother. He owns three travel agencies in the West End, you know. I'm too filled with loathing for the system to want to become a woman of substance within it.

EILEEN   Yeah, we can all see the Puritan in you Kamla!

KAMLA   Now, now, no religious labels please, ascetic will do. Look, if you want me to, I'll pick up the cake on my way back from Social Services.

EILEEN   That'll be a help. Thank you. *(Pause)* And Kamla, I must say this, don't rush Rajinder into anything, please.

KAMLA   There are professional guidelines on how to deal with child abuse, and, with respect, I'd like to keep to them, if I may. She's had a week to come to terms with this.

EILEEN   Not quite a week.

KAMLA   All right, I'll give her a few more days. If by Monday she doesn't come round, I will be getting in touch with Social Services, to notify them, that's my deadline.

EILEEN   Does it have to be set out like an ultimatum?

KAMLA   Yes, I'm afraid so.

EILEEN   Absolute deadlines make absolute disasters.

KAMLA   Some people need them.

EILEEN   Why do you want to be confrontational? Give her time, she'll come round.

KAMLA And if she doesn't?

EILEEN Then you could apply pressure later on. Savita's safe here, she's out of his reach. What's the point of going through a procedure, just for the heck of it? *(PRADEEP presses the entry phone buzzer again.)* Yes. Who is it please?

PRADEEP Could I see the lady of the house, maybe?

EILEEN No, you can't I'm afraid, she's out.

PRADEEP If you'd like to step out Madam I'd show you leaflets about our organisation. It's a bonafide charity, all very worthwhile work.

EILEEN I'm sure it is, it's just that I'm unable to contribute right now.

PRADEEP Not even fifty pence ma'am?

EILEEN I'm sorry, I said no. Is that clear or not?

PRADEEP God bless you all the same, madam and goodbye.

EILEEN *(Replaces the entry phone sharply this time with a sigh. Spotlight on PRADEEP)*

PRADEEP So this is the house... no dustbins out in the front... there must be an alleyway at the back... which makes life a bit easier. I'll try the back. I told you Rajinder, didn't I, the world isn't big enough to hide you from me. *(Exit PRADEEP.)*

KAMLA I can't believe that I should have to justify a duty... to a colleague.

EILEEN It's become some kind of a crusade, or a witch hunt...

KAMLA But she's letting him get away with it... and she shouldn't. He must be punished.

EILEEN Kamla that has to be less important than the well-being of Rajinder and Savita.

KAMLA Besides, Savita needs more help. I would like her to be a survivor, not a victim.

EILEEN Don't you see, love, this would hurt her too.

KAMLA No, it couldn't.

EILEEN How do you know?

KAMLA I'm going by the book and I expect others to do the same.

ACT THREE, SCENE 3
Int. night time. RAJINDER'S bedroom.

RAJINDER You're still awake Savita.

SAVITA I'll just finish this chapter and then I'll sleep.

RAJINDER It's late, you won't wake up in the morning, then. Go on now, just get yourself a hot drink, settle down in bed and say your prayers.

(Exit SAVITA. RAJINDER is praying softly.) Dar teray tayaan khaloti may kamli teray darbaar di. Sub da pala karo Guruji, hai arz teray guizaar di. *(F/X glass smashing in the distance. RAJINDER stops abruptly. Enter PRADEEP. RAJINDER is startled.)*

Pradeep!... so it was you...

PRADEEP   Didn't I warn you not to try to run away from me again?

RAJINDER   I had no choice.

PRADEEP   Come back home, I want you back. I'll forgive you if you return to me.

RAJINDER   I could never go back, not now, never.

PRADEEP   You've no right to do this, to steal my children from me   and run away like a thief in the night.

RAJINDER   That was the only way. *(Enter SAVITA, sees PRADEEP and screams.)*

PRADEEP   Shhh...

RAJINDER   Savita, be a good girl, go and lie down quietly in your bed. Don't be frightened, your father's come to ask me something, that's all.

SAVITA   I'll try to be quiet. Papaji, promise you won't hurt Mummy, please.

PRADEEP   Don't worry. Go to bed now, I'm only talking to her. I'm asking you, for the last time, Rajinder, come back to me.

RAJINDER   I can't. I know about you.

PRADEEP   So you won't come? You mean it, do you?

RAJINDER   Absolutely.

PRADEEP   Then your face away, Savita, so I can kiss your mother goodbye. *(Stabs her. RAJINDER gasps in shock and disbelief.)*

RAJINDER   Oh, God! Pradeep?

PRADEEP   This is for denying me yourself, and this for denying me my children. This and this and this.

(Noise and commotion. SAVITA begins to scream hysterically. Enter SONIA.)

SAVITA   Papa! What have you done to her! How could you? Mummy, Mummyji, say something, please Mummyji...

PRADEEP   I'm going home now. Tell the police when they come where I am.

SONIA   God, you crazy bastard! You've killed her, you murderer! Call a doctor. Someone phone please!

PRADEEP   This is not a murder, it is a death sentence, her punishment for taking away what was mine. Tell them when they come. She can't leave me, she's my wife. *(Exit PRADEEP. SONIA kneels beside RAJINDER, with her arm round SAVITA'S shoulder.)*

SONIA   Oh, Rajinder, why didn't you shout for help? I was only next door.

SAVITA   Is she going to die, Sonia? He said he was only kissing her goodbye. What are we going to do?

SONIA   Someone will be here to help us soon, I'm sure.

The End.

Running Dream

In 1988, I was asked to write a play for Second Wave Youth Group in Deptford — a play about three generations of women. I wasn't sure where to start so I started with myself and counted the generations back — my mother Agnes Cooke and my mother's mother Roselia Lagwa.

I soon discovered that within my own generation, (my brothers and sisters) there were two parts — a generation who travelled to England from Dominica and those who were born here. Three of my sisters and two brothers travelled to England when they were kids while four of us were born in England.

Those who travelled, remembered a world we English-born knew nothing about and as I got older I envied their memories. They spoke of a grand-mother who brought them up. My grandmother died before I met her and all I could imagine her to be was a shadow of a woman in a rocking-chair smoking a pipe in a country I knew very little about. Since then she has come to life in my dreams.

Thanks gran for the dream. Thanks mum for the language you have passed down because I know: 'We didn't just get here. We had a time before now — and sometimes I want to hold my time, my past, my history... I want to embrace it because it's mine'.

Trish Cooke

RUNNING DREAM

Trish Cooke

Running Dream had its first production at the Theatre Royal, Stratford East, London in March 1993. Directed by Olusola Oyeleye and designed by Andrea Montag.

CHARACTERS:
Sister 1
CLEMENTINE   **Marianne Jean Baptiste**
Sister 2
GRACE   **Sherlina Chamberlain**
Sister 3
BIANCA   **Cathy Tyson**
Their Mother
FLORENTINE   **Claudette Williams**
Their Grandmother
MA EFFELINE   **Corinne Skinner-Carter**

CHORUS OF FOUR OR MORE TO PLAY:
Their Father
WILLIAM   **Wilbert Johnson**
Shopkeeper
MA BELLE   **Mandy Lassalles**
Florentine's friend
TANTY PIPPIN   **Sharon D. Clarke**
Clementine and Grace's friend
DENNIS   **Haydn Forde**

AND CHORUS, VILLAGERS ETC...

PART 1

A score of music is undercurrent. The silhouette of a rocking-chair (a throne, an altar) magnified in size forms the back-drop on the stage. The chair begins to rock slowly. The sound of its rocking creates a rhythm – a slow unoiled regular croak. The sound of sea waves lapping gently accompanies this. Out of the sea sounds a low whisper emerges and a voice of an old woman personifies the croak of the rocking chair. EFFELINE is the name of the old woman. She is speaking in Dominican patois – a French Creole.

EFFELINE	Ah dou dou,	(Translation:	*My dearest*
	Ah dou dou		*My dearest*
	Tout sa ou dit		*Everything you say*
	Tout sa ou fe		*Everything you do*
	i èvè 'w		*It stays with you*
	Nous pasa lonbliye'y		*We will not forget*
	i èpi nou		*It stays with us*
	kon èspwi		*Like a spirit*
	kon èspwi		*Like a spirit*
	kon èspwi		*Like a spirit)*

She repeats this several times. A figure dressed in black comes out of the darkness and takes her place in the chair. Distant drum beats softly becoming progressively louder. The beat is light and quick, like running – playful running, a game of chase. The sound of children giggling is heard, followed by the sound of bare feet slapping the ground. Two children, CLEMENTINE and GRACE run on stage. CLEMENTINE is carrying her shoes around her neck. GRACE does not have any shoes. EFFELINE and the drum beat continue. The children giggle. The children do not acknowledge EFFELINE, and   EFFELINE looks through them.

CLEMENTINE   Djab ou la? (Spirit you there?)
GRACE   Otj'w djab? (Where you spirit?)
CLEMENTINE   Djab ou la?
GRACE   Oti' w djab?

(They run around the stage as if looking for something. They repeat the phrase as they look, running into each other and bouncing off each other. It is as if some sort of current is running through them. This continues. A slow, heavy panting is heard from all sides of the stage and the auditorium. The children do not react nor does EFFELINE. They carry on running around. Their movements are light and quick. A bed is

wheeled on to the rhythm of the heavy panting. BIANCA a young girl is pushing the bed. CLEMENTINE and GRACE playfully pull BIANCA into their game and begin to tease her.)

GRACE/CLEM *(almost a whisper)* Mwen rè'w gwaté patat. (I make you scrape patay.) Mwe fé'w manje kaka. (I make you eat ka ka.)

(They repeat this, directing it at BIANCA. FLORENTINE the middle-aged woman in the bed speaks heavily and slowly taking on the rhythm of the heavy panting which fades out as does the children's rhyme.)

FLORENTINE   Pa lonbliyé mwen. (Don't forget me.) Pa lonbliyé mwen. Pa lonbliyé mwen.

(From out of the shadows a CHORUS of faceless beings emerge repeating the phrase – 'Pa lonbliyé mwen'. They find their resting positions and remain as part of the background. One of the CHORUS is the drummer.)

EFFELINE   Pa onbliyé mwen.
GRACE/CLEM *(Kiss and part)* 'member me...
BIANCA *(To GRACE)* Remember me?

(Repeat and overlap. A coffin lowers onto the stage. FLORENTINE remains in the bed, GRACE, BIANCA and CLEMENTINE pick up the coffin and lower it down to the ground. Each of them jumps over the coffin, a ritual. After jumping they run around for another turn – a child's game.)

BIANCA   One
GRACE   Dé
CLEMENTINE   Twa
BIANCA   Four
GRACE   Senk
CLEMENTINE   Sis
BIANCA   Seven
GRACE   Ywit
CLEMENTINE   Nef
BIANCA   Ten!

(The women take the lid off the coffin inside is a white, blonde, blue-eyed doll. The rocking-chair moves. A baby cries – one of the CHORUS makes the sound)

EFFELINE Ah dou dou,   (Translation: *My dearest*
Ah dou dou   *My dearest*
Tout sa ou dit   *Everything you say*
Tout sa ou fe   *Everything you do*
i èvè 'w   *It stays with you*
Nous pasa lonbliyé 'y   *We will not forget*
i èpi nou   *It stays with us*
kon èspwi   *Like a spirit*
kon èspwi   *Like a spirit*
kon èspwi   *Like a spirit)*

(The drum makes the sound of a clock ticking. The undercurrent music stops. The ticking continues. The women take up the following positions: FLORENTINE sitting up in bed cradling a pillow in her arms. GRACE reading an airmail letter at the foot of the bed near a box of attic junk and old letters, air mail. BIANCA sitting on a chair. a pair of men's trousers at her feet. CLEMENTINE washing clothes.)

FLORENTINE *(Stirs in the bed, sings)*
Brown skin girl stay home and mind baby
Brown skin girl stay home and mind baby
If I sail on a sailing boat and I don't come back
Stay home and mind baby...
CHORUS *(Sings)* Away from home / Away from home
Away from home / Away from home
More than miles / Plenty miles
Away from home.
More than one / More than two
More than three / More than four
More than miles / Plenty miles
Away from home...

The sound of an aeroplane passing over head. GRACE and CLEMENTINE look up at the sky.

CLEMENTINE   Plane!

CLEM/GRACE   Plane bring my Mammy back to me. Plane bring my
Mammy back to me.

CHORUS   Run!

CLEMENTINE *(CLEMENTINE runs away from GRACE. As if washing
clothes. CLEM sings)*

Wash away my sorrow / Wash away my grief

Wash away that love / that once belonged to me.

Wash away my sorrow / Wash away my grief

Wash away that love / that once belonged to me.

CHORUS   Run!

CLEMENTINE *(Spoken)* Run away and leave me. Me Alone. I don't care.
You think I care. Me! I don't care love... See, what you do always come
back round, oh yes... So...

CHORUS   Run!

CLEMENTINE   Away!

CHORUS   Run!

CLEMENTINE   Back!

CHORUS   Run!

CLEMENTINE   Into... I'm still... here. *(Return to song)*

Wash away my sorrow / Wash away my grief

Wash away that love / that once belonged to me.

Oh... Wash away my sorrow / Wash away my grief

Wash away that love / that once belonged to me.

*The sound of drumming – like running. GRACE runs ahead of
CLEMENTINE who is sulking. They are both carrying blond, blue-eyed
dolls. CLEMENTINE'S doll has a broken leg which she is trying to fix.
GRACE notices MATCHES STICK, a mad man. GRACE mimics his funny
walk.*

GRACE *(Calling after him)* Matches Stick! Matches Stick! Look how he
walking Clem. *(They both do the MATCHES STICK walk, one behind the
other obviously following him. They stop.)*

CLEMENTINE   Matches Stick you rum sucker!

GRACE   Run he coming! *(They run away laughing. CLEMENTINE
goes back to trying to fix her doll. She kisses her teeth.)*

CLEMENTINE   Give me yours nah?

GRACE *(Hugging her doll close)* You mad! Mine don't break – yours
break, why I have to give you mine?

CLEMENTINE *(Thinks)* Come. *(GRACE approaches CLEMENTINE cautiously holding onto her doll.)*

GRACE What?

CLEMENTINE I don't want your doll nab I jus' want to see if it have a face like mine. *(GRACE takes a peek at her doll's face, keeping it well out of CLEMENTINE'S reach.)*

GRACE Yes it have a face. *(She looks at CLEMENTINE'S doll.)* Yes is the same thing.

CLEMENTINE So how you know that one is yours and this one with the mash up foot is mine?

GRACE Because your name was mark on that parcel. You think you smart Clementine but you don't getting mine doh!

CLEMENTINE Gimme it! *(CLEMENTINE tries to snatch the doll. GRACE runs. CLEMENTINE sits down running her fingers in the dirt. GRACE notices. She comes back and sits beside her.)*

CLEMENTINE Is O.K. Mine is prettier anyway... *(CLEMENTINE sees a cigarette box on the floor she picks it up. There is nothing inside but the silver paper.)*

You have money?

(GRACE searches her pockets. She finds a coin.)

GRACE Only that.

CLEMENTINE Let's go buy penny bread.

GRACE One penny bread! That's all the money can buy.

CLEMENTINE You want to see magic. *(CLEMENTINE covers the coin with the silver paper.)* We can get two bread and still get change. Come let's go by Ma Belle.

One of the CHORUS steps out and becomes MA BELLE. She is an old lady who cannot see too well.

CLEMENTINE *(Pushing GRACE ahead of her)* You go first!

GRACE Why me? Is always me?

CLEMENTINE You is the youngest.

GRACE I always the youngest.

CLEMENTINE *(Pushing her in)* Jus' go on!

MA BELLE Ki moun sa yé? *(Who is that?)*

(CLEMENTINE pushes GRACE forward. She gives GRACE the coin and hides.)

GRACE Man Belle sé mwen Florentine chil'.

MA BELLE Zanfan Florentine? *(Florentine's child?)*

(MA BELLE squints her eyes and looks hard at GRACE.) Clementine?

GRACE   Wi mwen sé Clementine. (Yes is Clementine)

(GRACE looks at CLEMENTINE hiding and giggles. CLEMENTINE throws the cigarette box at GRACE who coughs to cover up the sound.)

MA BELLE   What your mammy sen' you from Inglan? *(GRACE hands MA BELLE the doll.)*

GRACE   Sa. (This)

MA BELLE   Your Mammy sen' you yon bel ti pòpòt Clementine. (A   nice doll) *(CLEMENTINE still hidden looks at her deformed doll with disappointment.)* So what I can get for you Mamzel?

GRACE   Mwen lé dé gwo kapa pen souple? (Two penny bread please.)

MA BELLE   Dé gwo kapa pen? (Two penny bread?)

GRACE   Wi souplé Man Belle. (Yes please Ma Belle.)

(MA BELLE gets the bread and takes the coin.)

MA BELLE   How is Ma Effeline?

GRACE   I byen Man Belle. (She's fine Ma Belle.)

(CLEMENTINE signals for GRACE to hurry up. MA BELLE puts the coin between her teeth. GRACE takes the bread and starts to go.)

MA BELLE *(Calling after her)* Clementine!

CLEMENTINE *(From hiding place)* Wi Man Belle. (Yes Ma Belle.)

(GRACE hushes her.)

MA BELLE   Lamonne'w. You forget your change.

GRACE   Se sa. (Oh is that.) *(GRACE goes back for change.)* Mesi Man Belle. (Thank you Ma Belle.) *(CLEMENT/NE sneaks out of the shop and GRACE runs after her. MA BELLE returns to CHORUS.)*

CLEMENTINE   Bondyé, I think she catch us!

GRACE   What you have to open your big mouth for? *(GRACE mimics CLEMENTINE)* Yes Ma Belle! Ou fol nan!

CLEMENTINE   She call my name. Is you who give her my name. Is you that mad!

GRACE   Anyway take your money. *(GRACE gives CLEMENTINE half of the money and a penny bread. CLEMENTINE takes them and then notices the mad woman – VERON.)*

CLEMENTINE *(Calling after her)* Veron Tèt Chèch! (Veron Dry Head!)

GRACE/CLEMENTINE   Veron Tèt Chèch! Vèron Tèt Chèch!

(They run away.)

GRACE   But look mango modyé!

CLEMENTINE   Come let's get some.

GRACE   We'll dirty our clothes. *(CLEMENTINE kisses her teeth. She climbs up on GRACE'S shoulders and passes some mangoes to GRACE* *who has hitched up her skirt and is putting the fruit in the flap of her dress. CLEM gets down. They share the mangoes looking over their shoulders all the time to see if they are being watched. They sneak out then sit down outside their yard. GRACE brushes the dirt from beneath her feet as CLEMENTINE puts on her shoes.)*

CLEMENTINE   Let's play tikitok.

GRACE   No is too late! You know why!

CLEMENTINE   You scared Grace?

GRACE   No.

CLEMENTINE   Why you don't want to play?

GRACE   Is after six o'clock.

CLEMENTINE   Gracie 'fraid.

GRACE   I don't 'fraid. I jus' saying.

CLEMENTINE *(Deviously)* I want to play tikitok now.

EFFELINE   All you all right in the yard?

CLEM/GRACE   Yes Ma. *(CLEMENTINE begins to play pick-up.)*

GRACE   Clemo-i!

CLEMENTINE   Come nan! *(CLEMENTINE throws one pebble up in the air and picks up a handful of pebbles quickly. She then arranges the pebbles in single file.)* See. Nothing don't happen.

GRACE *(Looks up at the sky)* Full moon too.

CLEMENTINE   You is still a chil'

GRACE   No.

CLEMENTINE   So... *(CLEMENTINE gives GRACE the pebbles. GRACE starts to play the game. She is obviously afraid.)*

EFFELINE *(From rocking-chair)* Clementine! Gracie! Come bring your Uncle food for him. *(GRACE gets up quickly, glad to have an excuse to stop playing the game.)*

GRACE   Maman calling us.

CLEMENTINE   I hear her but I don't going. *(CLEMENTINE continues to play.)*

EFFELINE   Clementine! Gracie!

GRACE   I coming manman. *(GRACE runs and comes back with a pot of food. CLEMENTINE continues playing.)*

GRACE   Maman say we have to bring the food for Uncle.

CLEMENTINE   I don't going.

GRACE   I don't going me alone.

(CLEMENTINE shrugs her shoulders and continues playing.)

I don't going me alone.

CLEMENTINE   Go nah Grace I have a message to do.

GRACE   Which message? Where you going?

CLEMENTINE   Big people business. Go I coming.

(GRACE stands with the pot in her hands but does not move.)

CLEMENTINE   You 'fraid?

GRACE   No. *(CLEMENTINE looks at GRACE. GRACE still does not move.)*... I 'fraid.

CLEMENTINE   What you 'fraid?

GRACE   I jus' 'fraid!

CLEMENTINE   Chil'! *(CLEMENTINE kisses her teeth and leaves GRACE with the pot.)*

GRACE *(Shouting after her)* Is Robbie you going to look for! Robbie is your boyfriend! Clementine go fin' boyfrien'. Clementine go fin' boyfrien'. Kissin' under Manman bed! Kissin' under Manman bed!

CLEMENTINE *(V.O)* Chil' shet op!

GRACE   Then come!

CLEMENTINE   Go I'll catch you on the way back!

GRACE *(Singing/talking to herself)* I don't 'fraid cemetery where Mavis Auntie bury. I don't 'fraid soukouyan. They can't do nothing to me. *(repeat)*

(A creature in black comes out and follows GRACE. She is aware of something behind her but she does not turn around.)

Clementine think I 'fraid. But I don't 'fraid soukouyan. She try to frighten me but I will be good for her. *(GRACE jumps around to face the creature.)* Clementine!

CLEMENTINE *(With black cloth over her)* Sou kou yab ahhh ahhh!

(The creature sucks GRACE'S finger. GRACE drops the pot.)

GRACE   Soukouyan! Soukouyan!

(The creature runs away. CLEMENTINE catches up with GRACE. She is carrying the pot and she is breathless.)

CLEMENTINE   Sa ki tet la? Mwen tapé chodyè-a asou chimèn-an? (What happen I find the pot on the road?)

GRACE   Mwen wè yon soukouyan! (I see soukouyan!)

CLEMENTINE   It touché'w? (It touch you?)

GRACE   i sousé dwèt mwen. (It suck my finger.)

CLEMENTINE   Bondyé! Ou ni pou pisé anle dwèt la. (God! You have to wee wee on it.)

GRACE   Mwen ni pou pise anle'y? (I have to wee wee on it?)

CLEMENTINE   Ta lè mwen ké mènè potchanm Manman. (Wait I'll get Manman's potty.) *(CLEMENTINE gets the potty and puts GRACE'S finger in it.)*

GRACE   Mesi. (Thank you.)

EFFELINE   Gracie! Clementine!

Drumbeat – running. GRACE and CLEMENTINE run back to previous positions. GRACE at foot of bed, CLEMENTINE washing clothes. Drum beat stops. Spotlight on GRACE. Alert, bright. An awakening.

GRACE   An oil-lamp with the wick inside... My mother told me to find it like it was a matter of life or death. And I wanted to find it, wanted to please her. She said Effeline was dying – her mother, my Grannie, the lady who brought me up – and she wanted the oil-lamp to burn so Effeline could see through the spirit world... you know, the other life. *(GRACE reads from one of the air mail letters.)*

CHORUS *(Sing)* Whoooi huh whooooi huh huh whooooi whooooi
Whoooi huh whooooi huh huh whooooi whooooi

GRACE   I sen' you a letter. An' I get the reply. Ma Effeline is going to a different world.

CHORUS   Cross over the sea / But you can't get to me
Ma Effeline / It seem you going to a different world.
Whoooi whooooi whooooi
It seem you going to a different (world)
Whoooi whooooi whooooi
It seem you going to a different world.
(CHORUS continue singing quietly as GRACE speaks.)

GRACE   Is like I had to go, you know... back. Is like a big hole, like all the years I here, I missing. Ma Effeline, she was my past. My history. I had a time before now. And sometimes I want to hold my time, my past, my history you know.

CHORUS   And sometimes I want to hold my time, my past, my history you know.
And sometimes I want to hold my time, my past,
my history you know.

GRACE   Sometimes I just want to embrace it, because it's mine...

Drumbeat – sounds like running, for a moment the CHORUS become country people repeating odd phrases in patois. Market sounds, savannah sounds, odd words in Creole.

CHORUS   Vini dou'y (Come love)
Vini (Come)
Vini (Come)
Mondyé gadé non! (Come look nah!)

Pwan'y! (Take it!)

Vini vini (Come come)

Konmèn ou lé? (How many you want?)

Come my lady, come and see what I have!

Which one you want?

Ou lé a anchay dou'y (You want a load luvvy)

Anni pon 'chay sala non (Just take this load nah)

Mwen ké mété yon ti piti avè'y (I'll put a little extra one with it)

GRACE *(Takes the pillow from FLORENTINE'S bed and throws it to CLEMENTINE)* Catch! *(CLEMENTINE stuffs the pillow up her dress. She is pregnant. CLEMENTINE calls after GRACE who is a little ahead of her, then she runs to catch up with GRACE.)*

CLEMENTINE　Gracie! Gracie! Ma Effeline want you. She was in school today you know and Madam John Pierre say she don't see you. Ma Effeline going to burs' your arse chil'! Where you was?

GRACE *(Afraid)* Ma Effeline was in school today?

CLEMENTINE　Yes. She get de letter from Inglan. De passage pay for one chil' an' is not my name mark on it.

GRACE　　　I going Inglan?

CLEMENTINE　Look so.

GRACE　　　Ou faché èpi mwen? (You vex wid me?)

CLEMENTINE　How I can vex wid you? You is only a chil'.

GRACE　　　An' what you is?

CLEMENTINE　A big woman.

GRACE *(Teasing)* A 'big, 'big woman! *(GRACE runs away. CLEM chases after her.)*

GRACE　　　I going to see my Mammy! Mwen ka alé wè Manman mwen!

CHORUS　　Run!

FLORENTINE　How far? Over oceans?

CHORUS　　Run!

GRACE　　　Across skies?

CHORUS　　Run!

BIANCA　　Through land?

CHORUS　　Run!

CLEMENTINE　Through people?

CHORUS　　Through whiplash on pigmented skin

Through people

Through whiplash on pigmented skin

Through people with white teeth smiles and defiant eyes

(Pause)

Through whiplash / Through whiplash
Through whiplash / Throooooooooooooaaaaaaaaagh!
(From out of the words a deep cry forms. GRACE continues the cry and runs to the rocking-chair.)

GRACE   Aaaahhhhhhh Maman.

CHORUS   Don't beat me!

GRACE   Don't beat me Maman!

EFFELINE   Ola ou té yé jodi-a? (Where were you today?) *(Pause)*
Grace ou pa tann mwen? (Grace you don't hear me?) You was in school today Grace? *(GRACE does not answer)* Gracie?

GRACE   Wi Manman? (Yes Maman?)

EFFELINE   Remember las' week I sen' you school an' you go take a sea bath?

GRACE   Wi Manman.

EFFELINE   What I do to you Gracie?

GRACE   You take my clothes when I was in de water Maman, and when I come out I had to run through de savana showing all I have.

EFFELINE   Remember the beating I give you?

GRACE   Wi Manman.

EFFELINE   Go get me strap.

CHORUS   Don't beat me.

GRACE   Pa bat mwen Manman. (Don't beat me Maman.)

CHORUS   Pa bat mwen Manman. (Don't beat me Maman.)

CLEMENTINE   Don't leave me. Don't leave me.

GRACE   Manman.

CLEMENTINE   Don't leave me.

CHORUS   Don't leave me Manman. Don't leave me.

GRACE   I going away?

EFFELINE   In Inglan they does do fing different you know dat?

GRACE   How you mean Maman?

EFFELINE   In Inglan you don't go school an' Ma Effeline not there to take strap behind you. You know what dat mean?

GRACE   No Maman.

EFFELINE   It mean if you don't want learn nobody going care. You understan'? So. Wha' you fink I should do wid dat strap?

CHORUS   Beat.

GRACE   Beat me Maman?

CHORUS   *(Sigh)* Ahhh.

EFFELINE   Why you fink I should do dat?

CHORUS   Beat.

GRACE	Because I take sea bath when is school I should go?
EFFELINE	Where you should go?
CHORUS	Beat.
GRACE	School Manman.
EFFELINE	Ola? (Where?)
CHORUS	Beat. Beat.
GRACE	School.
EFFELINE	I don't hear wha' you say.
CHORUS	Beat.
GRACE	I said school Maman.
CHORUS *(Sigh)*	Aaahhhh.
GRACE	School.
EFFELINE	What you shouting for?

(CHORUS look at each other.)

EFFELINE	An' why you mus' to school?
GRACE	I to learn. *(Single regular slow drum beat)* Maman.
EFFELINE	An' why you mus' learn?
GRACE	I understan' de way of de worl' Maman.
EFFELINE	Sé sa... (Is dat...) *(EFFELINE hands GRACE a letter)*

Florentine sen' for you...Is time.

The drumming gets faster. The CHORUS make fet. Dancing and making merry as if celebrating something – blowing whistles etc.

CHORUS   She going away / And she not coming back
She going away to stay – Aieeeeee!
She going away / And she not coming back
She going away to stay – Aieeeeee!
We lose one more / We lose one more
She going away to stay – Aieeeeee!
We lose one more / We lose one more
Gracie going away – Aieeeeee Aieeeeee
*(The CHORUS turn away and sing to the tune of "I sen' you a letter".
They keep the tune going during the ritual.)*
CHORUS   Whooooooi huh whooooi huh huh whooooi whoooooi
Whooooooi huh whooooi huh huh whooooi whoooooi

*Drumbeat. GRACE travels, her hand above her head, holding the hand of an imaginary stranger. She runs to keep up. She looks back once.
CLEMENTINE and GRACE connect and then she turns and walks away.*

Ritual –CLEMENTINE finds her doll and bashes the broken leg on its head. FLORENTINE writhes on the bed. GRACE blows kisses to the sky. CLEMENTINE catches them on her side of the stage.

CHORUS   I keep blowing kisses to the sky.
    I hope you catch them,
    Catch the thought behind the sigh.
CLEM/GRACE   See the moon.
    (The moon appears. CLEMENTINE goes back to washing clothes, her eyes on the moon.)
CHORUS   See it?
    Makes you wonder / Don't it make you high,
    See, right now, / Right this minute,
    Me and you / You and me
    We're sharing the sky
CLEM/GRACE   *(Sing)* You and I / You and I
    You and I / You and I
CHORUS   Sharing this sky together.
    (GRACE goes back to earlier position at the foot of FLORENTINE'S bed with the airmail letters. CHORUS start giggling.)
    Spirits spy / Spirits fly. Spirit.
    Tie up and catch up by the light spirit
    Diab ou la? / Where you spirit?
    (They focus on FLORENTINE in a restless sleep in the bed.)
    Eh eh temperatures high tonight!
FLORENTINE   Vyé djab! Vyé djab! Kité mwen! Devil! Devil!
CHORUS *(Giggling whispers)* Hee hee hee. *(The rocking-chair moves.)*
    Hee hee hee.

EFFELINE	Ab dou dou,	*My dearest*
	Ah dou dou,	*My dearest*
	Tout sa ou dit	*Everything you say*
	Tout sa ou fè	*Everything you do*
	i èvè 'w	*It stays with you*
	Nou pasa lonbliyé 'y	*We cannot forget it*
	i èpi nou	*It stays with us*
	kon èspwi	*Like a spirit*
	kon èspwi	*Like a spirit*
	kon èspwi	*Like a spirit*

CHORUS *(overlap)* My dearest...
My dearest...
Everything you say
Everything you do
It stays with you
We cannot forget
Like a spirit
Like a spirit
Like a spirit

(FLORENTINE readjusts herself until she is sitting on the edge of the bed. She manoeuvres her left leg with her hand until her legs are wide open, her dress falling between the gap.)

FLORENTINE Sometime I wish I was a virgin you know. No is true if I was a virgin I would be alright. *(She grins)* A grown woman wishing dat eh... I does wish some things for true. When I lie down there... I does think some things. *(She chuckles)* I does go back on old things and say if I did do dat instead of dat... maybe I wouldn't have dat... you understand. *(She looks at her three children)* See if I was a virgin... If you don't do nothing you can't really make mistake and nobody can tell you nothing... It not something you can jus... *(Drum beat in the distance.)* I jus' –

WILLIAM Psssssss... pssssss...

FLORENTINE *(Waves the sound away)* Kité mwen djab! (Leave me devil!)

The moon glows. From out of the shadows WILLIAM appears.

WILLIAM Florentine-oi! Florentine-oi! You going far?

FLORENTINE Yes. *(FLORENTINE jumps off the bed, picks up a basket and runs ahead of WILLIAM.)*

WILLIAM Oh, how far you going?

FLORENTINE Far far.

WILLIAM Roseau far or Canefield far? Portsmouth side or Marigot? Which far far you going?

FLORENTINE None of your business far!

WILLIAM Ah, that far! *(They walk in silence)* You want company?

FLORENTINE No.

WILLIAM Oh that's alright then... *(FLORENTINE looks at him)* Me neither.
(They walk on.)
You want me to carry that basket for you?

FLORENTINE *(Suspiciously)* Why?

WILLIAM *(Backs off)* Don't bite me Papa I was just asking.

FLORENTINE *(On the attack)* I strong you know.

WILLIAM   I know. I never say you don't strong. I can see you strong, I was jus' asking that's all.

FLORENTINE *(FLORENTINE puts down basket)* Oh.
(She wipes her forehead. WILLIAM picks up the basket.)

WILLIAM   You shouldn't be so...

FLORENTINE   How I is? How I shouldn't be?

WILLIAM   Is like you want to fight me and I don't even know you well.

FLORENTINE   Well I know you well. You is William Cross, John Cross the school teacher is your fardhar. And I know what is on your mind too. And I see all the woman that follow you.

WILLIAM   How you know so much about me?

FLORENTINE *(Shrugs)* I don't blind.

WILLIAM   I don't blind too so how I don't notice you before?

FLORENTINE   Maybe your eyes was full already. Anyway you may as full them back because I don't like you.

WILLIAM   Why, what I do you?

FLORENTINE *(Embarrassed)* Nothing.

WILLIAM   You speak your mind all the time like that?

FLORENTINE   Most days yes.
(The rhythm of a calypso melody is heard, playing faintly. FLORENTINE is about to say something then stops herself.)

WILLIAM   Say it, don't be 'fraid... I heard most things already.

FLORENTINE   Not from me. You don't hear nothing from me Misyé.

WILLIAM   Is it? *(FLORENTINE looks at him. WILLIAM grins)* I hear everything you saying. I hear your song. I hear it loud and clear.
(The rhythm gets louder. FLORENTINE giggles and walks away. The chorus step forward, she tries to usher them back.)

CHORUS *(Sing)* Mister Mister
(FLORENTINE covers up her mouth and still tries to hush the CHORUS.)

WILLIAM   Yes my girl. What you saying?

FLORENTINE   I don't say nothing. *(Walks away embarrassed.)* Take me take... Don't let me go. Mister Mister I love you so.

WILLIAM *(Enjoying this)* Mamzèl Mamzèl.
(CHORUS push FLORENTINE forward.)

FLORENTINE   Wi Misyé.

WILLIAM   Sa'w ka di mwen? (What are you saying to me?)

FLORENTINE   Mwen pa di anyen. (I didn't say anything.)

CHORUS   Pon mwen Pon mwen (Take me, take me) Pa kité mwen (Don't leave me)
WILLIAM *(Overlaps with FLORENTINE)* Marnzèl Mamzèl
FLORENTINE *(Overlaps)* Misyé Misyé
FLORENTINE/WILLIAM   Mwen enmen'w (I like you)

The song is repeated. The CHORUS getting into more of a party spirit second and possibly third time round. The CHORUS are constantly pushing FLORENTINE closer to WILLIAM. Finally FLORENTINE gives in. FLORENTINE and WILLIAM kiss. The CHORUS having done their job break away and observe the scene. The moon glows. The CHORUS become village gossipers.

CHORUS 1   You know the moon is a man with a dirty face.
CHORUS 2   Is that a fact?
CHORUS   Mésyé Kwik
REST OF CHORUS *(Answer)* Kwak
CHORUS 1   They say... a woman was wid child.
CHORUS 2   Yes?
CHORUS 1   For a man who use to come to the woman house in the middle of the night.
CHORUS 3   No!
CHORUS 1   An' every night he did come and do his business wid her de woman never see his face.
CHORUS 4   Never see his face?
CHORUS 3   That's what they say...
CHORUS 1   Anyway one night de girl modder take watch an' she stan' up outside de house to find out who is de man dat come and trouble her daughter every night.
CHORUS 2   Bondyé.
CHORUS 1   De modder hold some ashes in her hand and wait for de man. When de man come she leggo de ash in his face –
CHORUS 3   What!
CHORUS 1   Next day now de modder look for de man wid de dirty face...
CHORUS 2   Why de ash stain?
CHORUS 1   Never come out!
CHORUS 3   Kaval!
CHORUS 4   They find him?
CHORUS 1   Yes and wid shame he...
CHORUS   ...run...

CHORUS 1   ... to the sky...
(CHORUS repeat story in background.)
CHORUS 1   Ou sav lalin sé yon nonm èvè yon vijay sal
CHORUS 2   Mésyé Kwik
REST OF CHORUS   Kwak
CHORUS 1   Yo di yon fanm té anset
CHORUS 2   Sa v wé?
CHORUS 1   Pou yon nonm ki vini akay fanm la tou lé swè
CHORUS 3   Sa pa vwé!
CHORUS 1   Èvè chak swè i vini jwé èvè fanm la, fanm la pa jènmen wè vijay li
CHORUS 4   Pa janmen wè vijay?
CHORUS 3   Sé sa yo di...
CHORUS 1   Kanmenm, yon swè Manman ti fi a doubout dèwò kay la, i gadé pou wè ki nonm sala ki vini anbèté fi – y tout lé swè
CHORUS 2   Bonodyé.
CHORUS 1   Manman – a pon yon ti tak oukou an lanmen-y èvè i wèspèyé pou nonm la. Le nonm la viwé i jèté oukou-a an vijay li!
CHORUS 3   Sa-w ka di-a!
CHORUS 1   Le denmen Manman – a gadé pa nonm la èvè vijay sal la
CHORUS 2   i pasa netwayé-y?
CHORUS 1   i pakka sorti
CHORUS 3   Kaval
CHORUS 4   Yo tappé-y
CHORUS 1   Wi èvè i tèlman hont i kouwi an syèl la jik jodi sé la i yé èvè vijay sal li. Kwik
REST OF CHORUS *(answer)* Kwak
CHORUS 1   Mésyé Kwik
REST OF CHORUS *(answer)* Kwak
(CHORUS all look at the moon. FLORENTINE breaks away from WILLIAM'S embrace and squats to wash clothes in the river. The CHORUS squat too as if washing clothes.)
WILLIAM   Florentine-oi! Florentine-oi! *(FLORENTINE ignores him)* Mmmmm mmmmm your head high today Madam. Eh, eh – so you and me is stranger now? *(FLORENTINE carries on washing clothes)* You making like you don't know me now. What happen you 'fraid the sky have eye? *(FLORENTINE wrings out the item of clothing she is washing and takes a step forward away from the CHORUS. The CHORUS link up and listen.)*
FLORENTINE   Man why you have to tell everybody my business?

WILLIAM   What? I never know I is secret. I make you shame?

FLORENTINE   No. Is jus' dat everybody have a story to tell about William Cross – how he run up and down wid all kind of woman. Some of dem say...

CHORUS 1 *(As gossiper)* He have two woman expecting for him you know.

CHORUS 2   Is true?

CHORUS 3   I hear it was three.

FLORENTINE   William, love me or don't love me, but don't do me so...

CHORUS *(Sing reprise)* Love me or don't love me but don't do me so.

FLORENTINE   Misyé Misyé. *(WILLIAM goes to touch her.)* Pa touche mwen. (Don't touch me) *(FLORENTINE pulls away.)*

WILLIAM   Marnzèl Mamzèl. Pa fe sa. (Don't do that.)

FLORENTINE   Them things that you doing... They making me vex. You saying one thing... And doing the nex'... So, love me or don't love me but don't do me so!

WILLIAM   I love you.

(The CHORUS go back into the shadows. WILLIAM sits FLORENTINE down and sits down beside her.)

You know what I want?

FLORENTINE   What you want William?

WILLIAM   Jus' a woman who can be my friend, you know, a woman who not afraid to stand beside me and let me be a man.

FLORENTINE   An' what about a woman who want to do thing for herself... You would want her?

WILLIAM   But you wouldn't have to do anything for yourself girl, I will take care of you.

FLORENTINE   I know dat but I is a woman dat like to *do* things. My modder say don't do dat and dat is the thing I want to do. Look at me...I fall down in love with you and nobody can take that away from me.

WILLIAM *(Teasing)* Rebel woman!

FLORENTINE   Dat's me. *(She sings)*

I can climb coconut tree / like any somebody

I can climb coconut tree / Man what you want from me

I can climb coconut tree / like any somebody

I can climb coconut tree / Man what you want from me

I feel like there's something waiting for me.

CHORUS   Life's jus' starting.

FLORENTINE   Something calling eager for me.

CHORUS   Life jus' starting.

FLORENTINE   I not a one to study book but if I see something I like I
     hook. Aiiiieeeeeeeeeeee!
FLORENTINE/CHORUS
     I can climb coconut tree / like any somebody
     I can climb coconut tree / Man what you want from me
     I can climb coconut tree / like any somebody
     I can climb coconut tree / Man what you want from me.
FLORENTINE   I not the same like everybody.
CHORUS   Life jus' starting.
FLORENTINE   So if you think dat this woman easy.
CHORUS   Time we parting.
FLORENTINE   I'll stand beside you, if you stand beside me. If is I do.
     That's the way it will be. Aiiiiiiiieeeeeeee.
FLORENTINE/CHORUS   I can climb coconut tree
     (Repeats to end)

CHORUS move back. WILLIAM and FLORENTINE laugh with each other.

WILLIAM   You know why I like you?
FLORENTINE   Why?
WILLIAM   Because you different.
FLORENTINE   What you talking about?
WILLIAM   You don't understand what I'm saying? People like to talk.
     They like to make you into who they say you is – not who you really is. I
     like you because you is you and you take me as I am.
FLORENTINE   I can't change the way you is.
WILLIAM   See what I mean. You'd be surprised at how many people
     want to change me... *(He looks at FLORENTINE.)* An' what you want
     Marnzèl Florentine? What you want in life?
FLORENTINE *(Taken aback)* Me? Want in life... I don't know... peace. Just
     peace.
     (WILLIAM puts his arm around her.)
WILLIAM   I hope you can find that wid me.
     *(The sound of sea waves lapping. The two of them look out to sea.
     WILLIAM looks troubled.)*
FLORENTINE   What?
WILLIAM   I want... I want to do something with my life, you know. All
     people take me for round here is good time. Good time William...
FLORENTINE   Not me.

WILLIAM   No – not you. You have something there. *(He looks afraid)* I never stick quite so tight before, to someone.

FLORENTINE   Chet up, you make me 'fraid.

WILLIAM   I make you 'fraid? Ou ka fè mwen ka ka a sou mwen! (You scare the shit outta me.) *(FLORENTINE laughs)* I serious. I've always been able to take control before, you know, but wid you anything could happen.

(FLORENTINE puts her head on his lap. Silence. He sighs. The sound of sea waves lapping gets louder.)

You think there's something more Florentine? Something more out there?

FLORENTINE   England you mean?

WILLIAM   England. America. Wherever you think is worth taking a chance like the rest of them?

FLORENTINE   I don't know. *(She looks at WILLIAM)* It depends on what you want.

WILLIAM   I want... I don't know what I want, but it's not here. There's got to be something more.

FLORENTINE   And you think England is that something.

WILLIAM   I don't know. It was just a thought.

FLORENTINE   What about me?

WILLIAM   I didn't say I was really going. I jus' say... Everybody going – I don't want to miss. If there's something out there I want my share.

FLORENTINE   And me now?

WILLIAM   I didn't say I was going. I jus' thinking, that's all.

CHORUS   Tell him

FLORENTINE *(Hesitates)* I'm expecting.

CHORUS   Bam!

WILLIAM   What you talking about?

FLORENTINE   Mwen anset. (I'm pregnant.)

WILLIAM   No!

(The sound of sea waves. WILLIAM looks out to sea.)

FLORENTINE   But I can't keep you. I know dat.

CHORUS   You like a bird. I want to hold you but if I hold you I might hold you too tight and cripple you, you know, stop you from flying...

WILLIAM   I love you.

(FLORENTINE hesitates.) Say it.

FLORENTINE *(Does not look at him)* Then don't go.

WILLIAM *(Quietly)* OK... I won't.

CHORUS   Aieeeeeeeeee! / Come likkle birdy
Let me hol' you / I won't hol' too tight

Squeeze you likkle breath away,

Won't make you die.

Jus' want to... / You is me...

Come / Come / Come let me...

Aieeeeeeeee...fly.

(They giggle)

And de belly grow and de belly grow bigger.

Seh de belly grow de belly grow fatter.

And de wind blow / De wind blow harder

It blow so hard / She fall down

BAM

She had anodder one / Seh wha?

She had anodder one / Awhoi!

And de man?

(WILLIAM and FLORENTINE separate.)

Which man? / Oh – William!

He gone – / To Englan'

(The moon glows. CHORUS whisper.)

They say the moon is a man with a *dirty* face.

EFFELINE *(Rocks in the chair)* Florentine-oi you wid chil' again?

FLORENTINE   Wi Manman.

EFFELINE   Florentine, ou pa las fè zanfan? (Florentine, you don' tired make children?)

FLORENTINE   William say he will sen' for me when he save enough money in Englan'.

EFFELINE   You and who he going to sen' for? All the woman who have children for William waiting for the same letter. Fanm ou sot wi! Woman you foolish! William don' worry wid you now. He gone!

FLORENTINE   Manman I going Englan'.

EFFELINE *(Smokes her pipe and rocks in the chair.)* Why you want to go England, ou lé William ba'w pli zanfan? (for William to give you more children?)

FLORENTINE   William will not give me more children Manman! Manman everybody say if you want to be somebody then Englan' is the place to be. Well maybe is too late for meself but I want my children to be somebody. I want my children to learn.

EFFELINE   Pwenmyè bagay, (First *you* must learn to respect yourself)

FLORENTINE   Give me a chance nah Maman. Let me make something of the mistake I do already.

EFFELINE   So how far you think you going to get wid a child and a big bouden? (belly)

FLORENTINE   You think me is a person can starve. Me? Ma Effeline child? Englan' call me Maman and I make my mind up I going.

EFFELINE   Ében alé, (Then go but leave the children with me)

FLORENTINE   How can I leave my children?

EFFELINE   If you mus' go then wait 'til the child born, then go England. Find your way, if that is what you want. I will look after the children for you 'til you ready then after I will send them for you. But don't go chasing William, girl. Have respect for yourself.

FLORENTINE   Yes Manman.

CHORUS   Hear de call. Florentine-oi Florentine-oi. Come a Englan' vini. Florentine-oi Florentine-oi. Come a Englan' come.

(The sound of sea waves lapping. FLORENTINE follows the call.)

First the ocean breathed / And it hissed and called her name
Beckoned her, coaxed her, tempted her
Gave her dreams wild wishes and hopes.
Made her leave her home / Throwing herself upon it
Floating... away.
But as she left / Her stomach turned
And jumped and called out silently
And she expelled the sour demon
Coming at her throat / Expelled her to the salt sea
And left unclad / Unarmed / Unprepared
She harboured in this no man's land
And longed for home.

CHORUS sing to the tune of 'I sen' you a letter'.

Whoooooi huh whoooooi huh huh whoooooi whoooooi
Whoooooi huh whoooooi huh huh whoooooi whoooooi

One of the CHORUS step forward as TANTY PIPPIN. FLORENTINE and PIPPIN behave as if on a boat. They are both being sick.

FLORENTINE   Whoooooooi whoooooi

TANTY PIPPIN   Whoooooi whoooo. He want to kill me! Cyril send for me so dat I would drown in this ocean. Son of a ba... Whoooooi! *(She is sick)* What dem people put in my food!

FLORENTINE   Pippin go lie down I will look after you.

TANTY PIPPIN   I like to be in the kitchen when stranger cooking... mmmmm... mmmmm. *(She clicks her throat, then looks hard at FLORENTINE)* Is me should be looking after you. Your modder leave you in bad hands. The hands of Judas. A traitor. What you think she will say when she find out is me dat give you de address of dat Satan William?

FLORENTINE   I did beg you to ask Cyril to look out for him when he reach Englan'.

TANTY PIPPIN   That is not the point. The law say you must respect.

FLORENTINE   Which law is dat Pippin?

TANTY PIPPIN   The law that say you must respect yourself. You see respect is a good word in life but it look like I forget it since I leave my island...

(TANTY PIPPIN is sick again.)

FLORENTINE   Quick give me the address before you change your mind.

TANTY PIPPIN   Is in my purse. Take it. I don't want the stain of the sin on my hands. Take it. *(She curses CYRIL as the boat rocks)* Kaval! Vyé neg! He sen' for me to come on boat and he know well I can't swim. He want me dead yes. Bondyé!

FLORENTINE   You lucky. Cyril sen' for you.

TANTY PIPPIN   What you going Englan' for FIorentine, really eh?

FLORENTINE   I want my babies to be somebody...

TANTY PIPPIN   Your babies? *(FLORENTINE looks out at the sea)*

FLORENTINE   Yes... *(TANTY PIPPIN goes back to CHORUS. The CHORUS hum calypso tune merrily as they push FLORENTINE in front of WILLIAM, who steps out of the CHORUS.)*

CHORUS *(Sing)* Mister Mister I love you so... *(CHORUS laugh)* Aiiiiiieeeee! *(A light drum beat like rain starting to fall is underneath WILLIAM and FLORENTINE'S words. The drumbeat builds up marking the tension between them.)*

WILLIAM   So is fight you come to fight. *(FLORENTINE says nothing)* Come let me take you home. Is not so them does carry on in this country. They keep their affair private.

FLORENTINE *(Shouting)* So is why you never button your fly if is private you want to keep it!

WILLIAM   Woman is not de place for... I have a room come.

FLORENTINE   You and who have the room?

WILLIAM   Me and a... friend. She... am... cook for me and the like.

FLORENTINE   In anodder woman place you taking me?

WILLIAM   So where you want me to take you? Woman shut up.

FLORENTINE   I don't going.

WILLIAM   Is what you mean you stan' up wid your face, humph humph you-not-going? Well stay nah! *(Pause. WILLIAM softens)* Is not easy Florentine... You think is easy?

FLORENTINE   You forget me.

WILLIAM   No...I jus' change track.

FLORENTINE   Why?

WILLIAM   Because I cannot look after you the way I want... You cannot see that?

FLORENTINE   How you know? I tell you I want you to look after me? I can take care of myself... and you too. I can do that William...

WILLIAM   ... yes. *(awkward pause)* So how de children?

FLORENTINE   Fine.

WILLIAM *(Points ahead)* Look my place there.

FLORENTINE   In anodder woman place WilIiam, how you expect me to stay?

WlLLIAM   Come meet her, she a nice woman. English you know. She treat me good. Since I come in this country she take me in.

FLORENTINE   William no.

WILLIAM   You come and look for me and now you find me. *(WILLIAM goes ahead of her)* I home. *(FLORENTINE hesitates then follows him in. The drumming builds. CHORUS voices join in.)*

CHORUS 1   La pli ka tonbé (Rain falling)

CHORUS 2   I fwèt (It cold)

CHORUS 3   Way-ya-yay (Goodness me)

CHORUS 4   Mi fwédi (It's freezing!)

(This is repeated three times. The fourth time it is said in English.)

CHORUS 1   Rain falling

CHORUS 2   It cold

CHORUS 3   Way-ya-yay

CHORUS 4   It's freezing!

(FLORENTINE is led back to bed by the CHORUS.)

FLORENTINE   I lose myself.

CHORUS *(They laugh)* I pèdi ko'y (She lose herself)

FLORENTINE   ... somewhere.

CHORUS   ... between the sky and the sea. Somehow.

FLORENTINE   I...

CHORUS   ... lost sight of –

FLORENTINE   ... me...

CHORUS   And de wind blow / de wind blow harder
It blow so hard / She fall down BAM!

She had anodder one? / She had anodder one.

(The CHORUS give FLORENTINE a bundle which she rocks like a baby. WILLIAM walks away into the shadows.)

You made mountains part when you caressed my thigh. I travelled on seas when I looked into your eyes. And now you turn away.

FLORENTINE *(Sings)* Brown skin girl stay home and mind baby

Brown skin girl stay home and mind baby

If I sail on a sailing boat and I don't come back

Stay home and mind baby.

(GRACE and CLEMENTINE sing, the distance between them is big.)

GRACE/CLEM *(Sing)* You and I / You and I / You and I /

You and I Sharing the sky... *(The singing is interrupted by a baby crying.)*

BIANCA   Aaaaaaaaaaagh. *(GRACE looks at BIANCA.)*

GRACE   She was like one of them tiny tears dolls that cried real tears... only *she* never really cried. She just made the noise.

BIANCA   Aaaaaaaaaagh.

GRACE   ... and I would take the 'kerchief and wipe her nose until the snot reach her temple. And it would stay there and dry up on her face until night time when I had to bathe her. And then she'd cry.

BIANCA   Aaaaaaaaaagh.

GRACE   ... and tell Mammy I do her mischievous.

CHORUS   Méchansté! (Mischievous!)

BIANCA   Mummy Grace pinched me!

GRACE   Chet up before I bite you!

BIANCA *(About to cry)* I'm telling!

GRACE   Tell nah! See if you don't find my foot in your stomach!

(BIANCA smiles.)

BIANCA   It's not my fault!

CHORUS   Sé pa fot-li. (It's not her fault.) *(CHORUS give BIANCA airmail letter. BIANCA gives letter to GRACE.)*

BIANCA   It's not my fault. *(GRACE snatches the letter.)*

GRACE   I tell you don't... *(GRACE beats BIANCA)* don't touch my things eh! Mmmm!

(GRACE sits at the foot of the bed and looks over her letters. Light drum beat. CHORUS join in as before.)

CHORUS 1   Lapli ka tonbé (Rain falling)

CHORUS 2   i fwèt (It cold)

CHORUS 3   Way-ya-yay (Goodness me)

CHORUS 4   Mi fwedi (It's freezing)

(This is repeated several times. The sound of street traffic merges into this. BIANCA picks up a satchel. The CHORUS put GRACE beside BIANCA. GRACE and BIANCA look as if they are waiting for a bus. They are both cold. GRACE looks at her watch.)

GRACE   There should be one coming. *(BIANCA sits down)* Get up from there.

BIANCA   I'm tired.

GRACE   You want to get piles! Get up!

(The CHORUS make the sounds of kids chanting from where they are in the shadows.)

CHORUS   Blackie! Golliwogs! Nig Nog!

GRACE/BIANCA *(In unison)* White Trash! White Trash!

CHORUS   Go back to where you come from!

GRACE   T'jou Manman'w! (Swear word)

BIANCA   English Rubbish!

GRACE   And what you is? *(BIANCA shrugs her shoulders.)*

BIANCA *(Shivering she looks over at the chanters)* I'm not... English. *(Pause)* Grace tell me about that place again. *(GRACE is trying to get warm – she puts her arm over BIANCA'S shoulder warming her sister up.)*

GRACE   Well, it hot!

BIANCA   ... and sweaty?

GRACE   Sometimes.

BIANCA   What else? Did you swim everyday?

GRACE   Most days if you want.

BIANCA   And Clementine?

GRACE   What, my sister... my sister always making mischievous. She not afraid to go any place and do anything. If my sister was here eh... you think them children would trouble us! You mad!

BIANCA   Ou fol!

GRACE   What you say?

BIANCA *(Embarrassed)* You mad.

GRACE   No, say it in patwa again...

BIANCA   Ou fol?

GRACE   È è Bianca ou ka vini bono (Eh, eh Bianca you coming good.)

BIANCA *(Pleased with herself)* Tar...

GRACE   What else you know?

BIANCA   Tjou manman'w, tjou papa'w! (Swear word)

GRACE   Don't let Mammy hear you sat dat nah!

BIANCA   I know what it means too...

GRACE *(Interrupts)* Hush your mouth! *(Pause)* You know what a salop is? *(BIANCA nods. GRACE holds BIANCA'S hand. They run to where the tormentors were calling from and shout together.)*

GRACE/BIANCA   Salop! Run! *(GRACE and BIANCA run. Drumbeat. The CHORUS join in.)*

CHORUS 1   Lapli ka tonbé.

CHORUS 2   i fwèt.

CHORUS 3   Way-ya-yay

CHORUS 4   Mi fwédi.

The CHORUS and drumming continue during ritual. Ritual: CLEMENTINE in the Caribbean shack lights a candle. She takes the doll from underneath her bed and bashes the leg against the head. FLORENTINE writhes in the bed. The sound of an ambulance siren. TANTY PIPPIN, a member of the CHORUS steps forward, GRACE and BIANCA stop in front of her.

GRACE/BIANCA   Good afternoon Tanty Pippin.

TANTY PIPPIN   Well is not so good... See all you Mammy not well but she'll be all right. They say is a stroke but she'll be O.K. You have to take care of all you Mammy. Have to help in the house, have to look after her... *(GRACE tries to push past TANTY PIPPIN into FLORENTINE'S bedroom. BIANCA does not try to enter.)*

BIANCA *(In spotlight)* I hate the smell of soft candle and bay rum. It makes me think of stuffy rooms, drawn curtains, potties full of piss.

CHORUS   Under the bed / Under the bed.

FLORENTINE   I never forget you Clementine. I just had to let go. Make you grow yourself, because it would have make me mad to think about you every day.

CLEMENTINE *(Talking to doll)* But I thought of you every day. Thought of you, thought of my sister. Every morning I making my trip to the post office and coming back without my letter. I did think may be it lose so I did keep writing all you asking when I was going to come and meet all you. And then I get a letter. Oh yes I get a letter. You tell me how I have a new sister and how you cannot afford to send for me... me and my child.

FLORENTINE   Mwen pate ni lanjan... I didn't have money.

CLEMENTINE   You run leave me Mammy. Well you won't run again.

CHORUS   Learn to stay / Learn to stay put
When the foot gone / You can't run again
Learn to stay / Learn to stay put
When the foot gone / You can't run again.

FLORENTINE   Ayiiiiiiiiii! Ayiiiiiiiiiii!
Ah timoun / Sa'w ka fè sa pou?
Oh child / Why you doing that for?
Kité mwen djab! (Leave me devil!)
Kité mwen! / Kité mwen djab / Kité mwen!

The sound of sea waves lapping gently, accompanied by loud sighs coming from the CHORUS. From this BIANCA'S light voice emerges. She is in her earlier position with the trousers.

BIANCA   Running eases the tension. Makes me feel at home with myself. Makes me relax with what I know to be me. *(CHORUS sighs)* The sound of breathing, you know... the sound of something coming from me, coming out of me... something that's mine. I don't know where I am going or why. I just want to –
CHORUS   Run!
BIANCA   I ran for the school / ran for the county
Wanted to run for the country
CHORUS   Which country?
BIANCA *(Hesitates)*... mine. I ran for myself – I don't know... ran for my life. Ran away – from my mother. She...
FLORENTINE *(To BIANCA)* ... loved you
BIANCA/CHORUS   Too much
BIANCA   Loved me
CHORUS   For everybody
BIANCA *(To FLORENTINE)* Loved me because you couldn't love yourself any more. And if you can't love yourself how can you love me?
CHORUS   And if you can't love yourself how can you love me? *(Pause)* She lost herself somewhere between the sky and the sea. Somehow she lost sight of –
BIANCA/CLEM/GRACE   Me!
BIANCA   I ran for my own good, ran for him. *(Pause)* I... loved somebody.
(CHORUS look at BIANCA)
I did. He made me feel like a human being.
(She looks at FLORENTINE)
Not merely an extension of you.
FLORENTINE   How many times.
BIANCA/CHORUS   What?
FLORENTINE   Did I say.

BIANCA/CHORUS What?
FLORENTINE Be careful?
BIANCA *(Controlled)* Must have been at least one million, mother.
CHORUS And how many times.
BIANCA Did I say – Let me live my life. See...
CHORUS Yeh?
BIANCA You'd had yours. *(Pause)* I lost someone – myself, and I thought I had found her, this person I thought I'd lost.
CHORUS Yeh?
BIANCA I thought I found her.
CHORUS Where?
BIANCA She was there.
CHORUS Where?
BIANCA Dead centre. Between his temples – his eyebrows, where the hairs nearly join.

Drum beat. Everybody is animated in their positions. EFFELINE in rocking-chair smoking her pipe. FLORENTINE in bed. GRACE at foot of bed. CLEMENTINE washing. BIANCA with trousers.

PART 2
Drum beat and CHORUS speak as everybody is animated in their positions. EFFELINE in rocking-chair smoking her pipe. FLORENTINE in bed. GRACE at foot of bed. CLEMENTINE washing. BIANCA with trousers. From this image the four women move to their next positions. EFFELINE in rocking-chair watching all. FLORENTINE in bed writhing. GRACE is massaging FLORENTINE'S limbs and rubbing her with bay rum. GRACE looks tired. CLEMENTINE with doll passing her hands above its body. BIANCA still with trousers watches GRACE.

CHORUS 1 Lapli ka tonbé (Rain falling)
CHORUS 2 i fwèt (It cold)
CHORUS 3 Way-ya-yay (Goodness me)
CHORUS 4 Mi fwèdi (It's freezing!)
(The CHORUS repeat this several times with the drumming.)
CHORUS Run! *(GRACE runs to BIANCA.)*
GRACE Hi, I had to get out of that house. That bloody woman!
BIANCA What's up now?
GRACE I've got to go home, Bianca, I've got to go home to Dominica!
BIANCA What's up Grace?

GRACE *(Almost in tears)* I got a letter right. Ma Effeline is sick – How long have I been here right, what do I have to do? What do I have to do to make her happy?

BIANCA   You do it to yourself Grace, I told you from time!

GRACE   I'm there for her all the time Bianca.

BIANCA   I know, you don't have to tell *me*.

GRACE   I just feel like I have to go to Dominica... It might be the last chance I get.

BIANCA   Go you silly bugger go! Don't worry about Mum. Tanty Pippin's here, I'm here.

GRACE   She just makes me feel like I'm leaving her... She makes me feel so guilty to leave her, like I'm leaving her with nobody. I'm always here for her Bianca. I don't have a life of my own.

BIANCA   Ah, take no notice of her. You know what she's like.

GRACE   She pisses me off. Bloody woman! *(Pause)* How are you anyway?

BIANCA   Ah – O.K.

GRACE   Sure?

BIANCA   Mmmmm. How much is it to go to Dominica now?

GRACE   I don't know... I don't care I'm going.

BIANCA   I can help you out if you want.

GRACE   Thanks sis... Are you sure you O.K? *(GRACE takes the trousers from BIANCA'S lap.)*

BIANCA   How do you know if you're having a nervous breakdown?... See I couldn't have one because I wouldn't know if I was doing it right.

GRACE   Baby... come here. *(GRACE hugs BIANCA)* What's happened?

BIANCA   He took all his things this morning.

GRACE   Oh, love.

BIANCA   But that's not it. I don't know how I feel. I don't know if I'm sad or relieved... I don't know how to react.

GRACE   Come 'ere. What – did he just go?

BIANCA   No. *(Pause)* I asked him to. *(Pause. BIANCA looks embarrassed.)*

GRACE   How's school?

BIANCA   Fine. *(Pause)* Boring! *(Pause)*... ah I'm just fed up. It's like I don't have any reasons any more. I don't know why I'm doing anything. I don't know why I'm here. *(Pause)* What's it all about Grace?

GRACE   We all go through it.

BIANCA   Do we? It just seems such a waste...everything was so right with me and Malcolm.

GRACE   Can't have been...

BIANCA   ... no. *(Pause)*... but he feels so safe.

GRACE   So what happened?

BIANCA   I don't know... there's got to be something more – more than just getting up in the morning and knowing what it's going to be like for the next forty years... same face... open your eyes and the same... no surprises...

GRACE *(Interrupting)* Some people would...

BIANCA *(Interrupting not having heard)* Is that what it's all about?

GRACE   I don't know.

BIANCA   Are we supposed to just accept that? Is that it?

GRACE   You're luckier than most.

BIANCA   So I've just got to accept this... Grace there might be something more!

GRACE   Yeh...and there might not... *(Pause)* Just get on with it Bianca – That's life... that's how it is.

BIANCA   Look you might want to waste your life looking after Mum but I want more.

GRACE   Yeh, you always want... Sometimes you just get on with it because you have to.

BIANCA   So what's the point of it all, if that's how it is? Everybody wants something... even Mum wanted something. She lived her life...

FLORENTINE *(In bed)* Kité mwen djab! Kité mwen!

BIANCA   What about you Grace?

GRACE   I don't know... home I suppose. I want to go home...
      (CLEMENTINE throws the doll on the floor. FLORENTINE reacts.)

FLORENTINE   Clemo... i

CHORUS   Hee hee hee *(Whispers)* Clemo... i

CLEMENTINE runs to pick up the doll. At first concerned, she then puts the doll under the bed matter of factly. Drum beat. A cock crows and an alarm clock rings. GRACE and BIANCA take these sounds as signals to move. GRACE picks up a suitcase and goes to CLEMENTINE'S Caribbean shack area. BIANCA picks up suitcase and stands outside FLORENTINE'S room ready to go in. The CHORUS sing to the tune of 'I sen' you a letter'.

CHORUS   Whooooooooi huh whooooooi huh huh whooooooi whooooi. Whooooooi huh whooooooi huh huh whooooooi whooooi.
      I sen' you a letter / An' get the reply
      Ma Effeline / is going to a different (world)
      Cross over the sea / but you can't get to me

Ma Effeline / It seem you go into a different (world)
Whoooooi huh whoooooi huh huh whoooooooi
It seem you going into a different (world)
Whoooooi huh whoooooi huh huh whoooooooi
It seem you going into a different (world)

The CHORUS hum the tune as FLORENTINE speaks and EFFELINE leaves the stage. The oil-lamp in FLORENTINE'S room lights up as EFFELINE leaves.

FLORENTINE I dreamed my modder passed away. She couldn't see me you know – couldn't make out my face... said the light was going like there was no tomorrow and yesterday... she say yesterday was hiding somewhere, I can't remember.

Lights up on FLORENTINE'S bedroom. BIANCA puts the suitcase down and comes inside the bedroom. She opens the curtain. An oil-lamp is burning on the dressing-table. FLORENTINE Coughing.

FLORENTINE I know you don't like this. I know dat. *(BIANCA goes out of the room.)* It's not Grace fault. Is like something jus' call her. She and Effeline was close. *(BIANCA comes in with a basin of water and a face cloth. She puts it down beside the bed.)* I don't want to make you late for work... Don't be vex BiBi. Ah BiBi pa fe sa! (Ah BiBi don't be like that!) *(BIANCA gives the face cloth to FLORENTINE. FLORENTINE washes her face.)* She wasn't going to go you know. Is me... I say go. *(BIANCA hands FLORENTINE a towel.)* Don't be like dat Bianca... I'm your mother. Mwen se Manman'w! *(BIANCA gets out a tube of ointment and rubs some into her mother's leg.)* You don't have to stay. Tanty Pippin say she'll stay wid me... if you cannot. I know you don't like the smell... *(BIANCA puts her hands in the basin of water and washes them.)* I glad you come though... It's been a long time since we spend time together, jus' you and me... *(Pause. BIANCA takes the basin.)* I don't want you to fink you have to do everything for me you know... *(BIANCA leaves with the basin.)* I know you have your life – *(Shouts after BIANCA)* You and fing O.K? *(Pause)* You don't want to talk to me? Is alright. I don't blame you. *(BIANCA comes back in with her coat. She puts lipstick on)* It not for long BiBi. Grace soon come back. *(BIANCA stands by the door. She does not look at FLORENTINE.)*
BIANCA Bye.
FLORENTINE Bye love. *(BIANCA leaves)* Bye.

Lights fade.

*Lights up on the inside of a Caribbean shack. CLEMENTINE goes inside,
ahead of GRACE, carrying a suitcase and opens the shutters. She then goes
into the kitchen. GRACE stands in the doorway carrying hand luggage. She
is looking around the room fondly. The rocking-chair is now empty. One of
the CHORUS steps forward as DENNIS. He comes inside with another
suitcase.*

DENNIS *(To GRACE)* You still don't remember me? *(GRACE smiles politely
and shakes her head.)*
GRACE   You look like somebody.
CLEMENTINE *(From kitchen)* Dennis get me some ice nah?
GRACE *(Looks at DENNIS trying to remember the face)* Dennis? Ti kwas
Dennis?

*(CLEMENTINE comes out of the kitchen with a container. She hands it to
DENNIS.)*

CLEMENTINE   An' tell everybody. *(She looks at GRACE with a smile)...*
tell them my sister reach... *(Spotlight on CLEMENTINE as DENNIS takes
the container, mutters.)* Sister... *(DENNIS gives GRACE a final smile,
then leaves.)*
GRACE   Dennis! Ti kwas Dennis... His face always crusty with dry
mango juice and his clothes always stain with yellow! Eh eh...
(CLEMENTINE looks her sister up and down.)
CLEMENTINE   Wè wè wè, look my sister! *(They hug loudly.)*
GRACE   Mèsyé Kwik
CLEMENTINE   Kwak
GRACE   Tim Tim.
CLEMENTINE   Bwa chèch! *(They laugh)* Turn around let me see you.
(GRACE spins) Mi boda! *(GRACE holds her bottom.)*
GRACE   You have it too!
CLEMENTINE *(She shakes her head.)* Mmm mmm not like that no sah!
GRACE   Effeline make sure she leave her trade mark.
CLEMENTINE   Shake it baby shake it! *(GRACE shakes her behind. They
laugh.)*
GRACE   I wish she could have jus' hold on, hold on jus' for me to see
her again and for her to know I turn out O.K...
*(GRACE goes to the rocking-chair and kneels down. She puts her head on
the seat. CLEMENTINE watches.)* It feels good to be back.

Lights fade.

Lights up on FLORENTINE'S room in England. FLORENTINE is staring into space. TANTY PIPPIN comes in with a pot of food and a tray and the phone.

TANTY PIPPIN   You must remind Bianca to keep the phone by your bed, I was trying to ring earlier.

FLORENTINE   È è Tanty, ou la? (Eh eh Tanty, you there then?)

TANTY PIPPIN   So... how she take to looking after her old mother? *(FLORENTINE tuts. TANTY teasing)* She don't like it!

FLORENTINE   It the worse thing that could happen.

TANTY PIPPIN   How's the feeling?

FLORENTINE   i la. (It there.) *(She fixes herself up on the bed.)* Foté do mwen suoplé Pippin. (Rub my back for me please Pippin.)

TANTY PIPPIN   *(TANTY PIPPIN massages FLORENTINE'S back)* So you don't know if Grace phone?

FLORENTINE   She don't have to phone I know already.

TANTY PIPPIN   Don't be foolish.

FLORENTINE   You think I have to have phone-call to know me Modder dead? *(Looking in pot)* What you cook?... ah latje bef. (... ah oxtail.)

TANTY PIPPIN   Ah you and your dream!

FLORENTINE   Don't laugh, love is dream that put us where we is.

TANTY PIPPIN   No dream carry me nowhere. If is dream that put you where you is I sorry for you. I don't waste my time on dream love, I too old for that. You carry on with your dreams. Your 'dream land'. Your 'dream boy' *(She tuts)*... run from life!

FLORENTINE   Pe tjou'w! (Swear word)

TANTY PIPPIN   *(Teasing)* William! William! William! Carry on with your stupidness.

FLORENTINE   Is dream that put us here!

TANTY PIPPIN   Dream bring us here! Which dream! You come here for dream? I come here for money!

FLORENTINE   *(Laughing)* You get your money? *(TANTY PIPPIN does not answer. She puts some food out on a plate humming to herself, 'Bridge Over Troubled Water'.)* Then don't bother cut your style on my dream. Is all I know an' is all I have and my dream never let me down yet.

TANTY PIPPIN   *(Singing to 'Bridge Over Troubled Waters' tune)*
Dream on silver bird, / Dream on by
Your time will come to fly...
(Teasing)
All your dreams will come your way.

The phone rings. FLORENTINE and TANTY PIPPIN look at the phone.
Lights fade.

Lights up on CLEMENTINE'S Caribbean shack. CLEMENTINE dusts the
rocking-chair carefully. CLEMETINE picks up MA EFFELINE'S pipe as if it
is a fragile person. CLEMENTINE sits down on the rocking-chair,
tentatively at first. GRACE comes in through the front door. She. catches
CLEMENTINE from the doorway. CLEMENTINE rocks comfortably as if
usurping the throne. GRACE shakes her head with disapproval. GRACE
coughs.

GRACE   I reversed the charges. *(CLEMENTINE gets up from the*
   chair and carries on cleaning it.)
CLEMENTINE   Oh. What she say?
GRACE   She sen' her love...
   (CLEMENTINE stops cleaning, registers what GRACE has said and then
   carries on cleaning the chair.)
CLEMENTINE   Dat all...
GRACE   No... no she say she know already.
CLEMENTINE   She know already... What she know?
GRACE   She say she dream it... She dream Ma Effeline dead already...
CLEMENTINE   What she know? She don't know nothing.
   (CLEMENTINE gets bottle of rum from under the bed, she wipes the dust
   from it. GRACE gets two glasses. They drink to MA EFFELINE.
   CLEMENTINE then flicks rum around the room blessing the space.
   GRACE fans herself.)
GRACE   Mi chalè! (Look heat!)
CLEMENTINE   What, you forget the heat! *(CLEMENTINE goes through*
   GRACE'S suitcase.) So what you bring for your old sister?
   (CLEMENTINE finds a dress and puts it on.) I can look pretty too you
   know. *(CLEMENTINE fixes her hair.)*
GRACE   Eh eh.
CLEMENTINE   Vini, mwen lé penyen chivé 'w! (Come let me do
   something with your hair!) *(GRACE sits between CLEMENTINE'S legs.)*
GRACE   Mind you tear my dress! *(CLEMENTINE gives GRACE a*
   dirty look and opens her legs wider. She greases GRACE'S scalp and
   begins to comb her hair)
CLEMENTINE   You 'member Mavis, *ugly* Mavis, face like a mongoose.
GRACE   Yeh...
CLEMENTINE   She married now.
GRACE   Eh eh.

CLEMENTINE   Yes child! She marry a business man pa pa. De man in oil child. Grace, pouki ou kité chivé'w chèch kon sa? (Grace why you let your hair go so dry?)

GRACE *(Feeling her hair)* It dry?

CLEMENTINE   Look like England steal my sister. When you go your hair was your back and your face was pretty pretty pretty.

GRACE   So my face ugly now?

CLEMENTINE   No... It jus' looking long, like you live your life already...

GRACE   Yes I live it what you want me to do wait for you... I didn't mean it so. It so it come out...

CLEMENTINE   Is alright. *(Pause)*

GRACE   Anyway, Mavis now, where she find dis business man? In her oil bed?

CLEMENTINE   Ou two hadi! (You too rude!) He was taking a tour my dear.

GRACE   Oh a tour. Still it don't matter how you put it is the same thing.

CLEMENTINE   Ki sa? (What?)

GRACE   She catch her fortune.

CLEMENTINE *(Distantly)* Mmmm mmmm...

GRACE   And where you was when Mavis make the move? Why you never come out in your pretty dress too?

CLEMENTINE   I was... busy.

GRACE   Busy wid what? I mean who... You and Robbie was still playing games under Maman bed? *(CLEMENTINE hits GRACE on the head with the comb.)*

GRACE   'member when Ma Effeline catch you? She push de broom under her bed and put her hand in front of her eyes.

GRACE/CLEM *(Mimicking)* Soti soti soti! (Get out, get out, get out!) *(They laugh.)*

GRACE   'member... *(singing)*
Down to the carpet you must go / Like a blackbird in the... air.
(CLEMENTINE joins in. They relive it.)

GRACE/CLEM   Rise up stand up on your feet / And choose the one you love the best
When you marry you tell me so
Firs' the boy second the girl / Sunday after Sunday school
Kiss kiss and say goodbye...

They laugh, look at each other and hug. Lights fade.

Lights up on FLORENTINE'S room in England. BIANCA comes into FLORENTINE'S room. She is wearing her coat.

BIANCA   Hi, everything O.K?
FLORENTINE   Mwen la. (Fine.) *(BIANCA notices phone near bed.)*
BIANCA   Anybody ring?
FLORENTINE   Grace phone.
BIANCA   She reached O.K?
FLORENTINE   Mmmm... mmmm. Ma Effeline passed away in her sleep...
BIANCA   Oh... *(She gives her mother a gentle hug)* You O.K?
FLORENTINE   Sé lavi. (Is life love.) Oh and thing phone...
BIANCA *(Looks at FLORENTINE)* Malcolm?
FLORENTINE   Yes, Malcolm.
BIANCA   Did he leave a message?
FLORENTINE   No. You two O.K?
BIANCA   Yeh... Tanty leave any oxtail?
FLORENTINE   i pa té jè. (It wasn't much.) You did want nah? The
    Chinese open... *(BIANCA looks distant)* School was alright today?
BIANCA   O.K. *(BIANCA looks at the burning lamp)* Does that thing
    have to be burning all the time now?
FLORENTINE   Yes... until she find her way. Is a custom. You don't
    understand but is a custom.
BIANCA *(Teasing)* What would happen if I blew it out?
FLORENTINE   Anyen. (Nothing.)
BIANCA   Nothing?
FLORENTINE   Well maybe, I don't know... Is jus' lost... lost spirit, you
    know like when you don't know where you going...
BIANCA   A lost soul...
FLORENTINE   Is dat!
BIANCA   How do you know if she's found the light?
FLORENTINE   Mwen pa sav. (I don't know) I jus' hoping...
BIANCA   And if she doesn't find it... *(giggling)* is she just floating
    around sort of...?
FLORENTINE   Is so they make us believe but I don't know... I don't
    know... I used to think I know everything but Bibi your Mammy getting
    old and I not so sure again... but I used to be young and sure at one time,
    but the things I was sure about was the things I ended up being not so sure
    about and the things I wasn't sure about was the things I wish I had been
    sure about because then I might not be where I am today... *(BIANCA
    laughs. FLORENTINE laughs with her.)* You understand what I'm saying?
    (She holds BIANCA'S hand.) He's a man, you know, and you have to let

him be his own person because... he cannot be anybody else... *(She turns BIANCA'S face to face her own.)*... and you self can only be you...

Lights fade.

Lights up on Caribbean shack. GRACE is unpacking. CLEMENTINE is helping her.

GRACE   Your boys mus' be big now!

CLEMENTINE   Wait... *(CLEMENTINE takes the Bible from under her pillow. From it she takes out two photographs hidden between the pages)* Look Philip – handsome eh? and George favour his father eh? They with Robbie now in the States – I should be happy – they studying...

GRACE   No chance of you and Robbie...?

CLEMENTINE   he go to the States it was to find work... He find wife... Look like everybody forget me when they leave.

GRACE   Is not forget they forget... Is jus'

CLEMENTINE   What?

GRACE   Anyway I never forget you. *(CLEMENTINE turns the volume up on the radio – Cadance music.)*

CLEMENTINE   'member this one! *(CLEMENTINE dances like MA EFFELINE)* Is so Maman dance! *(GRACE joins in.)*

GRACE   Is not so is so. You forget man!

CLEMENTINE *(Impressed)* Eh eh you can still move.

GRACE   Now that's something you cannot forget!

CLEMENTINE   Is true you cannot lose that easy.

GRACE   Easy? You think England easy? England not easy love. Clementine you don't know cold. When cold hold you you can lose anything... but not easy!

CLEMENTINE   Anything?

GRACE   I tell you everything God give you can go wid one wind up your skirt!

CLEMENTINE   You sure it not your brain that freeze off...

GRACE   You think is joke. You don't see how my hair drop. I hear some man say it make their thing come small small small.

CLEMENTINE   What!

GRACE   Cold is serious business man I telling you.

CLEMENTINE   If is so bad why you never come home? *(Pause)*

GRACE   I never know how... and England is a place can hold you back. You play games with yourself... with your mind... You never do what you plan to do... always something holding your back. Like here you want to bathe eh? You get up you go in river you bathe... You want to eat, you pick a fruit, whatever you find you eat. Over there you want to bathe you must have money to heat up water and to eat... you may as well forget it if you don't have money... Clemo-i is a different world. If you don't have money you stay put.

CLEMENTINE   Is the same wherever you is.

GRACE   Is not the same nah. When you poor in England you poor. When you don't have money here is rich your rich. Is den when you eat food. Look at you and your bananas now, you plant your banana, cut them, package them, sell them. Is your life, you well happy.

CLEMENTINE   Yes I well happy... You defrost yet. You sure your brain don't melt? Look like you was in England too long for true.

GRACE   I change?

CLEMENTINE   A little... no your face a little fuller maybe... I don't know you must change. What about me?

GRACE   You don't change nah. You could never change! You still adventurous?

CLEMENTINE   Is an adventure to get out of bed on a morning?

GRACE   Could be?

CLEMENTINE   Then I adventurous. *(CLEMENTINE laughs)* I make the most of things that's all... *(GRACE finishes with the clothes. They start to straighten the bedspread.)*

GRACE   You know when you lose something Clem and no matter where you look you cannot find that thing.

CLEMENTINE   Like the time you clean Ma Effeline pipe and you don't know where you put it...

(GRACE picks up the pipe and smells it.)

GRACE   Mmmm... mmmm I use to dream of this smell. I use to love clean that pipe... Well when I lose it I did know it wasn't far because I never left the room with it. I know I would come across it again... *(She smiles at CLEMENTINE)* one day.

Lights fade.

Lights up on FLORENTINE'S room in England. BIANCA is still by the bed.

FLORENTINE *(Shivering)* Pon bayrum... Ia ban mwen. (Take the bay rum for me.) *(BIANCA gives the bay rum to her mother and is about to leave.)* Ou pa ka foté mwen? (You not going to rub me?)

BIANCA   I... I've got some work to do... books to mark. *(BIANCA takes the bay rum reluctantly and rubs FLORENTINE'S neck and head quickly.)*

FLORENTINE   I ever tell you about when I first come to this country?

BIANCA   Yeh, Mum yeh...

FLORENTINE   I wasn't much older than you – and I came here – like I
had a itch inside of me to see what the world had to offer. I always like
that... I always looking for something. *(BIANCA puts the top back on the
bottle. FLORENTINE holds her hand to stop her from leaving.)* You know
when I was small it was my brother used to take care of me... take me all
about put me on his shoulder and jus' walk. Mammy use to be working in
the distillery in town. Everybody I know, all the children about same age
like me is their Grannie used to bring them up and when I ask my Mammy
why I never have a Grannie she never mix her words, she say her mother
was dead and my Daddy mother never believe I was his on account of my
skin being so black. Is then I learn the meaning of the word bastard.
(BIANCA hesitates then fixes FLORENTINE'S pillow.) And me and my
brother Jessop, we would sit on the road late at night and he would talk to
me. My brother Jessop, he brought me up... tell me to be strong in life.
Jessop. Jessop was my first mother. He didn't know woman. He was a
mako. What you call them again? Homo what?

BIANCA   ... sexual?

FLORENTINE   Yes is so he was and some people did laugh... but I did
love him more than anything in the world – his gold teeth smile, the way
he walk... Everything about him I respected. *(BIANCA smiles. She gets
comfortable on the bed.)* He used to call me 'Lagwa', the fight, because I
was the only twenty-one year old woman he know that didn't have
children yet. I *was* a fighter, a real how you call it? Tom boy? I had no use
for a man. I was strong. I could do most things a man could do but
Mammy, Mammy did want me to be like other woman. Make children, be
a wife ha... Well I make children, did all the things I had to do, played the
part... but all I wanted to do was –

BIANCA   Run?

FLORENTINE   You know me because you is me. *(Pause. FLORENTINE
looks at BIANCA and smiles.)* So, you and thing...

BIANCA   Malcolm.

FLORENTINE   Yeh... how's it?

BIANCA   I don't know.

(The CHORUS pull BIANCA away from FLORENTINE.)

FLORENTINE   Sometimes it make sense to jus... let go.

CHORUS   And run! / For if we never ran.
We would never feel the breeze against our cheeks
Or hear the gentle buzz of summer flying past our ears
And oh... / What a loss that would be.

FLORENTINE   I forget. I didn't forget nah I jus'...

BIANCA   Forgot. Wrapped up in him.
CHORUS   She forget herself.
BIANCA   I didn't forget I just...
CHORUS   Forgot.
BIANCA   That before I met him I was somebody else. Not quite whole but somebody. There was a yesterday. There was a time before now and I came from somewhere, once...
CHORUS   She didn't forget / She just –
BIANCA   Forgot.
          (CHORUS giggle. FLORENTINE laughs in bed. The rocking-chair moves.)
CHORUS   Ou pa ni pou lonbliyé ko'w. (You shouldn't forget yourself.)
GRACE/CLEM   i lonbliyé ko'y *(GRACE and CLEMENTINE giggle.)* i lonbliyé ko'y
FLORENTINE/GRACE/CLEM/BIANCA   She forgot herself.
CHORUS   Remember –
FLORENTINE/GRACE/CLEM/BIANCA   Me.

Cadance music is playing in the background. The drummer leads. Spotlight on BIANCA.

CHORUS   Hear de call / Bianca-oi Bianca-oi vini!
          Come girl come / Come girl come
BIANCA   I didn't know what I was looking for. I didn't know what I would find.
FLORENTINE   Peace...
CHORUS   ... of mind. Peace of mind...

Cadance music gets loud. CHORUS make fète. They dance, blow whistles. Celebration. As the revelling comes to a close, lights fade. The moon appears. The sound of sea waves lapping. BIANCA follows the call.)

CHORUS
          First the sky appeared / dispelling from it rays of hope,
          tormenting my mutancy, / ridiculing my peculiarity,
          and I felt that I did not belong.
          I searched for the root / but she had drowned in the ocean,
          the stem of our tree had wilted in the breeze,
          We, the branches, had lost our way / So I searched for a new seed to give me reason, / and above the rotting earth

I found her still growing in the shade
(BIANCA looks at CLEMENTINE)
Her eyes were bright and she could see beyond my return...

CLEMENTINE looks at BIANCA. After a pause they both turn away. Lights up on Caribbean shack.)

CLEMENTINE   I hear a bus outside.
GRACE *(Looking at watch)* Is her? *(CLEMENTINE beckons for GRACE to join her at the door.)*
CLEM/BIANCA My eyes –
BIANCA   ... daring to stare –
CLEM/BIANCA ... at me with such distaste. My nose –
CLEMENTINE   ... turning on its end –
CLEM/BIANCA ... and scorning me –
CLEMENTINE   èvè djèl mwen – (and my mouth)
BIANCA   ... my mouth
CLEM/BIANCA ... mine.
CLEMENTINE *(To GRACE)* You never tell me she was pretty so.
    (GRACE runs out to meet BIANCA. DENNIS puts suitcase indoors.)
DENNIS   I catch all you later I have a message to do!
CLEMENTINE   O.K. Dennis thank you eh! *(DENNIS goes back to CHORUS. GRACE and BIANCA are hugging. CLEMENTINE distances herself from them.)*
GRACE   You reach!
BIANCA *(Screaming with delight)* Grace! Look at you, you've caught the sun.
GRACE *(Fussing over BIANCA)* You must be tired...
    (GRACE looks at CLEMENTINE and ushers her to meet BIANCA.)
GRACE   Look your sister!
CLEMENTINE   *(She introduces herself)* Hello. Clementine.
BIANCA   Hi... *(BIANCA and CLEMENTINE hug. CLEMENTINE pulls away quickly and busies herself)*
GRACE   So what you say Clem?
CLEMENTINE *(Distantly)* Girl you mus' be thirsty all that travelling...
    (CLEMENTINE leaves. Pause. GRACE goes to BIANCA'S suitcase and drags it further into the room.)
GRACE   Child what you bring, the bag heavy eh!
BIANCA   All sorts. I wasn't sure what clothes to bring so I just brought most of my stuff.

GRACE   You mean all of it. I'll have to borrow man. We'll go out the weekend eh?

BIANCA *(Excitedly)* There's places to go?

(CLEMENTINE enters with a glass of red drink.)

CLEMENTINE *(Sarcastically)* No, people does just sit down in the house... *(GRACE looks at CLEMENTINE. Politely)* Mi bwè 'wo. (Look your drink.)

BIANCA   Thank you. *(Pause. GRACE picks up a duty free bag.)*

GRACE   What's in here? *(GRACE looks inside the bag.)*

BIANCA   Perfume... for Clementine. *(GRACE gives the perfume to CLEMENTINE.)*

GRACE   Oh, that's nice...

CLEMENTINE   Mesi. (Thank you.) *(CLEMENTINE takes the perfume and puts it down somewhere.)*

GRACE   Mum send anything?

CLEMENTINE *(Mumbles)*... yon pòpòt. (... a doll.)

GRACE   What you say?

CLEMENTINE   I said a doll. A real English doll.

GRACE   Clementine!

CLEMENTINE   Only this one have two strong foot, with fancy shoe, fancy high heel shoe that make click click on my floor.

GRACE   What happen since the child reach you...?

CLEMENTINE *(Politely)* Drink your drink... *(BIANCA takes a sip.)*

BIANCA   What is it?

CLEMENTINE   Blood!

GRACE *(Looking at CLEMENTINE)* Sorrel. Is a Christmas drink.

CLEMENTINE *(Laughing)* England don't have Christmas drink like us?

BIANCA   No. It's... nice. Aaaaaagh! *(CLEMENTINE brushes away an insect with her foot.)*

CLEMENTINE   It won't bite... Is only a bug!

GRACE   She's not used to –

BIANCA   I could do with a bath.

GRACE   They jus' turn off the water but we full some bucket at the back in the yard.

BIANCA   You joking?

GRACE *(Laughing)* It's O.K. the water's clean, we collect it from the tap before it went off.

BIANCA   But it's dark out there... Oh, it doesn't matter.

GRACE   What you mean, come I'll full a basin for you. *(GRACE gets up)* Come.

BIANCA   It's O.K. I said. (*CLEMENTINE laughs. BIANCA looks uncomfortable. She scratches her knees.*)

GRACE   Don't scratch it love.

CLEMENTINE   Drink your drink.

GRACE   It will get sore – is de mosquito. (*BIANCA takes a sip from her drink.*)

CLEMENTINE   They like new blood. Drink up. (*CLEMENTINE laughs. She touches BIANCA'S hair.*) Dry like coconut. Veron Tèt Chèch! 'member de mad woman they use to chain up sometimes her head dry dry dry? (*Drum beat*)

GRACE   O.K. Clem, hush now.

CLEMENTINE   You don't remember her?

GRACE   Yes, yes but you don't have to go on so.

CLEMENTINE   I cannot talk then? I only talking. You know I hear some people talking the other day, they say Veron Tèt Chèch was never mad you know, is people that do her that because she was well-to-do. She had more money than them go on with her fancy clothes and thing so they make her mad. And Matches Stick he did only walk mad when the spirit take him. Remember how we did know when to call him and know when he alright? Was somebody that put something in his food or drink or... Eh, eh Bianca drink your drink nah. (*BIANCA looks at the glass*) Yes, somebody was jealous of his things. And Peggy remember Peggy, Grace? Fanm-Ia ki té ka – (The woman who use to –)

GRACE   Stop it now.

CLEMENTINE   kouwi an savann-lan èvè i té ka hélé! (run through the savana screaming!) One minute she was a well-to-do lady, nice high heel, nice little slim back. She had a white pair I did like dat shoe.

GRACE   Take no notice Bianca. I don't know what happen to her.

CLEMENTINE   I just – (*looks at BIANCA*) talking. You don't mind. (*DENNIS comes out of the CHORUS and stands in the doorway.*)

DENNIS   Psssss!... pssssss! (*The women turn and see him*) Hi (*to CLEMENTINE*) Zanfan'w-nan? (Your child nah?)

BIANCA   No, I'm her sister.

DENNIS   È è, ou ka palé patwa?

BIANCA   Yes my mum speaks it all the time.

CLEMENTINE   Wait a minute, wait a minute. (*GRACE laughs*) You talking patwa?

BIANCA   A bit... I understand it more than speak it.

GRACE   Eh, eh something shock Clementine tonight!

DENNIS   Madam Anglé, vini, mwen ka moutjwe'w toupatou.
(Hey English come let me show you the sights.)
CLEMENTINE   Which sights? Leave the girl, let me talk.
BIANCA *(Gets up)* I wouldn't mind some fresh air. *(Steps outside)*
CHORUS   Aieeeeeeeeeeee! *(The CHORUS make the sound of loud sighs.
This leads to the sound of sea waves lapping. The full moon looks
brighter. DENNIS and BIANCA sit down.)*
DENNIS   First time here? *(BIANCA nods)* So you don't know
Clementine? *(BIANCA shakes her head)* You don't talk much...

The sound of sea is louder.

BIANCA   I'm enjoying the peace.
DENNIS   It's O.K., nothing special.
BIANCA   It's special.
DENNIS *(Pleased)* You think so?
BIANCA *(Takes a deep breath)* If I could bottle this I would be rich.
DENNIS   And if I could put you in a bottle I think I would be a
millionaire.
CHORUS *(They sing)* Mamzèl Mamzèl / Wi Misyé...
BIANCA   I've heard it all already. *(The CHORUS back off)* I'm not
interested.
DENNIS   Pardon me?
BIANCA   I'm married with six kids.
DENNIS   That doesn't –
BIANCA   Look, really I just want to sit here. I just want to take this all
in.
DENNIS *(Backs off)* O.K.

*BIANCA looks out at the sea. GRACE steps out of the shack. She looks up at
the moon then looks for some pebbles. She finds a handful and starts to play
pick up. DENNIS and BIANCA do not notice her.*

BIANCA   Where does it all start... and where does it end?
GRACE   It just goes on and on. *(They acknowledge GRACE.)*
BIANCA   On to where?
GRACE   You don't tired worry about stupidness?
BIANCA *(Looks at Dennis)* Sorry.
DENNIS   That's O.K.
BIANCA   Everything must be straight-forward for you though.

DENNIS *(Laughs)* Hey Grace, your sister not easy doh! *(To BIANCA)* Why you say that?

BIANCA   Because this is yours.

DENNIS   What? You're joking. The only thing that is mine is what you see in front of you. I make no claims on this island.

BIANCA   You were born here.

DENNIS   Grace too.

GRACE   Hey, leave me out of all you politics! *(Continues playing her game.)*

DENNIS *(To BIANCA)* So because you were born in England you would say England is yours?

BIANCA   That's my point, it's not.

DENNIS   Well, this ain't mine either.

BIANCA   So, don't you ever want something solid to hold on to, something you can say is yours? Some beginning, somewhere?

DENNIS   No.

GRACE   Your head don't hurting you Bianca?

DENNIS *(To GRACE)* She always so serious?

GRACE *(Kisses her teeth and carries on playing)* I don't know what wrong wid her she jus' want to burs' her brain.

DENNIS   Relax man.

BIANCA   O.K., O.K. *(BIANCA sighs)*

DENNIS *(Teasing)* Problem, problem, problem! Don't England have any doctors?

BIANCA   Look I've finished. I'm not saying anything else. *(BIANCA and DENNIS look out at the sea. GRACE continues playing pick-up. Pause. BIANCA looks at DENNIS and smiles. He laughs. Pause.)* What's that noise?

DENNIS *(Listens)* I don't hear...

BIANCA   That high-pitched... screaming. *(He listens)*

GRACE   She means the crickets.

DENNIS   Oh, the crickets. I accustom to hearing it so much that I can't even hear it.

GRACE   Is true but when you been away... you notice. *(BIANCA screams as a firefly passes. GRACE grins, DENNIS chuckles.)*

GRACE/DENNIS *(To BIANCA)* Firefly.

BIANCA   Oh.

The sound of sea waves lapping. DENNIS and BIANCA look out to sea. Lights up slightly inside the shack. CHORUS emerge from out of the shadows. They are whispering and giggling.

CHORUS   Djab! Djab! Djab! *I* Djab ou la? / Oti'w djab? (Devil where you?)

Djab ou la? / Oti'w djab?

CLEMENTINE *(Excitedly)* Gracie! Vimi! (Gracie! Come!) *(GRACE runs inside)* You know what I have under the bed Grace – you'll die when you see! *(CLEMENTINE takes the doll from underneath the bed. It has one leg. The other leg is nowhere in sight.)*

GRACE   You still have that old thing? Where de foot?

CLEMENTINE   I burn it.

GRACE   Why you burn it for?

CLEMENTINE   It wasn't going nowhere. What it want foot for! *(Picks at the doll's eyes and laughs)* What it have eyes for, it don't see nothing?

England. FLORENTINE in the bed in England rubs her eyes.

FLORENTINE   Aieeeeeeeeee!

(WILLIAM steps out of the CHORUS and stands at the bedroom door. He coughs. Still rubbing her eyes) William?

WILLIAM   Hello, Florentine...

FLORENTINE   Sé' w? (Is you dat?)

WILLIAM   Is me.

FLORENTINE   Bondyé kité mwen djab! Kité mwen!

WILLIAM   Florentine...

FLORENTINE   Is really you William?

WILLIAM   Yes is me! Sa ki wivé 'w? (What happen to you?)

FLORENTINE   Somebody put something on me. Run my bath for me – get the blue – put the blue in the water.

WILLIAM   Mwen ké kiyé yon doktè ba'w. (I'll call the doctor.)

FLORENTINE   I don't want the doctor I want bath. Put blue in the water!

WILLIAM   Calm down Florentine! *(He begins to dial.)*

FLORENTINE   Who you phoning? *(She throws a pillow at him)* I tell you I don't want doctor, you don't hear. Something not right. May be my modder calling me – Maybe is my time...

WILLIAM   Don't talk like that... I have to talk to you.

FLORENTINE   Talk?

WILLIAM   I came tonight to talk to you, about something that's been on my mind for a long time...

FLORENTINE   Oh... Paée non. (Oh... Then talk)

WILLIAM   I was jus' passing...

FLORENTINE   Passing? Passing through? Passing over? Passing water? Get to the point!

WILLIAM   Give me chance. I wanted to talk to you about... going home. *(Silence. FLORENTINE laughs a hard deep laugh. The CHORUS join her. The laughing taking over their whole bodies until they are empty.)*

FLORENTINE *(Serious)* That's nice, that's very nice. Jus' like that eh?... about going home... yes, husband talk to me about going home. *(He turns to leave. With sarcasm)* Don't. I thought you wanted to go home. Go pack – pack everything for me. I don't want to leave anything, you hear, even my coat I want because snow could fall in Dominica tonight, things changing yes... Me and my husband, we going home! *(WILLIAM starts to walk away)* I don't finish yet... You know how long I waiting for you to say that to me? But you never... never so much as show your face since Bianca born but is today you come and lay down the law!

WILLIAM   Mwen paté ni lanjan... I didn't have the money... I never proved myself FIorentine... Can't *you* understand that?

FLORENTINE   When did you ever have to prove to me William? Did I tell you I wanted you to prove something to me? All I wanted was for you to be there... To care William, I had to do it on my own.

WILLIAM   You think it was easy for me, knowing that?

FLORENTINE   So why you never phone? Why you never come and see if we O.K.?

WILLIAM   I didn't have anything to give you.

FLORENTINE   I didn't need for you to give me anything. I would have settled for just you.

WILLIAM   I know... but I didn't want you to just settle... that would never have been enough.

CHORUS   Aieeeeeeeeee! / Come likkle birdy
Let me hol' you / I won't hol' too tight
Squeeze you likkle breath away,
Won't make you die. / Just want to...
You is me... / Come / Come
Come let me... / Aieeeeeeeee! /...fly.

FLORENTINE *(Holds her hands on her eyes)* Aieeeeeeeeee!

WILLIAM   What you want me to do?

FLORENTINE   Mwen pa sav... I don't know... *(He goes close to her.)*

Caribbean shack.

GRACE   Maybe that doll see everything.

CLEMENTINE *(Bitterly)* And maybe it forget what it see.

GRACE   And you now you'll never forget?

CLEMENTINE   Grace, why I have to forget for?

GRACE   Because you're getting bitter Clem!

CLEMENTINE   Well, maybe I have reason.

GRACE   You don't have reason – no more reason than anyone of us so stop it, stop it now!

CLEMENTINE   i sanm ou lonbliyé la'w soti! (It's like you forget where you come out!)

GRACE   How I can forget? I know where I come out Clem, and it nice to come back to but it not my home again. I remember all the good times we had but they're memories you know... They're just what we used to be... and now we're different people.

CLEMENTINE   Mammy left us.

GRACE   I can't even remember Mammy at home, and if you honest you can't either. Ma Effeline brought us up. I only got to know Mammy when I went to meet her in England, and we didn't miss her when she went away because we had everything. We had each other, we had everybody all around. You still had that when I left, you still had everybody around. I had nobody Clem. Can't you understand what you're jealous of is nothing? I had nobody. I lived for your letters too.

CLEMENTINE   Mammy left me...

England. WILLIAM is stroking FLORENTINE'S head.

FLORENTINE   William... William what you come back for?

WILLIAM   When you run so far forward you forget what you running from you start to think maybe you should stop and look...especially when you think you getting somewhere and you turn and see you still in the same place...

FLORENTINE   I know dat.

WILLIAM   I always thought there was something there, for me, on the other side, so I ran to take it. I never stopped to see that what I was running to reach I already had.

FLORENTINE   I tired... William... Mwen las.

WILLIAM   You see nobody ever made me feel 'fraid like you. Is like you had my life in your hand and you could have done anything to me...

FLORENTINE   I would never have hurt you.

WILLIAM I love you. You know dat. I never lie.
FLORENTINE Is too late William... I tired.
WILLIAM Let me run your water.
FLORENTINE No. I'll bathe in the morning.

Caribbean shack. GRACE tries to take the doll from CLEMENTINE.

GRACE Gimme it!
CLEMENTINE Is mine.
GRACE I know is yours – I want to see.
CLEMENTINE Why you want to see it for? *(GRACE snatches it.)*
GRACE 'Cos it cause you too much pain already. Is jus' a doll and you put so much meaning, so much anger, so much hatred, in this...
(The sound of sea waves. GRACE is about to throw the doll out to sea. CLEMENTINE sprints towards her.)
CHORUS No! *(Silence. BIANCA and DENNIS look towards shack.)*
DENNIS Ou fini goumen? (All you finish fighting?)
(GRACE and CLEMENTINE say nothing. The tension is held between them.) Right. Good. *(He gets up to go. To BIANCA)* Hey res' yourself here girl and don't let them sisters of yours bully you. Bonswe. (Goodnight)
(He goes quickly back into the shadows. BIANCA looks at GRACE and CLEMENTINE who are focused on each other. The doll is out of CLEMENTINE'S reach.)
CLEMENTINE Is mine Grade. *My piece* of what you had. *My piece* of what all you had. Yes it break up and ugly but it mine.
EFFELINE it rest Clemoi.
GRACE Let it rest Clemoi.
(The sound of sea waves. GRACE looks out to sea. The drummer begins the rhythm of 'Wash Away'.)
EFFELINE Ah dou dou / Ah dou dou
Tout sa ou di / Tout sa ou fè
i èvè 'w / Nou pasa lonbilyé 'y
i èpi nou / kon èspwi
kon èspwi / kon èspwi
(As MA EFFELINE speaks GRACE lowers the doll to the sea and begins to wash it.)
CHORUS *(Sigh)* Ahhhhhhhhh!
(CLEMENTINE and BlANCA watch GRACE.)
(Whisper) Wash / Wash / Wash
Wash / Wash / Wash.

England. The sound of sea waves, the drumming, and the CHORUS 'wash'
continue through this scene. WILLIAM is stroking FLORENTINE'S head.
She is drifting into sleep but turning her head from side to side.

FLORENTINE *(Mumbling)...* my piece of what you had... my piece. Mine!
    My piece... mine. My peace... my peace... my peace.
CHORUS   My peace of mind.

Caribbean. The sound of sea waves lapping becomes louder as does the
CHORUS 'wash'. GRACE is still washing the doll. CLEMENTINE and
BIANCA still watching her.

CLEMENTINE *(Sings)* Wash away my sorrow / Wash away my grief
    Wash away that love / that once belonged to me
    Wash away my sorrow / Wash away my grief
    Wash away that love / that once belonged to me.
CHORUS *(Overlap with song)* Yo ka gadé kont Manman yo
    Yo ka gadé kont Manman yo / Yo ka gadé kont Manman yo
    Yo ka gadé kont Manman yo / (They looking after their mammy)

England. FLORENTINE'S head stays still. WILLIAM puts his head to
FLORENTINE'S nose. He listens to her heart and leaves his head on her
chest as he cries.

Caribbean. Semi-darkness, the sound of sea waves. GRACE stops washing
the doll and lays it to rest in the sea. She puts her arms out to her sisters.
CLEMENTINE hesitates and then moves towards GRACE. Lights fade
gently. The moon glows on the doll in the water. From out of the sea sounds,
the creak of the rocking-chair emerges followed by the low croak of MA
EFFELINE'S voice. The rocking-chair moves.

EFFELINE   Ah dou dou / Ah dou dou

Drum beat. The CHORUS emerge from the shadows. The drummer leads
BIANCA, GRACE and CLEMENTINE off. WILLIAM pushes the bed on which
FLORENTINE is lying and the rest of the CHORUS follow. Lights down.

Curtain call. The CHORUS come back on and make fête.

CHORUS *(Sing)* If I sail on a sailing boat and I don't come back,
    stay home and mind baby...

Brown skin girl stay home and mind baby
Brown skin girl stay home and mind baby
If I sail on a sailing boat and I don't come back
Stay home and mind baby...

The song is repeated and picks up momentum as the CHORUS dance and make fête.

The End.

aurora metro press

Founded in 1989 to publish and promote new writing, the press has specialised in new drama, fiction and work in translation, winning recognition and awards from the industry.

New drama
I have before me a remarkable document... by Sonja Linden
ISBN 0-9546912-3-7 £7.99

Harvest by Manjula Padmanabhan
ISBN 0-9536757-7-7 £6.99

Under Their Influence by Wayne Buchanan
ISBN 0-9536757-5-0 £7.99

Trashed by Noël Greig
ISBN 0-9546912-2-9 £7.99

Lysistrata - the sex strike by Aristophanes, adapted by Germaine Greer and Phil Willmott **ISBN 0-9536757-0-8 £7.99**

Anthologies
Black and Asian plays introduced by Afia Nkrumah
ISBN 09536757-4-2 £9.95

Theatre Centre plays for young people, introduced by Rosamunde Hutt
ISBN 09542330-5-0 £12.99

The Classic Fairytales retold for the stage by Charles Way
ISBN 09542330-0-X £11.50

Young Blood, plays for young performers edited by Sally Goldsworthy
ISBN 09515877-6-5 £10.95

Seven plays by women, female voices, fighting lives
ed. Cheryl Robson **ISBN 0-9515877-1-4 £5.95**

A touch of the Dutch: plays by women ed. Cheryl Robson
ISBN 0-9515877-7-3 £9.95

Mediterranean plays by women ed. Marion Baraitser
ISBN 0-9515877-3-0 £9.95

Eastern Promise, *7 plays from central and eastern Europe*
eds. Sian Evans and Cheryl Robson **ISBN 0-9515877-9-X £11.99**

www.aurorametro.com